Tell It Like It Is

Tell It Like It Is

Women in the National
Welfare Rights Movement

It Is

Mary E. Triece

The University of South Carolina Press

© 2013 University of South Carolina

Published by the University of South Carolina Press
Columbia, South Carolina 29208

www.sc.edu/uscpress

Manufactured in the United States of America

22 21 20 19 18 17 16 15 14 13
10 9 8 7 6 5 4 3 2 1

Library of Congress Cataloging-in-Publication Data

Triece, Mary Eleanor, 1967 –
    Tell it like it is : women in the national welfare rights movement / Mary E. Triece.
        p. cm.
    Includes bibliographical references and index.
    ISBN 978-1-61117-153-2 (hbk. : alk. paper) — ISBN 978-1-61117-154-9 (pbk. : alk. paper)
1. Welfare rights movement—United States—History. 2. Women—Political activity—United
States—History—20th century. 3. Public welfare—United States—History—20th century.
4. National Welfare Rights Organization (U.S.)—History. I. Title.
    HV91.T75 2013
    361.973—dc23
                                        2012035735

Contents

Illustrations

Acknowledgments

During the fall of 2005, with my newborn daughter in tow, I interviewed three working-class women to explore how their work as mothers affected their experiences in the workplace and as activists.

It was in my conversation with Minerva Pérez Vargas that I was first introduced to the concept of welfare rights organizing. When I asked what this group was about, Ms. Pérez Vargas responded plainly that welfare rights activists "would call [the Department of Human Services] out on their shit." Her forthright response embodied the spirit of welfare rights activists who employed a variety of strategies and actions between 1967 and 1972 in order to give lie to racist welfare discourses underpinning public policies that made it difficult for welfare recipients to raise their families in a dignified manner. By "calling out" welfare bureaucrats and politicians on their repeated use of timeworn stereotypes, these mothers attempted to set the record straight; they sought to "tell it like it is."

I am thankful to Ms. Pérez Vargas for introducing me to what I discovered to be an influential facet of the civil rights movement that has yet to receive its historical due. Six years later I was most fortunate to be able to interview another mother activist—Jacqueline Pope—whose work as a founding member of the Brooklyn Welfare Action Council was an inspiration for me as I wrote this book.

The following study of welfare rights activism came to life as I culled the archives of the National Welfare Rights Organization at the Moorland-Spingarn Research Center at Howard University. I am particularly grateful to Joellen El Bashir, curator of manuscripts, for making work with the collection manageable and enjoyable. My research was also facilitated by the assistance of Bill Barrow, special collections librarian at the Michael Schwartz Library at Cleveland State University, and by Joseph LaRose, applied arts bibliographer at Bierce Library at the University of Akron.

I would also like to acknowledge individuals who enabled me to see this project through to publication, including Jim Denton, my acquisitions editor at the

University of South Carolina Press, and the anonymous reviewers who provided valuable suggestions for strengthening the project.

And finally at the University of Akron I was fortunate to receive a summer faculty fellowship in 2007, which enabled me to continue the study of mothering and activism sparked by the conversations I had with Minerva Pérez Vargas and others in 2005.

Introduction

I would hope that a wise Latina woman with the richness of
her experiences would more often than not reach a better
conclusion than a white male who hasn't lived that life.

Sonia Sotomayor, as quoted in "A Latina Judge's Voice,"
New York Times, May 15, 2009

All the degrees in the world can't help someone who [has] never
been really hungry to know how much an empty stomach hurts,
or what it's like to live in a fourth-floor, cold-water walkup flat
with no heat, no plumbing, and rats and roaches.

Betty Meredith, *Examination of the War on Poverty:*
Hearing before the Subcommittee on Employment,
Manpower, and Poverty, 90th Congress, 1967

Separated in time by more than three decades, the statements by Sonia Sotomayor,
then an appeals court judge, and Boston area community activist Betty Meredith
are strikingly similar in their emphasis on the power of firsthand experience in
shaping one's perceptions. In more academic terms, both women referred to the
"epistemic advantage" (Alcoff 2006, 96) they gained by virtue of their standpoint.* In her speech to an audience at the University of California, Berkeley,
School of Law, Sotomayor asserted that "our experiences as women and people
of color affect our decisions." And she noted that "although struggle . . . does
not create a Latina identity, it does inspire how" she lives her life (Sotomayor).
Likewise in her testimony before the U.S. Congress, Meredith explained that only
those who had lived the experience of poverty could understand what it was like,
which by extension put them in a better position to make decisions concerning
welfare policy. The controversy that ensued in the wake of both women's statements reveals the importance of studying how women—and in the case of this
book, poor, mostly black women—make claims to knowledge in public forums
dominated primarily by white males.† Welfare recipients of the late 1960s and

---

* Bat-Ami Bar On (1993) uses the term "epistemic privilege."
† During confirmation hearings following her nomination to the U.S. Supreme
Court, Sotomayor was taken to task by senators for her "wise Latina" statement,

early 1970s were enmeshed in what Nancy Fraser (1989) refers to as the "politics of needs interpretation" (146). Part of their task as speakers was to unmask or give lie to the ways welfare practices acted hegemonically as they "construct[ed] women and women's needs according to certain specific—and, in principle, contestable—interpretations, even as they len[t] those interpretations an aura of facticity that discourage[d] contestation" (146). Welfare righters persisted in efforts to define their own needs and to represent themselves in the context of welfare debates that relied on racist narratives and tropes such as the "welfare chiseler" and the "welfare queen."

It is worth noting that poor black mothers occupied a conflicted position at the intersection of capital and care. Conscripted by a racist workplace and hegemonic gender norms, welfare recipients negotiated the dueling roles of worker and mother. Speaking as women discriminated by a capitalist welfare state that positioned them exclusively as (failed) mothers (Fraser 1989, 153), they established themselves as credible workers deserving of decent jobs. From their position under the slave-era legacy of forced employment for black women, they situated themselves as deserving mothers who had a right to remain home with their children. The following chapters explore the rhetorical strategies and direct actions women used as they negotiated varying needs and contradictory demands while asserting claims to knowledge about poverty and life on welfare that stood in contrast to prevailing understandings promoted in political and popular discourses.

On a theoretical level *Tell It Like It Is* engages in ongoing ontological and epistemological debates regarding language, knowledge, truth, and reality. As the posthumanist turn in the humanities has taken the idea of a knowable reality and a knowing subject out of currency, the present study (1) explores the possibilities of agency even as social actors are constrained—and motivated—by deeply entrenched structures and (2) emphasizes the relevance of lived experience (what Marx (1888) referred to as "sensuous human activity") for making claims to knowing and for establishing the credibility of those claims in the context of debates characterized by power differentials. From the days of slavery to present day Supreme Court nominations, subaltern groups have sought out the rhetorical possibilities for asserting knowledge claims to those in power. McBride (2001) notes of slave narratives, "One of the crises of witnessing slavery is the very problem of how to narrate slave experience to an audience outside that epistemological community of slaves" (85). Welfare rights activists faced much the

---

which incidentally was often taken out of context. Meredith's and other welfare rights activists' assertions that they "knew better than" the senators to whom they presented statements during congressional hearings often provoked curt and sometimes overtly demeaning responses from members of congress.

same rhetorical dilemma as they attempted to shape public policy debates over public aid in the late 1960s and early 1970s.

"The only real hope for Welfare mothers is to be 'organized'"

These were the sentiments of Jacqueline Pope (1971), welfare rights organizer. The National Welfare Rights Organization (NWRO) came into being in 1967 in a field of local welfare rights organizations that, across the country, had been advocating on behalf of welfare recipients for the better part of the 1960s. Formation of the NWRO came on the heels of nationwide marches in June 1966 by welfare recipients demanding decent benefits and dignified treatment. These marches were coordinated with a previously planned Walk for Decent Welfare, in which recipients walked 150 miles from Cleveland to Columbus, Ohio, to call attention to the need for welfare reform. With the assistance of George Wiley and the Poverty/Rights Action Center, welfare recipients and middle-class allies came together in 1967 to form the National Coordinating Committee and a constitution for the newly formed organization (Bailis 1974; Nadasen 2005).

By the late 1960s the welfare rights movement had gained a respectable following—approximately thirty thousand dues-paying members at its peak— and yet "compared to other struggles of the 1960s, the welfare rights movement has been essentially glossed over" (Nadasen 2005, xiv).* Studies by historians such as Felicia Kornbluh (1997, 2007) and Anne Valk (2000) have added to our knowledge of how NWRO activists have communicated their needs in public settings. Kornbluh showed the extensive political actions of New York's City-Wide Coordinating Committee of Welfare Groups (2007) and explored the language of rights used by NWRO activists as they enacted a politics of consumption in their campaign for store credit (1997). Valk's analysis shed light on the ways welfare rights activists in Washington, D.C., employed the trope of motherhood in order to "bolster their moral authority . . . and question the antifamily values inherent in welfare policies" (2000, 51).

Other scholars have focused on organizational issues such as recruitment, internal conflicts, and external obstacles, for example in the Massachusetts Welfare Rights Organization (Bailis 1974); the Brooklyn, New York, Welfare Action Council (Pope 1989); and the Minnesota Welfare Rights Organization (Hertz 1981). Accounts such as those by Davis (1996), Nadasen (2005), Piven and Cloward (1979), West (1981), and White (1999) focus on the NWRO as a movement,

---

* Also according to Nadasen the movement "had an estimated following of somewhere between 30,000 and 100,000" (xiv). West states that according to her own analysis of NWRO documents, there were 24,500 dues-paying members in 1969, and the numbers declined after that (1981, 50).

examining the group's activities, leadership, and relationship to other women's organizations and broader structures, with less emphasis on rhetorical strategies per se. Scholarship has also focused on how poor women and welfare recipients have been represented in mainstream media (Entman and Leff 1991; Gans 1995; Hancock 2004; Jewell 1992; Komisar 1977; L. Williams 1995; Zucchino 1997); however little work has been conducted within communication studies to bring to light the ways that poor women on welfare represent themselves.

Scholars studying the formation of welfare policies throughout the twentieth century have also focused on how welfare bureaucrats, social workers, and politicians have spoken on behalf of women (Abramovitz 1988; Asen 2001, 2002, 2003; Fraser 1989; Gans 1995; Gordon 1995; Hancock 2004; Handler and Hasenfeld 1991; Mink 1995, 1998; Neubeck and Cazenave 2001; Quadagno 1994; Zarefsky 1986). Of note is Nancy Fraser's (1989) study of how the "tacit norms and implicit assumptions" undergirding the patriarchal capitalist welfare state have contributed to discussions of how women were rhetorically constructed in policy debates.

Like Fraser, who focuses on the hegemonic or dominant discourses shaping welfare policies and recipients, the communication scholar Robert Asen (2001, 2002, 2003) studies how poor women were imagined in welfare policy debates by political decision makers. In "Women, Work, Welfare," Asen (2003) explores the changing rhetorical construction of welfare recipients from the "mother as caregiver" in early 1900s mothers' pensions debates to the "mother as paid worker" in 1960s debates. He notes that Nixon administration officials "did not imagine the poor mother ... through detailed depictions. They did not present vignettes or stories of poor women struggling at the margins of the paid labor market, nor did they share testimony from poor women" (303).

An important piece missing from larger accounts of welfare policy debates is how welfare recipients spoke *for themselves* in these debates, specifically from their position as poor black mothers systematically categorized as the "undeserving" poor. Of importance—and not fully developed in Asen's (2003) account of welfare policy formation—black women have historically been denied the status of "mother as caregiver," since slave-era stereotypes have categorized black women as "employable" and as "undeserving" mothers. In addition, although Nixon-era politicians did not offer narratives of poor women's struggles, welfare recipients provided *their own* stories to Congress as they testified a number of times between 1968 and 1973 in their attempts to shape public discussions of welfare policy.

Tell It Like It Is draws on archival resources as well as other scholarly accounts of the NWRO in an effort to understand how welfare rights activists represented themselves and their needs in the welfare policy debates taking place in formal political arenas. The analyses in chapters 2 through 5 rely on documents of the NWRO archived at the Moorland-Spingarn Research Center at Howard

University and the William Whitaker Collection at the Ohio Historical Society, which include pamphlets, flyers, position statements, convention materials, and the like. The organization's official organ, the *Welfare Fighter*—published between the years 1969 and 1972—also lends considerable insight when examining the organization's public discourse. Subscriptions went out to individuals as well as organizations from across the country—including the National Organization for Women (NOW) and various churches and community groups—who requested the paper. The following study also draws on the congressional testimony given by welfare recipients in the late 1960s and early 1970s, providing the first in-depth look at the ways poor black women represented themselves in this elite political forum. Thus the analysis covers welfare righters' rhetoric in both group-created and group-controlled spaces (for example national and local meetings, and flyers and pamphlets distributed to recipients) as well as broader publics, such as congressional hearings, where viewpoints were articulated in contrast to narratives that prevailed in the public imagination. Typical of counterpublics, welfare rights activists "oscillat[ed] between protected enclaves ... and more hostile but also broader surroundings" in order to test their ideas against those of the "reigning reality" (Mansbridge 1996, 57; see also Brouwer 2001; Squires 2001). In addition to employing the typical rhetorical means for dissemination of their views, this group also drew from contemporaneous civil rights activism as well as the history of women's community-based activism in their confrontations with entrenched economic structures existing outside their discourse.

In order to understand the welfare policy debates and activism of the 1960s and 1970s, we must trace their roots to the formation of welfare legislation in the early part of the twentieth century. This historical backdrop demonstrates the ways welfare policies are inextricably linked to economic conditions and are shaped by dominant understandings of race and gender.

The History of Welfare Policy and Activism

Welfare policy debates have always been about much more than providing public assistance for those in need. These debates and the resulting legislation have been at root about maintaining white privilege, supporting the patriarchal family, and sustaining corporate interests. Scholars of welfare policy have explored the ways that public assistance is expanded or contracted in accordance with the needs of the labor market (Abramovitz 2000; Piven and Cloward 1971). From sixteenth-century European pauper policies to present U.S. welfare legislation, those in power have exerted social control by instilling a traditional work ethic and "restor[ing] people to work roles" (Piven and Cloward 1971, 8). Others have noted that racism has been embedded in welfare legislation from its beginnings (Neubeck and Cazenave 2001; Quadagno 1994). Welfare policy is also "targeted not only at the poor, but equally at the nonpoor, through the symbols it conveys about what behaviors are deemed virtuous or deviant" (Handler and Hasenfeld 1991, 11). In short the story of welfare policy is one that reveals much about how race, class, and gender hegemony are upheld and contested both materially and rhetorically.

In the Progressive Era spirit of the early 1900s, white middle-class reformers campaigned for mothers' pensions, which were intended to help single mothers in need. The assumptions underlying the push for mothers' pensions—which provided the basis for Aid to Dependent Children (ADC) in 1930s New Deal legislation—cemented understandings of ideal motherhood for decades to come. Mink (1995) explains, "Welfare's premises were that the health of the polity depended on the quality of its children; that the preparation of the child for citizenship depended on the quality of home life; that mother care was the linchpin of the family" (3). Public assistance targeted "deserving" mothers, primarily widows. Never-married, divorced, and in most cases deserted mothers were not eligible. The goal of mothers' pensions, in the eyes of the reformers who initiated them, was to ensure that mothers were raising their children to be good American citizens. "Maternalist reformers fashioned universalizing policies, building a welfare state that linked the uplift of women's material conditions through social provision to the uplift of mothers' character and quality through Americanization" (Mink 1995, 28). With such assumptions officials regularly scrutinized recipients of mothers' pensions. States enacted "suitable" home policies, "established regulations for continuing eligibility," and in some cases "incorporated regular investigation of recipients to enforce moral and cultural dimensions of 'Americanism': celibacy, temperance, English and citizenship training, 'American' cooking, and maternal domesticity" (38). Many of these controlling and invasive policies remained in practice well into the 1960s and became the target of welfare rights activists in the NWRO.

The distinction between "deserving" and "undeserving" poor has been a mainstay in welfare legislation from the early 1900s and plays a significant role in disciplining citizens who do not behave in accordance with the moral and materials needs of the socioeconomic system. Indeed the social construction of various populations—from big business to minorities to mothers—as "deserving" of either benefits or burdens plays a role in policy formation (Schneider and Ingram 1993). With regard to public aid, mothers were subcategorized according to race thus perpetuating discriminatory welfare policy. Since the goal of mothers' pensions was to ensure the full-time domesticity of (deserving) mothers, waged work outside the home was strongly discouraged, even stigmatized, by maternalists despite the fact that many mothers had to work outside the home to supplement their pensions. A different view was taken however when it came to the needs of poor black mothers who were stereotyped as "employable" and as "ill-suited to domestic motherhood by a long history of toil outside the home" (Mink 1995, 51). Racist images of black mothers—as lazy, immoral, promiscuous—ensured they were labeled "undeserving" (Neubeck and Cazenave 2001, 45). From its inception then the mothers' pension program was an "'elite' program" for "gilt-edged widows" (Bell 1965, 19, 9).

In 1935 mothers' pensions were federalized in Title IV of the Social Security Act, a move that "honored motherhood in principle but regulated mothers in practice" (Abramovitz 2000, 64), particularly black mothers. ADC was shaped by race stereotypes of the "employable" and "promiscuous" black woman as well as the notion that black families needed less than white families (Mink 1995, 142; Neubeck and Cazenave 2001, 46). The legislation enabled the "deserving" mother (that is the white widow) to stay home with her children and ensured that black mothers remained available as a source of cheap labor, for instance as agricultural workers in the south and domestic and unskilled industrial workers in urban areas (Abramovitz 2000, 64–66; Mink 1995, 132–33; Neubeck and Cazenave 2001, 47–59). Congressional leaders from the south lobbied to remove language that would have outlawed racial discrimination, and they ensured that nationally set aid standards were eliminated, giving states control over a large pool of workers desperate to take any job available (Neubeck and Cazenave 2001, 47). The words of a welfare program supervisor in 1939 encapsulate the racist sentiments of the time that were reflected in welfare legislation: "The number of Negro cases is few due to the unanimous feeling of the staff and board that there were more work opportunities for Negro women and to their intense desire not to interfere with local labor conditions. The attitude that 'they always have gotten along,' and that 'all they'll do is have more children' is definite" (Bell 1965, 34–35). Strikingly similar statements circulated in political and popular discourses well into the 1960s as welfare rights activists created a movement for welfare policy justice.

The Social Security amendments of 1939 broadened coverage of Old Age Insurance (OAI) to include the widows and children of insured men. This change led to the stigmatization of ADC since now "undeserving" mothers—never-married, divorced—were left on ADC, as "deserving" widows were covered by OAI. Furthermore, since many black men were not eligible for Social Security benefits, their widows and children did not qualify for OAI and were forced to remain on ADC, the payments of which were half of OAI payments (Abramovitz 2000, 66).

Beginning in the early 1940s politicians and the media launched an attack on ADC, which would continue into the 1960s and beyond. The attacks stemmed from concerns over the "competing demand for women's unpaid labor in the home and their low-paid labor in the market" (Abramovitz 2000, 69). During periods of tight labor (for example after World War II), welfare programs such as ADC were constricted in an effort to expand the pool of cheap labor, meaning especially the labor of poor black women.* Such efforts were particularly intense in the south, where states restricted ADC payments so as to ensure black women's labor during the harvest season (71). For example Louisiana, Arkansas, and Georgia had "farm policies" that enabled them to deny ADC to black women whose labor was needed in cotton and tobacco fields (Abramovitz 2000, 71; Neubeck and Cazenave 2001, 57–58). Southern states, concerned about rising welfare costs, lamented that public aid was "conducive to [black people's] idleness" and prevented them from getting and keeping a "legitimate" job (Bell 1965, 64). The Public Affairs Research Council noted that in Louisiana "public assistance results in reducing the unskilled labor supply in employment where women and older children form a principal part of the labor supply" and that the racial makeup of ADC (two-thirds of ADC recipients were nonwhite) negatively influenced public perceptions of the program (65). In addition Neubeck and Cazenave (2001) have observed that ADC eligibility policies such as compulsory work rules and residency requirements affected poor black families disproportionately (61–62).

To justify racist welfare policies that controlled black women's waged labor, politicians—with the support of the popular press—rhetorically constructed ADC recipients as lazy and immoral "chiselers" who collected public assistance to subsidize their lavish lifestyles (Abramovitz 2000, 69; Komisar 1977, 72–73; Patterson 2000, 106). In 1949 the *Saturday Evening Post* carried a series of articles about welfare "chiselers" who spent their ADC payments on "maids, radios, television sets, cars and jewelry" (Komisar 1977, 72). Throughout the 1950s the mainstream press sounded the bell about supposed welfare fraud even as thorough investigations were revealing few to no instances of cheating (Bell 1965, 62). With regards to the issue of welfare fraud, Bell notes that "economic and racial conflicts were so intertwined as to be inseparable" (63). Racist assumptions about work and black womanhood—namely the idea that black women were more "employable" than white women—were woven into these discourses (Bell 1965, 64). The "chiseler" theme was popular with editors, businessmen, and politicians for decades to come (Komisar 1977, 73).

Changes in the needs of the labor market were accompanied by changes in family structure during the 1940s and 1950s. Divorce rates and births by unmarried women increased for both white and black women between 1940 and

---

* Throughout the 1940s and 1950s, welfare rolls and expenditures expanded or contracted in relation to the economic conditions of the period. During wartime the rolls declined, while depressions and recessions (for example 1930s, 1953–1954, 1957–1958) led to an increase in enrollment (Abramovitz 2000, 68). Piven and Cloward (1971) go further in saying that relief rolls are expanded during times of economic distress not only to address basic needs, but also to serve as a form of social control.

1950. These trends were seen as threats to the traditional male-headed family and prompted passage of rules such as the suitable home and man-in-the-house policies, which enabled the close scrutiny of poor women's personal lives, from their sexual behavior to the ways they raised their children. These rules affected black families disproportionately and represented a form of "camouflaged welfare racism" in the period following World War II (Neubeck and Cazenave 2001, 59–60).

Through the late 1950s and early 1960s, rhetorics that scapegoated poor black mothers became more prominent and further justified racist welfare policies. Alarmist rhetoric came from all corners as psychologists, sociologists, and politicians attributed youth delinquency and criminal behavior to the rise in single female–headed households (Abramovitz 2000, 73; Patterson 2000, 98–99). The increase in births outside of the traditional male-headed household (for both white and black women) led to accusations of promiscuity and welfare abuse targeted to black women. In 1951 the Georgia state welfare director proposed "limiting aid to children of unwed Negro mothers." He further stated that "70 percent of all mothers of more than one illegitimate child are negroes. . . . Some of them finding themselves tied down with one child are not averse to adding others as a business proposition" (Bell 1965, 67). A decade later, in 1960, the outspoken racist governor of Louisiana, Jimmie H. Davis, stood before the state legislature and similarly decried the "existing policy regarding public assistance to unwed mothers who have proved by their past conduct that they engage in the business of illegitimacy in the same way that a cattleman raises beef" (Neubeck and Cazenave 2001, 72). Statistics on out-of-wedlock births belie such statements. A mere "one half of 1 percent of all ADC mothers in 1959 had six or more children born out of wedlock" (W. Bell 1965, 210). And a majority of black mothers with "illegitimate" children had only one born out of wedlock (210). The historian James T. Patterson (2000) notes that although illegitimacy was an issue, it was "clearly not going to break the bank: only one-eighth of all children on AFDC [Aid to Families with Dependent Children] in 1961 were illegitimate" (108).

The gendered and racialized panic over welfare was formalized politically in Daniel Patrick Moynihan's 1965 report *The Negro Family: The Case for National Action,* in which the author explicated the current state of the black family. The document, a little over fifty pages in length, addressed a number of issues facing black families in the 1960s, including unemployment and poverty. The original twelve-page memo (on which the longer report was based), directed to Secretary W. Willard Wirtz of the Department of Labor, even addressed funding for birth control clinics as part of the country's poverty programs (Patterson 2010, 21). However aware of the need to "enlist . . . the support of conservative groups for quite radical social programs," Moynihan emphasized family issues (Moynihan qtd. in Patterson 2010, 21). The report's controversy grew largely out of the author's description of the black family as a "tangle of pathology" with the black female head of household as the source of dysfunction. According to the report, the "weak" and "disorganized" family structure in many poor black families will eventually become the "source of most of the aberrant, inadequate, or anti-social behavior" among black youth (Moynihan 1965, 76). The report cites numerous studies underscoring that the environments in "broken homes"—that is female-headed homes—have negative effects on black male youth (76–86). Regardless of the politician's intentions, the report led to a scapegoating of the female-headed black family and an eliding of economic and social structures that posed serious obstacles to survival in black communities (Schram 2005, 263).* As one journalist noted, the report was "fast becoming the scriptural basis for several new brands of bigotry, even without the consent of its authors" (Farmer 1965, 411).

It is important to note that the Moynihan report did not go unchallenged. For instance many pointed out that black women have historically relied on kin networks and "domestic exchange" and that the black family was more accurately characterized by cooperation than disorganization (Patterson 2000, 101). The outspoken newspaper columnist James Farmer (1965) wrote two scathing editorials in the *Amsterdam News* in December 1965 painting the Moynihan report as a "massive academic cop-out for the white conscience" and an insult to the "intelligence of black men and women everywhere" (410–11). Farmer denounced the report for blaming the "roots of poverty and violence in the Negro community upon Negroes themselves," a "straw-man logic" that has "been the fatal error of American society for 300 years" (410–11).

In addition to the Moynihan report, high profile debates in the 1960s launched welfare into national awareness, where it remained as a political football well into the 1990s. The controversy in Newburgh, New York, in 1961 was characterized by blatantly racist public comments made by city officials, which "helped to further imprint welfare reliance as a racial phenomenon in the public mind" (Neubeck and Cazenave 2001, 92). Like other American cities both then and now, Newburgh underwent substantial economic upheaval in the 1950s as industries relocated to areas where it was cheaper to do business. Many of the city's more well-off white families left the city for better opportunities. Racial discrimination ensured that poor black families remained segregated in the city's most downtrodden neighborhoods and were locked in the lowest paying jobs. The economic downturn coupled with the changing demographics of the city resulted in a backlash against the city's poor black population.

Newburgh councilman George F. McKneally was quick to blame the black community for its poverty. He accused "jobless southern Negroes" of migrating to Newburgh to take advantage of welfare. He openly scapegoated African Americans for the city's economic and political woes, stating that the "colored people

---

* See James T. Patterson's (2010) book *Freedom Is Not Enough* for a nuanced study of the Moynihan report and the black family from the 1960s to the twenty-first century.

of this city are our biggest police problem, our biggest sanitation problem, and our biggest health problem. . . .We cannot put up with their behavior any longer. We have been too lenient with them. They must be made to adhere to the standards of the rest of the community" (Neubeck and Cazenave 2001, 80). Efforts to punish the city's black population culminated two years later in a "thirteen point program" initiated by city manager Joseph Mitchell. Among other things the plan stipulated that no one would receive aid for more than three months out of the year; that cash payments would be replaced by vouchers for food, rent, and clothing; that women who had a second child out of wedlock would be removed from the rolls; and that children found living in "unsuitable" homes would be removed and placed in foster care. While it appeared race neutral, the thirteen-point plan would disproportionately impact poor black children. It is revealing of racist intent that McKneally said of the plan, "This is not a racial issue. But there's hardly an incentive to a naturally lazy people to work if they can exist without working" (Neubeck and Cazenave 2001, 88). The Newburgh plan sparked discussions beyond the city as editors and letter writers voiced their opinions in major papers. Senator Barry Goldwater said of the plan, "I don't like to see my taxes paid for children out of wedlock. I'm tired of professional chiselers walking up and down the streets who don't work and have no intention of working. I would like to see every city in the country adopt the plan" (Patterson 2000, 105).

Senators had further opportunity to comment on the welfare system in 1962 when Senator Robert Byrd (Dem. W.Va.) launched hearings on welfare fraud in Washington, D.C. The hearings were significant insofar as they created a national spectacle that stigmatized welfare recipients and delineated normative behavior for poor people. The hearings furthered racialized public assistance, making welfare a "black issue" in the public imagination. An investigation on fraud in the D.C. area showed that a little over half of the cases examined were ineligible. Of those the majority were in violation either because the mother was employable or because the family violated the restrictive man-in-the-house rule (Neubeck and Cazenave 2001, 101). In other words policies based on racist assumptions aimed at controlling poor black women's behaviors resulted in the detection of "fraud." During the D.C. hearings Byrd invoked stereotypes of "lazy, shiftless, dishonest, and irresponsible African-American men who were involved in predatory relationships with immoral, sexually promiscuous African-American women" (Neubeck and Cazenave 2001, 97). Byrd stated, "I cannot recall one instance in which a child has grown up to amount to anything where liquor in the home, and the mother's illicit relations with paramours are the order of the day. And seldom, if ever, do the lazy and slothful ever get anywhere. It is about time therefore, that we stop encouraging indolence and shiftlessness, and that we quit furnishing money, food, and rent for indecent mothers and paramours who contribute nothing but illegitimate children to the society of this Federal City, most of whom end up roaming the streets and getting arrested for various crimes" (Neubeck and Cazenave 2001, 99).

What Byrd ignored and welfare recipients emphasized time and again was that public assistance hardly contributed to slothfulness. Indeed the idea of "welfare dependency" was a misnomer; public assistance funds were never enough to enable poor families to make ends meet. Poor mothers—particularly black mothers deemed "undeserving" of public aid—have relied on a variety of sources of income, including charities, boyfriends, kin, unreported earnings, and the fathers of their children (Neubeck and Cazenave 2001, 100). Unfortunately the reality of poor women's lives went unnoticed because welfare recipients did not testify at the Byrd hearings. Remarkable is that recipients did testify before Congress numerous times in the late 1960s, often giving political leaders an earful as they "gave presence" (Perelman 1982) to their lives from the perspectives of those who lived it.

Policies of the Kennedy and Johnson administrations in the early to mid-1960s also contributed significantly to understandings of poverty and public assistance in this decade. Rooted in the Progressive Era approach of the maternalists, the policies of both presidents emphasized the need for increased "opportunity" for poor families trapped in the so-called "cycle of poverty." The cycle-of-poverty view framed poverty as a matter of culture rather than economics: Poor people lacked the proper values and skills that would enable them to take advantage of what the system had to offer. On this view then the solution was to educate, Americanize (as in the case of early twentieth-century reformers), or otherwise make available opportunities for success. Worthy of note is that this perspective sidetracks issues deeply rooted in legal and economic systems that by design marginalize certain groups (Jim Crow for example and capitalism, with its built-in recessions, depressions, and unemployment). Toward these ends Kennedy supported a "service strategy," which emphasized rehabilitation in the form of family services while decreasing cash handouts (M. Brown 1999, 207; Patterson 2000, 127). The approach appealed to conservatives who bristled at the idea that poor folks were getting "free money," and it appealed to social workers and other liberals who sought to uplift the poor through a variety of programs.

The services approach influenced the architecture of Johnson's Great Society and his War on Poverty launched in 1964. Again the underlying idea was not to redistribute income or jobs but rather to provide "opportunity," the sine qua non of the program (M. Brown 1999, 232; Patterson 2000, 131). Zarefsky (1986) explains that the "War on Poverty was in many ways the apex of the liberal reform efforts of the 1960s, clearly embodying the assumptions of the liberal argument: society was benign; 'fine tuning' could provide opportunities for those left out, without seriously threatening the interests of the well-to-do; opportunities would translate into results; . . . an expanding economy made it possible to alleviate poverty without redistribution of income or wealth" (20).

Workfare programs were also a hallmark of welfare policies put in place in the 1960s, exemplified by the 1967 Work Incentive Program (WIN) and Nixon's controversial Family Assistance Plan (FAP) of 1969. In stark contrast to mothers' pensions advocates of the early twentieth century, who bent every effort to keep mothers in the home as caretakers, workfare policies now pushed mothers into the workforce. WIN required all recipients of AFDC except mothers of preschool children to register for job training. The program could hardly be called a success from the recipients' perspective since there were not enough jobs available once women completed the program. By 1972 fewer than 2 percent of those eligible for the program were actually employed (Patterson 2000, 170). Those who did have jobs often did not make enough to raise themselves out of poverty (J. Jones 1985, 308). And typically for such initiatives, workfare programs subsidized low-wage jobs that employed primarily poor black women. In congressional hearings one official stated that under WIN "welfare recipients are made to serve as maids or to do day yard work in white homes to keep their checks. During the cotton-picking season no one is accepted on welfare because plantations need cheap labor to do cotton-picking behind the cotton-picking machines" (Quadagno 1994, 128).

When in 1969 Nixon presented his FAP, the plan elicited applause from supporters, who called it the most important legislation since FDR's New Deal, as well as accusations from detractors, who called the legislation antipoor and anti-black. FAP would guarantee a minimum federal income of $1,600 per year for a family of four. The bill was intended to help both the working and nonworking poor by allowing families to keep up to $60 per month of their income without losing benefits. Noteworthy is that FAP would help poor families in the south, whose benefits would increase under FAP.* Critics of the proposal, particularly those in the NWRO, pointed out that the guaranteed minimum was still far below the level determined necessary to support a family of four. The 1969 poverty line for a family of four was $3,743 per year as determined by the Social Security Administration or $6,960 if referring to statistics put out by the Bureau of Labor Statistics—well above FAP's proposed annual income (G. Fisher, 1992; Patterson 2000, 155). FAP opponents, especially welfare rights activists, also criticized the bill's workfare aspects, which to them called to the surface the ways that economic exploitation was imbricated with race and gender oppression. That is labor imperatives that relied on black women as a source of cheap labor stood in contradiction to assumptions of ideal motherhood that stipulated women with young children stay home to care for them. Thus poor black women faced a double bind: If they adhered to the role of good mother, they were labeled lazy; if they demonstrated the proper work ethic, they were labeled bad mothers.

---

* See Patterson (2000) and Quadagno (1994) for fuller discussion of the legislation and its positive and negative repercussions.

It is worth noting that stereotypes of the "welfare chiseler" and the "welfare queen" have gained prominence at key historical moments in order to justify draconian policies such as cutbacks on cash assistance and implementation of forced-work requirements (Albelda et al. 1996; Collins 1991; Gans 1995; Hancock 2004; Zucchino 1997). Piven (2002) notes that welfare program rollbacks go hand-in-hand with other big business tactics such as union busting and downsizing, all of which are manifestations of a "class politics" in which businesses are using "public policy to shore up private profits" (30). Late twentieth- and early twenty-first-century economic and political developments point to the ways that poverty and economic growth are related. For instance "worker productivity has increased dramatically since . . . 2001, but wages and job growth have lagged behind. At the same time, the share of national income going to corporate profits has dwarfed the amount going to wages and salaries" (Pugh 2007). Race and gender factor keenly into this picture of poverty in that nearly two-thirds of the severely poor are female and blacks make up a disproportionate share of the poor.

Furthermore at a time when social programs remain vulnerable to further cuts, increasing numbers of families are falling into poverty and are likely to rely on public assistance (Pugh 2007). And insofar as welfare benefits, past and present, are linked to work performed outside the home, recipients are forced to accept any job regardless of how dangerous, menial, degrading, or low paying. Thus as Abramovitz (2002) points out, "Both the welfare poor and the working poor must deal with issues that arise for them as workers, caretakers, and welfare state beneficiaries" (176).

The accumulation of corporate profits at the expense of workers' well-being is justified in part by blaming or scapegoating poor people, especially poor black women, through stereotypes that personalize poverty and divert attention from entrenched economic and political structures that profoundly influence employment opportunities and quality of life in the home. Even into the 1990s the image of the "welfare queen" was palpable in congressional debates over the Personal Responsibility and Work Opportunity Reconciliation Act, eventually signed by then-president Bill Clinton in 1996 (Hancock 2004, 89). It is not surprising then that while labels hold discursive sway and can impact people's lives in material ways, they are not always—sometimes not nearly—accurate in the sense that they do not concord with the reality of the situation, object, person, or group at hand. In the late 1960s and early 1970s and again in the 1990s, widespread misconceptions and stereotypes of the poor served as a popular backdrop for political debates and publicized discussions of welfare (Neubeck and Cazenave 2001).

At the heart of welfare debates then were the related issues of women's roles in the marketplace and in the home. Black women in particular occupied a tenuous position at the intersection between capital and care. The complex relationships among care work, marketplace labor, and women's roles therein remain important issues in the context of contemporary global capitalism and will be taken up in the conclusion of the book.

Black women's activism during the building of the welfare state has a long history, only some of which will be recounted here. I wish to highlight a few themes in the efforts of the early to mid-1900s that are sustained in the activism of 1960s welfare righters. In the late nineteenth and early twentieth centuries, black women's exclusion from white women's clubs and associations led them to form their own associations, such as Mary Church Terrell's National Association of Colored Women and the National Council of Negro Women, founded by Mary McLeod Bethune (White 1999). In their own efforts, black women foregrounded the need to address the ways that race, gender, and economic exploitation worked together to keep black women in impoverished conditions. Describing early 1900s welfare activism, Gordon (1995) points out, "Black reformers could not separate welfare from civil rights agitation, any more than they could separate the defense of black womanhood from the defense of the 'race.' Race issues were poverty issues, and women's issues were race issues" (132).

Like white middle-class reformers of the period, black women often took a maternalist approach to address various social issues (Gordon 1995, 126). However their brand of maternalism differed from that of their white counterparts in a number of ways. First black welfare activists were more open to mothers' employment outside of the home—indeed such work was quite often a necessity within the black family. Thus these women put effort into establishing day nurseries and kindergartens for their children, and they argued for better wages and working conditions (Boris 1993, 225; Gordon 1995, 136–37). Activist Sadie Alexander "criticized the view that domesticity should be a married woman's ideal. She saw that in an industrial society the work of the housewife would be increasingly seen as 'valueless consumption' and that women should 'place themselves again among the producers of the world'" (Gordon 1995, 137). With widespread acceptance of women's paid work outside the home came an emphasis on education. Black welfare activists viewed education as an antipoverty program that would help poor black women and men alike.

While black welfare activists worked to ensure that black women were treated fairly in the workplace, they also argued for black women's right to choose domesticity.* Their claims to ideal womanhood can be seen as a counterhegemonic stance that challenged the racist construction of "woman" and "mother" (Boris 1993, 217). Black women who had always been expected to toil in the fields or work as domestics for white families were denied the choice to stay home to care for their own children. When race is considered, it becomes apparent how the "institution of motherhood" is "molded" "to serve the interests of elites." In

---

* It is significant that the two departments in the National Association of Colored Women were "Mother, Home, Child" and "Negro Women in Industry."

contrast black women have struggled to "retain power over motherhood so that it serves the legitimate needs of their communities" (Collins 1994, 52–53).

Indeed the issue of self-definition has framed black women's struggles to control their lives as mothers and as paid workers. Patricia Hill Collins (1991) explains, "Black women's lives are a series of negotiations that aim to reconcile the contradictions separating our own internally defined images of self as African-American women with our objectification as the Other" (94). Thus black women's acts of countering stereotypes and asserting their own standpoints is a central theme throughout decades of speaking out, from the writings of Maria Stewart in the 1800s to the testimony of 1960s welfare activists. In particular Gordon (1995) notes, "Resistance to sexual slander lay at the heart of the black women's welfare vision" (130). Black women's vulnerability to sexual assault and the image of the jezebel that justified such exploitation led black activists to devote considerable energy to upending the image of the immoral black woman (Collins 1991; Gordon 1995, 130). And by emphasizing their morality, activists fashioned black women as morally fit, deserving mothers. Still by emphasizing their status as mothers, black women did not eschew their roles as paid workers. "Black women had incorporated both traditional (homemaking) and nontraditional (paid employment) roles into their personal ideologies of work, without needing to identify themselves exclusively in terms of either one role or the other the way white wives often did" (J. Jones 1985, 305). They at once legitimized their positions as (potential or actual) wage earners deserving of meaningful and well paying jobs and affirmed their place in the home as capable mothers who deserved state assistance to help them raise their children. Theirs were fitting responses to a system that placed them in an untenable position requiring them to fulfill the needs of capital both in and outside of the home.

The civil rights movement of the mid-1950s and 1960s represented a continuation of the struggles forged by women in the first part of the twentieth century. Black women played pivotal roles in civil rights organizations such as the Student Nonviolent Coordinating Committee (SNCC), where women canvassed door-to-door and attended meetings at a much higher rate than men (J. Jones 1985; Payne 1995, 266; Robnett 1997). Their courage was unparalleled. Organizers in the Mississippi Delta faced beatings, electric cattle prods, and jail time for taking part in demonstrations (Payne 1995, 270). Jo Ann Gibson Robinson—largely obscured by history until the publication of her memoir in 1987—epitomized such bravery as she and other women in the Women's Political Council of Montgomery laid the foundation for the Montgomery bus boycott of 1955–1956 as early as 1949. Hundreds of domestic and service workers sustained the 381-day boycott, which resulted in a Supreme Court ruling that outlawed segregation on busses. Despite their role as the backbone of the southern civil rights movement, many of these women have been all but lost to history. Civil rights activism is commonly reduced to "stirring speeches—given by men—and dramatic demonstrations—led by men" (Payne 1995, 276). The indispensable organizational work performed by women such as Fannie Lou Hamer, Ella Baker, Lula Belle Johnson, Laura McGhee, Susie Morgan, and Ethel Gray is often devalued or rendered invisible much like traditional women's work within the home.

In the midst of civil rights activism rose the voice of Black Power, a phrase coined by SNCC activist Stokely Carmichael at a 1966 rally (Joseph 2006). The Black Panther Party (BPP) and Malcolm X embodied the Black Power movement, which advocated direct confrontational protest tactics even as it worked for "bread-and-butter issues that impacted the everyday lives of all Americans" (Joseph 2010, 161). Not part of most historical accounts, black women such as Gloria Richardson, who were "provoked to act" by the "urgency of harsh daily realities," enacted black militancy toward the goals of economic and political equality years before Black Power became part of the national lexicon (R. Williams 2006, 83). Black women formed their own groups such as the Third World Women's Alliance (TWWA), the Black Women's Caucus of SNCC, and the Combahee River Collective, which spoke to their unique position at the intersection of race and sex discrimination (Springer 2006; Ward 2006). Contemporary black feminists Gloria Hull, Patricia Bell, and Barbara Smith captured black women's position in the title of their 1982 book *All the Women Are White, All the Blacks Are Men, but Some of Us Are Brave.*

It is interesting that black women activists served as role models for white women attracted to civil rights activism in the mid-1960s (Echols 1989, 27). Yet despite their involvement in groups such as SNCC and SDS, white women were dissatisfied by the sexism they experienced at the hands of male leaders such as SNCC's Stokely Carmichael, who sardonically asserted that women's place within the movement was on their backs (Echols 1989, 31). Incensed by their marginalization, white women refueled a women's movement that had seen little action since the early 1900s. For their part black women saw little relevance in a women's movement that centered on the right to work outside the home, since black women had always labored outside the home. When it came to diversifying the movement, white women's "attempts at outreach too often remained token in nature" (Echols 1989, 291).

History has been slower to recognize the coordinated efforts of poor, black, single mothers on welfare who organized on their own behalf throughout the 1960s, taking pages from civil rights activism while propelling Black Power activism into the early 1970s. Although SNCC and SDS turned attention to organizing around welfare issues (Echols 1989, 28; Jackson and Johnson 1974, 17), there is ample evidence to suggest that it was the firsthand experiences and acumen of poor mothers themselves that motivated them to organize local welfare rights organizations (WROs) at least five years prior to the formal founding of the National Welfare Rights Organization (NWRO). Welfare recipients were fed up with the disrespect and discrimination they experienced at the hands of welfare administrators, and they were tired of seeing their children go without basic necessities day after day. Johnnie Tillmon, who would later become the first chairperson of the NWRO, formed Aid to Needy Children (ANC)–Mothers Anonymous in Watts, California, in 1963. Tillmon was much like the other women who participated in local WROs. She had worked for years in a laundry but was forced to quit due to health problems. She struggled to support her children on paltry AFDC payments. Tillmon was not an experienced organizer or speaker when she formed ANC–Mothers Anonymous, but that did not stop her from appealing to other mothers to join her in confronting welfare officials head-on to secure the rights guaranteed to them by law.

From ANC–Mothers Anonymous in Watts to Mothers for Adequate Welfare in Boston, local WROs across the country staged sits-ins and mass demonstrations in the first part of the 1960s (J. Jones 1985; Kornbluh 2007; Nadasen 2005). Time and again in describing what motivated them to act during this period, women emphasized the ways anger stemming from their daily experiences (for example entire families living in one-room apartments, children without adequate clothes for school, and so on) prompted them to hone a critical consciousness, or as Archer (2000) says, to transform the "Me" to "I." In addition close proximity to other women enabled them to talk with one another—in kitchens, church, or other neighborhood gathering places—and to develop an awareness of the collective nature of their experiences—to transform the "I" to "We." * Events in the summer of 1966 catapulted welfare rights efforts into a national movement. Welfare rights organizations across the country organized local actions in coordination with the Ohio Steering Committee for Adequate Welfare's planned Walk for Decent Welfare in June 1966. On June 20, 1966, one hundred supporters, including welfare mothers and their children, ministers, and members of SDS began the 155-mile walk from Cleveland to Columbus. Forty of them arrived in Columbus ten days later and were met by over two thousand others who joined in the protest for fair welfare. Thousands more recipients turned out in protests staged in cities coast to coast.

WROs continued to press administrators through the use of creative tactics. Women in New York staged a sit-in at the welfare department; Cleveland women organized a buy-in at a local department store where recipients shopped for goods for their children then informed cashiers to charge the bill to the welfare department; and in Baltimore women held a cook-in in which they prepared a welfare-budget-style meal for the mayor (Piven and Cloward 1967). These events marked the "birth of a movement," according to Columbia University professors Frances Fox Piven and Richard Cloward, two middle-class allies who were described as "instrumental in the organization of the national movement for welfare rights" (West 1981, 24). Cloward and Piven (1966) drafted a position paper,

* See Nadasen 2005, 27, and J. Jones 1985, 2.

"The Weight of the Poor: A Strategy to End Poverty," that centered on creating a crisis within the welfare system thus forcing it to collapse. In their subsequent book, *Poor People's Movements* (Piven and Cloward 1979), they describe the two-pronged approach to their plan. First large-scale efforts would go toward getting millions of eligible families on the welfare rolls, thus addressing immediate needs for aid. Second the resulting expansion in relief would "set off fiscal and political crises in the cities, the reverberations of which might lead national political leaders to federalize the relief system and establish a national minimum income standard" (276). Social science scholars and activists alike took Piven and Cloward's proposed strategies (1966, 1971, 1979) to task for the emphasis on the efficacy of disruptive protest (Albritton 1979; see Piven and Cloward, 1979; West 1981). Contrary to their contemporaries, Piven and Cloward (1979) invested less hope in poor people's organizing efforts due to their limited resources and political influence, instead stressing the power poor people could wield through direct "disruption of the welfare system itself" (281–94, 285).

Welfare rights activists, including Piven and Cloward, found an ally in George Wiley, a Syracuse University chemistry professor, national director of the Congress on Racial Equality (CORE), and leader of the Poverty/Rights Action Center, who was attracted to the idea of building a poor people's movement. With recipients active in the actions of summer 1966, Wiley organized the first national welfare rights meeting in order to establish a foundation for the formation of a national organization. In a workshop held at the August 1966 meeting, recipient attendees established four goals: (1) adequate income "to live dignified lives as American citizens, above the level of poverty," (2) dignity—"the same full freedoms, respect, and . . . rights as all American citizens," (3) justice—a system "that guarantees an adequate income to all persons in need, through a fair . . . impartial process," (4) democratic participation "of recipients in the policy decisions under which they must live" ("The Report of Workshop 2"). To put it simply, activists demanded jobs, adequate income to raise their children, and a voice in the policies that affected their lives. In December 1966 the Poverty/Rights Action Center held a Washington Welfare Recipients Training Conference. The daylong event included workshops as well as a discussion entitled "Tell It Like It Is." The claim to epistemological advantage implied in the title as well as the themes emphasized throughout these two meetings resounded in welfare activists' public discourse from the early 1960s forward.* The NWRO held its first national convention August 25 to 28, 1967, in Washington, D.C. By this date there were over five thousand dues-paying members and over one hundred affiliated

---

* Exhortations to "tell 'em where it's at," "tell it like it is," and "give it to 'em straight" abound in welfare rights activists' discourse. The official newspaper of New York's City-Wide Coordinating Committee was *Tell It Like It Is.*

local groups (*NOW!* newsletter 1968).* Over the following two years, the organization grew steadily, with paid membership reaching 22,500 to 24,500 by 1969. The race and sex composition of the elected officials reflected the organization's commitment to maximum feasible participation by the poor. AFDC recipients, most of whom were black, occupied leadership positions at the local, state, and national levels. Johnnie Tillmon—the Watts mother who organized ANC–Mothers Anonymous—became the national organization's chairperson. In contrast to the formally elected leaders, the NWRO's staff was not composed of welfare recipients; most were middle-class white males. The staff ran the daily affairs out of the national office in Washington, D.C., and assisted in organizing local affiliates. Not unlike other social movements of the twentieth century, the NWRO experienced tension between middle-class allies and the welfare recipients who formed the heart of the organization. West (1981) notes that "dominance by the nonpoor, in a movement that called for empowerment of the poor . . . became one of the weakest links in the coalitions and cooperative efforts between different groups within NWRO" (77).

Studying the publicly engaged struggles of poor black mothers who were welfare recipients contributes to the ongoing discussion of the relationships among economy, state, politics, and social struggle. Through both rhetoric and direct actions, women confronted the state as it touched their lives through welfare policy. They called attention to the ways that social policies affected their lives as workers in the economic sphere of paid labor, as they were forced to accept low-paying, primarily domestic jobs, and in their homes, where their personal lives were monitored and controlled by caseworkers. The following chapters explore how these activists cultivated a collective agency that linked welfare policy to the economy. Their efforts suggest the continued relevance of class relations in shaping the lives of ordinary people, and they point to the ways that modern capitalist relations of exploitation impact the economy, state, public, and domestic spheres.

* *NOW!* is the title of the NWRO official newspaper that predated the *Welfare Fighter.* It does not refer to the National Organization for Women.

The Relevance of Reality

They always find some people who have expertise about
poverty but who aren't poor. Well, I ask you, if you're not
poor, how can you really know anything about poverty?
Lola Sanford, member Milwaukee County WRO, 1972

The story of women's struggles for welfare rights engages issues of representation
and by extension epistemological questions regarding truth and reality. The following chapters explore how a group of women—marginalized by their sex, race,
and economic standing—represented themselves publicly in opposition to prevailing stereotypes that shaped public policy decisions affecting their personal
and work experiences.

Tell It Like It Is intervenes in theoretical debates over agency and draws on insights from social movement studies and feminism in order to explore how welfare rights activists made claims to knowledge in public settings. In this chapter
I establish the theoretical assumptions underlying the analysis of welfare rights
rhetoric in chapters 2 through 5. I specifically argue for the explanatory power
of historical materialism as scholars continue to study modes of oppression and
possibilities for rhetorical intervention. Historical materialism, on my view, enables scholars to affirm the human capacity to alter oppressive circumstances
without subscribing to a naïve account of subjectivity that ignores discursive and
structural constraints on the actor. This chapter also introduces a conceptualization of agency as dialectical, a process cultivated through development of critical awareness, encouraged by the collectivization of firsthand experiences, and
mobilized through public expression. Each phase of agency development is then
explored in subsequent chapters.

Historical Materialism and Standpoint

Lola Sanford of the Milwaukee County WRO, whose words opened this chapter,
expressed with no small degree of frustration the ways her daily experiences provided her (and others on welfare) a keener insight on the material conditions of

poverty than that afforded to those with no firsthand experience with economic struggles.* Indeed recipients' repeated claims to "tell it like we have lived it" and "tell 'em [politicians] where it's at" suggest vital relationships among experience, consciousness, and rhetoric that deserve closer scrutiny. Historical materialism, the theoretical framework that undergirds this study, provides a necessary foundation for understanding the ways individuals living in specific economic conditions come to an awareness of their position vis-à-vis economic structures and political systems, articulate the collective nature of their oppressive conditions, and act to alter them. Marx and Engels's (1846) concept of historical materialism posits a dialectical relationship between experience and consciousness: "Circumstances make men just as much as men make circumstances" (59). The material conditions of society shape, delimit, and motivate discourse (both hegemonic and counterhegemonic) and action. This study is also guided by the understanding that race and gender shape the way that economic standing—poverty, employment, and unemployment—is experienced.

The process of "intersectionality" (Collins 1998)—or the ways that class is contoured by sex and race—may be seen in the history of welfare legislation, which has been shaped with an eye toward sustaining the interests of business and has impacted poor black women in unique ways, as detailed in the previous chapter. Engels's observation made in 1890 resonates here: "We make our history ourselves, but, in the first place, under very definite assumptions and conditions" (761). Corporate capitalism and the welfare state limited poor women's ability to earn a decent living and care for their children. And yet those same circumstances also gave rise to anger and frustration often leading recipients to form local welfare rights groups and articulate their demands in public settings. Rhetorical efforts—for example conversations among fellow recipients, participation in local welfare rights groups, and attendance at welfare rights marches and rallies—mediated the relationship between experience and consciousness and often motivated recipients to shape their own histories by confronting and at times successfully altering a racist welfare system.

As a framework for understanding social movements, historical materialism recognizes the human capacity to transform the world while steadying our focus on real structures that both constrain and motivate human action. Contradictions between recipients' lived experiences and prevailing ideologies purporting to describe those experiences often fostered the development of a critical consciousness, which was then publicly articulated in the form of arguments warranted by what I term *reality referencing*. Reality referencing is both a strategy

---

* Sanford's sentiments are quoted in *Welfare Mothers Speak Out,* a collection of essays written by women in the Milwaukee County Welfare Rights Organization (Tarantino and Becker 1972, 94).

and an epistemological stance that calls up the interplay among experience, consciousness, and rhetorical invention. Reality referencing foregrounds the ways that actually existing life conditions influence communication and struggles for social change and vice versa.

As a strategy reality referencing lent authority to activists' arguments as they pointed to daily experiences shaped by economic structures and political systems (for example hungry children, inadequate heating, substandard housing) that existed in contradistinction to and despite prevailing racist narratives that painted a quite different picture (such as the myth that welfare mothers lived high on the hog off of public assistance). Reality referencing, described later in the chapter, sheds light on the process by which marginalized groups warranted their public claims to knowing what life on welfare was really like: They sought to "tell it like it is."

In addition reality referencing calls up the connectedness between firsthand experience and common understandings of oppression and resistance as explained by both feminist and Marxist scholars. Nearly forty years ago the communication scholar Karlyn Kohrs Campbell spotlighted the role of women's experiences in their development of a feminist consciousness and a "feminine style" of speaking. Campbell (1973) explains that women's liberation rhetoric moves "from personal experience and feeling to illuminate a common condition that all women experience and share" (81). Specifically through participation in consciousness-raising groups, women realize personal experience as political, as shared experience arising out of a patriarchal system that determines unequal gender relationships. Likewise an emphasis on personal experience and anecdotes characterizes a feminine style of speaking often used by women as they create identification and empower their sisters to act on their own behalves.

Scholars in Marxist studies, communication studies, and across disciplines have used the term *standpoint* to explain the role of experience—particularly as shaped by class, race, sex, sexual identity, ethnicity—in influencing worldviews and motivating action. Georg Lukács's explanation of standpoint derives from a Marxist understanding of the relationship between proletariat and bourgeoisie. He explains that although the "objective situation" facing both worker and capitalist is the same, "the 'vantage point from which it is judged' has altered, only 'the value placed on it' has acquired a different emphasis" (1968, 150). Consciousness of one's surroundings—and thus the way one judges or values those surroundings—differs "thanks to the different position [that is standpoint] occupied by the two classes within the 'same' economic process" (150).

For feminists standpoint theory has been at the center of fundamental debates concerning the shape of and possibilities for feminist politics. Viewed as the originator of feminist standpoint theory, Nancy Hartsock (1983a, 1983b) draws on the work of Lukács and Marx to define the term as a "specific kind of epistemological device" derived from "'sensuous human activity'" or the "striving . . .

to meet physical needs" first and foremost (Hartsock 1983b, 118–19).* To be more specific, standpoint theory is based on the premises that "material life . . . not only structures but sets limits on the understanding of social relations" (232). One's position in relation to the production and distribution of necessary resources influences one's access to those resources and in turn shapes one's interests in either maintaining or challenging the current socioeconomic structure.

Standpoint theory therefore calls forth the intimate connection between knowledge and power. Echoing Lukács, Hartsock (1983b) states, "If material life is structured in fundamentally opposing ways for two different groups, one can expect that the vision of each will represent an inversion of the other, and in systems of domination the vision available to the rulers will be both partial and perverse" (232). Sandra Harding (1993) similarly points out that "one's social situation enables and sets limits on what one can know; some social situations— critically unexamined dominant ones—are more limiting than others . . . and what makes these situations more limiting is their inability to generate the most critical questions about received belief" (54–55). Thus although standpoint theory sees knowledge as perspectival, it does not view all perspectives as equally valid. The perspectives derived through firsthand experience with oppression lend greater critical insight—or provide what Alcoff (2006) refers to as "epistemic advantage" (96)—regarding social relations and systems that perpetuate domination and human suffering. Julia Wood (1992) explains that researchers "who operate from a standpoint posture begin by discovering the conditions that structure and establish limits on any particular person or group of people" then explore how individuals come together to confront or alter those conditions (15).

It is important to note that standpoint—or critical consciousness of one's circumstances—is not ready-made but rather is a reflective process. In her recent work on "visible identities" such as race and gender, Linda Alcoff (2006) draws on the literature of hermeneutics to shed light on the relationship between experience and interpretation of the world, what she refers to as "situated reasoning" (94). Alcoff explains that when individuals begin to reflect on their surroundings—what Engels (1890) refers to as the "assumptions and conditions" of life— their world becomes meaningful; it becomes what Hans-Georg Gadamer refers to as the "life-world" as opposed to the "world of bare existents" (qtd. in Alcoff 2006, 95). The "very process of trying to reach an understanding of something brings to the forefront one's personal experience, from which one draws in order to make sense of the thing" (Gadamer qtd. in Alcoff 2006, 95). Rhetoric plays an essential role in the reflective process as messages—conveyed in conversations with friends and kin, related in consciousness-raising sessions, read in pamphlets, and heard in speeches—raise awareness, confirm one's perceptions, or challenge one to think in a more critical manner.

---

* Hartsock is quoting from Marx's *Theses on Feuerbach.*

It is important to recognize the debated nature of the status or knowability of experience (Jay 1998). The feminist historian Joan W. Scott (1991) finds the use of experience as evidence problematic, claiming it "take[s] as self-evident the identities of those whose experience is being documented and thus naturalize[s] their difference" (777). For Scott the use of experience as the "origin of knowledge" obscures the "constructed nature of experience," and leaves aside issues of "how one's vision is structured" (777).

Alcoff usefully describes experience as a "constitutive feature" of our interpretations of the world, yet not "all-determining" (Alcoff 2006, 96). Our ability to critically reflect upon our circumstances "is always and necessarily partial" (96; see also Butler 2005, 84). Humans hold the capacity for critical reason and doubt, as when we sense a contradiction between "our actual beliefs and beliefs that we have had proposed to us" (Alcoff 2006, 96). Yet we cannot "stand completely outside of all traditions. . . . Our ability to negate, and even to reflect on and identify, aspects of the traditions within which we stand is always and necessarily partial" (96). As Julia Wood (2005) explains, the adoption of a standpoint is a politicized process that occurs when individuals gain an ability to critically reflect on their position within society. Likewise language is not a mechanism that reflects reality as a mirror does. To theorize the interplay among experience, consciousness, and rhetoric requires opening ourselves to the ways that actually existing life conditions influence communication and struggles for social change and vice versa.

Work among standpoint theorists has been diverse, with studies focusing on the impact of standpoint on reception of cultural texts (Droogsma 2007; Harris and Donmoyer 2000; Kinefuchi and Orbe 2008;) and production of cultural texts (Ellingson 2000); while others have grappled with the "commonality-diversity" problematic—recognizing differences among women even as they speak of a common women's experience (Bell et al. 2000; Dougherty and Krone 2000; Hallstein 2000; Harding 1991; J. Wood 1992). Black feminists have challenged tendencies toward reducing the female experience to a white experience highlighting black women's unique position as "outsider-within" (Collins 1986, 1991; hooks 1984,1989). As she relates her experiences as a black girl growing up in a southern town segregated by train tracks, bell hooks (1984) explains the outsider-within status. She and her family could cross the tracks to work; they could "enter that world" of white prosperity but could "not live there," she explains. "We had always to return to the margin, to cross the tracks, to shacks and abandoned houses on the edge of town" (ii). And yet such experiences provided a unique perspective. "We looked both from the outside in and from the inside out. . . . This sense of wholeness, impressed upon our consciousness by the structure of our daily lives, provided us an oppositional world view"—a view marked by both race and class (ii).

Collins (1986) explains how black women's outsider-within position "has provided a special standpoint on self, family, and society for Afro-American women" (S14; see also 1991). A black feminist standpoint emphasizes self-valuation and self-definition; calls attention to the interlocking nature of race, gender, and class oppression; and highlights black women's culture. In her book *Fighting Words* (1998), Collins suggests an intersectional approach that reveals the complexity of the interlocking axes of race, class, and gender oppression. Yet Collins does not advocate a total decontextualization of black women's experiences that would erase the ways that black women as a group are discriminated against systematically. For Collins intersectionality "operates as a new lens that potentially deepens understanding of how the actual mechanisms of institutional power can change dramatically even while they reproduce long-standing group inequalities of race, class, and gender" (1998, 206).

The present study of welfare rights activism aligns with the insights of scholars whose views on "standpoint" are more comfortably housed within a Marxist theoretical framework (Cloud 2006; Hartsock 1983a, 1983b; Lukács 1968). In order to understand welfare rights activism, a historical materialist framework must grapple with the ways that "visible identities" (Alcoff 2006) such as race and sex complicate women's relationship to the labor process. As explained earlier, poor black women occupied a unique position within the capitalist welfare state, which constrained them as mothers, workers, and clients, often in incompatible ways (for example to be a "good" worker necessarily required one to ignore her presumed duties of "mother" and vice versa; to be a "good" client necessitated docility or restraint in situations that may have benefited from militancy in demanding free school lunches and the like).

It is important to note that a historical materialist understanding of standpoint emphasizes how one is positioned in relation to the economic system and how one's location vis-à-vis access to necessary resources impacts the perspectives, values, and so on of both dominant and subordinate groups. Dominant ideologies hold hegemonic sway to the extent that they strongly influence the economic, political, and cultural conditions under which all groups live (Collins 1991, 26; Hartsock 1983b, 232). Thus for oppressed groups to express their (counterhegemonic) viewpoints in a public forum can be a challenge since a good deal of work goes into the suppressing of such perspectives. But much is at stake in such expressions since the potential for collective resistance is tied to one's ability to represent one's self and define one's needs. What we need is an examination of how oppressed groups *engage a collective agency* that challenges class, race, and sex oppression since, as Hartsock notes, such expressions carry "a historically liberatory role" (1983b, 232; see also Collins 1991, 28).

Debating Agency

Debates over agency grapple with the tension between the notion of the autonomous actor and the recognition of external structures that constrain actors—what Aune (1994) describes as the complex relationship between "subjective agencies and objective structures" (143). The course of thought in this area envelops the ideas of thinkers from Marx to Derrida and Foucault. In this section I provide a brief overview of the work of scholars in communication, feminism, and cultural studies who have addressed the status of the subject and the possibilities of agency. Their theories are variously underpinned by poststructuralism, postmodernism, and various strains of humanism. My aim in providing this theoretical trajectory is to further demonstrate the explanatory power of historical materialism for feminist critical studies and practice and for understanding the role of communication in attempts at social change.

In reaction to the Enlightenment's rational human who acts consciously upon his or her free will, poststructuralist and postmodernist scholars emphasize the influence of discourse in constructing contingent subject positions.* In *The Archeology of Knowledge,* Foucault (1972) explains, "Discourse is not the majestically unfolding manifestation of a thinking, knowing, speaking subject, but, on the contrary, a totality, in which the dispersion of the subject and his discontinuity with himself may be determined" (55). The deconstructionist theorist Jacques Derrida explains the ever-changing, always-in-process self as a result of a "play of differences." For Derrida there is no self, no identifiable referent. He explains, "No element can function as a sign without relating to another element which itself is not simply present. This linkage means that each 'element'... is constituted with reference to the trace in it of the other elements of the sequence or system. This linkage ... is the *text,* which is produced only through the transformation of another text. Nothing, either in the elements or in the system, is anywhere simply present or absent. There are only, everywhere, differences and traces of traces" (qtd. in Culler 1982, 99).

The French theorist of the "postmodern condition" Lyotard asserts that a "*self* does not amount to much;" but rather should be understood as "located at 'nodal points' of specific communication circuits" (1991, 15). According to Lyotard social bonds are constructed through "language games." The feminist scholar Wendy Brown (1995) problematizes the concept of the "postmodern," noting the lack of consensus regarding the "configuration of this condition, its most striking markers, implications, and portents" (30). On Brown's view feminists would be unwise to leave postmodern theory untapped; rather, they should consider "appropriating and navigating for radical political projects [postmodern theory's] peculiar (dis)organization of social, political, and economic life" (31).

Summarizing a feminist adaptation of Foucaultian thought, Biesecker (1992) has written, "Given that subjects emerge at the heterogeneous intersection of *multiple* and, presumably incompatible, interpellations—race, gender, and class—they

---

* Jean-François Lyotard's well-known tract *The Postmodern Condition,* first published in 1979, provided a reference point for studies positing the postmodern "incredulity toward metanarratives" (1991, xxiv).

cannot be made to cohere as Subjects. Hence, by reading the subject itself as a site of multiple and contestatory inscriptions, one can . . . locate a reservoir of revolutionary potential in the gaps, fissures and slippages of the nonidentical 'I'" (152).

Within the field of communication studies, scholars have theorized agency with attention to postmodernist challenges to the Enlightenment's subject who acts freely and self-consciously. Gaonkar (1997) argues against the "ideology of human agency" implicit in traditional understandings of rhetoric, which embraces "a view of speaker as the seat of origin rather than a point of articulation, a view of strategy as identifiable under an intentional description, a view of discourse as constitutive of character and community, a view of audience positioned simultaneously as 'spectator' and 'participant,' and finally a view of 'ends' that binds speaker, strategy, discourse, and audience in a web of purposive actions" (32, 33). Drawing on the work of Derrida, Lacan, and Foucault, Lundberg and Gunn (2005) suggest refiguring "agent" and "agency" to "subject" and "effect" so as to avoid "reducing agency to the self-transparent human agent" that "possesses" agency (88). Geisler (2005) turns attention to teaching concerns in the context of the contemporary postmodern rhetor. Recognizing the nonexistence of an autonomous agent who knowingly affects her world, Geisler suggests intervention at the points of rhetorical engagement and participation (112).

On the postmodernist/poststructuralist view, options for agents—who are dispersed and discursively constructed—come down to ad hoc or localized actions, what Foucault (1978) describes as a "plurality of resistances" that are "distributed in irregular fashion" (96). Biesecker (1992) refers to a kind of "'getting through' or ad hoc 'making do' by a subject whose resources are necessarily located in and circumscribed by the field within which she operates" (155). Borrowing the term *techne* from classical rhetoric, Biesecker retools the concept to mean a "bringing-about in the doing-of on the part of an agent that does not necessarily take herself to be anything like a subject of historical or . . . cultural change" (156). Hardt and Negri (2000) conceptualize agency as a type of "nomadism" whereby boundaries established on the basis of nation, race, ethnicity, and so on are transgressed. "Through circulation the common human species is composed, a multicolored Orpheus of infinite power; through circulation the human community is constituted" (362). Drawing on the work of Hardt and Negri, communication scholar Greene (2004) asserts the study of agency "requires the abandonment of the dialectical interface between structure and change" (198). Given the pervasive nature of capital (or "empire" to use Hardt and Negri's terminology), which "gobbl[es] up every domain of social action," (200), Greene refigures agency as "communicative labor," a "form of life-affirming constitutive power that embodies creativity and cooperation" (201). Greene (2006) also suggests a view toward how the "general intellect and communication might achieve escape velocity from their articulation to capitalism and/or the administrative apparatus of the state" (92). Central in all of these accounts is an abandonment of the view that collective, interest-driven resistance against an identifiable set of systems remains viable, indeed paramount to struggles for equality and justice.

In addition to studies that discursify agency or decenter the subject altogether are pieces that valorize the actor's ability to influence her surroundings or create new identities through resistant readings of cultural texts, willpower, or positive thinking. Texts as diverse as television dramas, soap operas, game shows, and romance novels have been examined for "semiotic excess," multiple meanings, or "unresolved contradictions" that allow oppressed groups "to take the signifying practices and products of the dominant, to use them for different social purposes, and to return them from where they came, stripped of their hegemonic power" (Fiske 1986, 406; Fiske 1987, 1989; McRobbie 1994; Radway 1984). Foss, Waters, and Armada (2007) put forward the concept "agentic orientation" to describe a "rhetorical mechanism . . . that provides various options for the enactment of agency" (206). Grounding their study in social constructionism or the idea that people construct reality through symbols, the authors state that the "choice of agentic orientation dictates the outcomes that agents experience in their lives rather than the strength, power, or persistence of material structures" (219).

It is interesting to note that while communication scholars have theorized agency, few of their studies look at how actual people—individually or in groups—affect or act upon their surroundings in the context of socioeconomic constraints.* This lacuna in studies on power and resistance may well be a logical outcome of theories that embody the discursive turn. As Fisher and Davis (1993) point out, "If men and women are discursive constructions, the focus is not on what they are actually doing but rather on how masculinity and femininity are produced and function within a system of signs. Interaction disappears, absorbed in a symbolic order which determines the form in which our thoughts may be expressed" (10). Likewise Hartsock (1990) notes, "Foucault's is a world in which things move, rather than people, a world in which subjects become obliterated or, rather, recreated as passive objects, a world in which passivity or refusal represent the only possible choices. . . . Subject [is] a kind of effect" (167). In short one may argue that the very premises of posthumanist thought lead to a worldview disconnected from the lives of real people. For instance what does Greene's suggestion of achieving "escape velocity" (2006) look like and how might it be enacted? Similar questions might be what are the possibilities and

---

* Notable exceptions include sociological studies anthologized in *Negotiating at the Margins,* edited by Sue Fisher and Kathy Davis. In fieldwork on homelessness, Rob Rosenthal (1993) viewed "homelessness as a process framed by the dialectic between agency and constraints" (207). Rosenthal explains that constraints "limit agency, they shape agency, but they certainly did not preclude agency among the homeless people I came to know" (207).

consequences of Hardt and Negri's "nomadism" (2000) for Palestinians in the Israeli-controlled West Bank and Gaza Strip? For Mexicans hoping to cross the Mexico-Texas border for work in the U.S.? For Muslims living under post–9/11 scrutiny in American cities and suburbs?

In contrast to studies undergirded by poststructuralism or social constructionism are those concerned about the implications of theories that erase the notion of a more or less coherent actor or that valorize the subject without adequate attention to material constraints. As some feminist theorists have asked: "Why is it, just at the moment in Western history when previously silenced populations have begun to speak for themselves and on behalf of their subjectivities, that the concept of the subject and possibility of discovering/creating a liberating 'truth' become suspect?" (Di Stefano 1990, 75; Hartsock 1990). Some note the perils for feminists of adopting a poststructuralist or postmodernist notion of subjectivity based on difference and deconstruction (Alcoff 1988; Hartsock 1990; McRobbie 2009). As Alcoff points out, "If the category 'woman' is fundamentally undecidable, then we can offer no positive conception of it that is immune to deconstruction. . . . If gender is simply a social construct, the need and even the possibility of a feminist politics becomes immediately problematic" (420).

Bordo (1990) refers also to the posthumanist conception of the disconnected self as an "epistemological fantasy of *becoming* multiplicity—the dream of limitless multiple embodiments, allowing one to dance from place to place and self to self" (145). Anticipating Hardt and Negri's notion of the nomadic multitude, Bordo asks, "What sort of body is it that is free to change its shape and location at will, that can become anyone and travel everywhere? If the body is a metaphor for our locatedness in space and time and thus for the finitude of human perception and knowledge, the postmodern body is no body at all" (145).

In response to the posthumanist challenges to agency, some scholars advance theories that emphasize a tension or dialectic between the agent as both influencing and influenced by her environment. Leff (2003) argues that the "humanistic approach entails a productively ambiguous notion of agency that positions the orator both as an individual who leads an audience and as a community member shaped and constrained by the demands of the audience" (135). Villadsen (2008) states that rhetorical agency "focuses on the constellation of individual and structural aspects that in the interaction between the speaking agent and the situational conditions are relevant for rhetorical meaning making and action" (27). Feminists have long debated the ways "women construct their own lives [but] . . . do so within determinant conditions" (Fisher and Davis 1993, 3) with a starting point being the "experience and point of view of the dominated" (Hartsock 1990, 158). Scholars have examined experiences ranging from campus union organizing (Gregg 1993), and dress codes for women (Arthur 1993), to the lives of battered women (Gordon 1988, 1995), concluding that women's resistance is a product "of subjective *and* material positions, discursive *and* socioeconomic realities" (Gregg 1993, 172, 173), and that agency, although not an entirely discursive construction, is nonetheless "malleable" and shaped in part by the particular historical moment.

Still present on the twenty-first-century landscape of "posts," studies grounded more specifically in Marxist historical materialism emphasize the dialectical relationship between a society's economic system and its cultural, legal, and political discourses. Such scholars remain troubled by the political consequences of posthumanist theories that elide the importance of the means of production in shaping lived experience and the potential for shared identity along class lines (Archer 2000; Cloud 2006; Cloud, Macek, and Aune 2006; Triece 2001, 2007; E. Wood 1986). The sociologist Margaret Archer begins her study of human agency noting that we are born into positions that grant us varying degrees of access to scarce resources. "Because of the pre-existence of those structures which shape the situations in which we find ourselves, they impinge upon us without our compliance, consent or complicity. The structures into which we are born and the cultures which we inherit mean that we are involuntarily situated beings" (2000, 262). Archer distinguishes between the "Me," which is the object of society and the "I," which has the capacity to reflect on one's placement in the world vis-à-vis others. She explains that what the "I" reflects on are the "day-to-day manifestations of objective and externally determined life-chances. The most basic of these reflections is an early recognition of constraints and enablements" (264).

Cloud (2006) emphasizes the "capacity to mobilize critical consciousness by invoking contradictions between experience and ideology, and by articulating together people who share a real relationship of class, across their differences, as the basis of political, not just economic, action. The process is dialectical, as contradictions in experience and consciousness create the possibility of contradicting the capitalist system and its rulers" (338). In their critique of "agentic orientation," Gunn and Cloud (2010) suggest "materialist dialectics" as a framework for understanding agency. From this grounding "class position and the experience of exploitation combine to form an epistemological potential in the dialectical contradiction between the lived experience of exploitation and the mystifications of ideology" (71).

Social movement studies provide another vantage point from which to explore agency. Traditional movement studies have been agent-centered, based on the presumption of a more or less self-aware actor who intentionally asserts herself publicly. In his pioneering article "The Rhetoric of Historical Movements," Griffin (1952) centered movement studies on rhetorical components used by people "dissatisfied with some aspect of their environment" and who "make efforts to alter" it (184). Subsequent studies have located the study of protest in its rhetorical strategies (Bowers and Ochs 1971); its use of feminine style (Campbell 1973, 1986); its stages (Griffin 1952; Railsback 1984); its functions (Lake 1983;

Stewart 1980); in terms of its leadership (Simons 1970); and its uses of confrontation or coercion (Haiman 1967; Scott and Smith 1969; Simons 1972), to name just a few.

Other studies (McGee 1980; Condit 1987; Condit and Lucaites 1991) take a decidedly discursive turn in their emphases on meaning formation to the exclusion of agency within a material context. McGee's defining article urges a view of social movements not as phenomena but as a "set of meanings," which point to a theory of "human consciousness" (1980, 125). Drawing on the work of McGee, Condit and Lucaites (1991) examine changes in ideographs and narratives in order to provide a history of "collective consciousness" (1). Condit (1987) studies changes in the public vocabulary surrounding civil rights between 1939 and 1959, noting a "positive re-characterization of Blacks" and "inclusion of Blacks under [the ideographs] <law> and <Constitution>" (14). Condit's study cannot explain however the persistence of Jim Crowism and high unemployment and poverty in black communities, all aspects of a material context that is elided in her discourse-centered study.

Concerned about the erasure of the human subject and the negation of material constraints inherent in the meaning-centered approach, others have drawn on the work of Gramsci and his concept of hegemony as a way to capture the complex relationship between "subjective agencies and objective structures" (Aune 1994, 143; see also Cloud 2005; Gitlin 1980; Lears 1985; Murphy 1992; Triece 2001, 2007). Gramsci developed a "more flexible approach" to the Marxist base and superstructure model, understanding the relationship not as "linear causality but circular interaction within an organic whole" (Lears 1985, 569). His work provides a way to study both dominant and subversive discourses that sustain or challenge prevailing power structures. And it is important that "unlike liberal notions of consensus, Gramsci's vision acknowledges the social and economic constraints on the less powerful, then aims to see the ways that culture collaborates with those constraints" (Lears 1985, 572).

To exemplify, Murphy (1992) examines Kennedy administration responses to and media coverage of the 1961 Freedom Rides to show how dissent was domesticated through rhetorical strategies that placed the rides "in a dominant system of meaning that dismissed them as counterproductive" (67). Other studies examine protest rhetoric for narratives and images that countered hegemonic understandings of worker struggle and exploitation and locate such analyses in a material context thereby pointing to the importance of coercive tactics that go beyond words (Cloud 2005; Triece, 2001, 2007). Studies of workers in the labor movement and women in the housewives' movement in the early part of the twentieth century underscore the importance of strikes, sit-ins, and walkouts, efforts that involved either bodily presence or absence. "To the extent that workers engaged or withdrew their labor power, they forced owners concerned about profits to give in to their demands" (Triece 2007, 37). Likewise, but on a more pessimistic note, Cloud (2005) argues that the lack of pickets and strikes by protesting workers at Staley Manufacturing in 1993 played a role in the workers' defeat. Cloud concludes that the "consequences of speaking loudly but carrying a small stick . . . call our attention to the limits of symbolic agency . . . and thus to questions about the overemphasis on discursive power in organization communication and social movement research" (511).

In the context of posthumanist challenges to subjectivity, the question of agency remains relevant in social movement and feminist studies. How do we "salvage a workable notion of humankind" (Archer 2000, 18) and still acknowledge the impact of discursive and material forces that impact workplace and community well-being, shape identities, and "determine . . . not only what is considered to be 'true,' but also who can speak and with what force" (Campbell 2005, 3)? The analysis in *Tell It Like It Is* is premised on a historical materialist perspective, which draws attention to important economic forces—namely capitalism— motivating both dominant and vernacular voices in welfare policy debates.

A Case for a Dialectical Understanding of Agency

In this study I argue that agency is not a "thing" possessed by individuals; rather it is "situated intervention" (Gunn and Cloud 2010, 72) that emerges in the dialectical struggles between subjectivity and structure (Cloud 2006; Cloud, Macek, and Aune 2006). As a form of engagement shaped by a specific historical moment, I suggest viewing agency as cultivated through a dialectic between "subjective agencies" and "objective structures" (Aune 1994, 143). First of all agency is cultivated through *development of critical awareness* as when we experience a reality gap (a contradiction between lived experiences and prevailing descriptions of those experiences) or when we engage in dialogue with others who persuade us to view our life circumstances in a particular way, for example as the result of particular oppressive forces. Second agency is further encouraged by the *collectivization* of our experiences, that is when individuals gain an understanding of their experiences of oppression and need for resistance as collective. To put it another way, collectivization is the process by which a class in itself is transformed into a class for itself, to paraphrase Marx. And third agency is mobilized through the *public expression*—by rhetoric and bodily actions—of demands for change.

Critical Reflection

Agency first develops when individuals begin to reflect upon and critically examine their life circumstances, particularly from the standpoint, that is taking into consideration material conditions, of the oppressed or marginalized. Recall the earlier discussion regarding the difference between the "Me," the object of society, and the "I," which has the capacity to reflect on one's placement in the world according to hierarchies of class, sex, race, and so on (Archer 2000, 264). In earlier work I used the term "reality gap" (Triece 2007) to home in on the process by which ordinary people come to understand the mechanics of their oppression and formulate a method for challenging that oppression. A reality gap is the space between prevailing, widely accepted ideologies that describe or interpret our experiences and the lives of ordinary people as they are experienced day in and day out. This gap may give rise to "contradictions or paradoxes that . . . provide an opening for social critique and change" (Triece 2007, 2). Another way to put it is that "contradiction is the rhetorical situation for oppositional politics" (Cloud 2006, 339). Direct experience with injustice often led to an "aha" moment for NWRO activists. Other times reflection was prompted by persuasive attempts by movement or organizational leaders who reached out to others in an effort to broaden the movement and draw connections among women's experiences.

Collectivizing Experiences

Next agency develops as individuals realize the connectedness of their experiences, that is as they gain an understanding of their own experiences of oppression and of need for resistance as collective. This awareness can develop in a number of ways. Through organizational newspapers and newsletters, church groups, as well as conversations with neighbors, relatives, and friends, individuals read and hear stories of others in similar situations, and therefore they gain an understanding of the political nature of their personal lives. For example housewives in the 1930s may have been relegated to the domestic sphere, but in conversations at stores and on front stoops, these women developed a political consciousness. In her study of women in Lawrence, Massachusetts, in the late 1800s and early 1900s, Cameron (1993) noted that "anger directed at the greedy landlord, the cheating grocer, or the unjust employer can, in the process of female exchange and mobilization, generate into a coherent attack upon an entire system of exploitation, what one former Lawrence [textile] striker called 'the powers that prey'" (112). And in the spirit of consciousness-raising groups of the early 1970s— the goal of which was to "create awareness that what were thought to be . . . individual problems are common and shared" (Campbell 1973, 79; Campbell 2002)—welfare recipients in a sewing class used their time together to share experiences and forge ties. As one member noted, "That sewing class really was the beginning of Clark County Welfare Rights" (Orleck 2005, 101). In these different cases "a class in itself—complex and composed of diverse persons of varying beliefs"—was transformed "into a class for itself" (Cloud 2006, 338).

Public Engagement

The development of critical consciousness occurs largely in "protected enclaves" (Mansbridge 1996). Activists also engaged themselves publicly in more hostile settings where they spoke out as a group. Collective public expression of one's needs and concerns, particularly contra images and narratives promoted through corporate media and by political and economic elites, provides the means by which marginalized groups direct agency toward the task of social change. Welfare righters (1) established credibility as decision makers, (2) created "presence" as workers and as mothers, (3) negotiated the contradictory positions demanded by capital and care work, and (4) enacted "militant motherhood" through direct actions (Tonn 1996). As I will demonstrate in the following chapters, activists' arguments were warranted by statements denoting "epistemic advantage"— again what I term reality referencing; that is data and claim were linked by the idea that firsthand experience with an event or process or situation gives one a clearer view of that reality.

Reality Referencing and Agency

In proposing the concept of reality referencing, I should elaborate on my choice of the word *reality* since, in the wake of a discursive turn in communication studies influenced in part by postmodernist and posthumanist theorizing, the word has arguably lost much currency (Cloud 1994, 141; Ebert 1996). On the one hand I am not arguing that individuals reference reality directly, since it is widely agreed there is no one-to-one correspondence between language and the things language describes. Furthermore I am not suggesting that reality— however one wishes to conceive it—stands ready to be interpreted in some "correct" or straightforward manner. Rather within the historical materialist framework explained earlier, I emphasize the dialectical relationship between experience and consciousness with rhetoric mediating that relationship. When activists made reference to their daily experiences living on welfare, they were insisting on the superiority of their claims to knowing and were establishing a ground upon which to judge competing claims.

Reality referencing functions much like testimony in that it provides a "sense of autobiographical truth and voice" for poor women and it functions counterhegemonically in public discourses surrounding controversial issues such as welfare policy reform (Avant-Mier and Hasian 2008, 330). Also, like testimony, reality referencing allows for self-representation, which in turn establishes the speaker as an agent capable of enacting change (Beverley 2005).

Yet the term *reality referencing* pointedly calls into question posthumanist doubts of a knowing subject capable of acting upon her surroundings. In the context of a speaking situation in which audience members wielded the power to define the welfare experience and to propose who would received aid, recipients insisted on the superiority of self-representations and firsthand accounts of life on welfare. Recipients' repeated phrases (expressed with overt frustration at times) such as "we are saying it the way we have lived it" and "I am on welfare now and I know what I am writing about" call out the relationship between experience and consciousness. Again this is not to say that recipients' experiences were unmediated or unproblematically reflected in their arguments, but rather to insist that some claims to knowing provide greater insight and are more sound for determining social policy. In other words reality referencing enabled speakers to establish their credibility and give presence to the welfare experience, both of which established the grounds for a "reality test" necessary for assessing knowledge claims and making decisions regarding which claims would hold sway (Cloud 2006, 331; see also Triece 2007, 2).

First welfare rights activists emphasized their credibility as decision makers, a rhetorical move essential for making their counternarratives convincing. Here again reality referencing plays a role since, activists argued, it was their experience with poverty that enabled them to "tell it like it is." By referencing a reality, activists established a basis upon which to compare prevailing conceptions and misconceptions of life on welfare and their own experiences of need, which, they argued, would guide policy formation in a more just way.

Second by referring to their daily lived experiences or the reality they faced day-to-day, activists created "presence" for their experiences as workers. Perelman (1982) explains that "choosing to single out certain things for presentation in a speech draws the attention of the audience to them and thereby gives them a *presence* that prevents them from being neglected" (35). Creating presence is particularly important for speakers who are "evoking realities that are distant in time and space" (35) as was the case when welfare rights activists argued their positions to welfare administrators, middle-class "allies," mayors, representatives, and senators. The strategy of creating presence enables speakers to draw attention to and establish the importance of their issues. On the other hand, without presence, issues may "become abstract, almost nonexistent" (36). Perelman quotes writer Stephen Spender, who aptly explains the importance of creating presence or foregrounding one's reality. Spender notes, "Nearly all human beings have an extremely intermittent grasp on reality. Only a few things, which illustrate their own interests and ideas, are real to them; other things, which are in fact equally real, appear to them as abstractions . . . . Your friends are allies and therefore human beings. . . . Your opponents are just tiresome, unreasonable, unnecessary theses, whose lives are so many false statements which you would like to strike out with a lead bullet" (Spender qtd. in Perelman 36).

Note the assumption in this statement regarding the existence of a reality that does not disappear in the absence of discourse about it. That is language shapes the ways we think about and act upon certain events, issues, or groups. But it does not change the status of something as "in fact equally real." Indeed welfare rights activists saw as one of their most formidable tasks that of making their daily experiences as poor black mothers "real" to the policy makers whose decisions so profoundly affected their lives. Reality referencing challenged stereotypes by premising arguments on the notion that some articulations of reality ring truer than others.

Next welfare rights activists negotiated the double bind they faced as poor black mothers by emphasizing their right to choose between the work of a stay-at-home mother or a decent job outside the home. In the context of white society's control and commodification of black women's bodies, recipients' calls for dignity and self-determination in the home can be viewed as upending the traditional white patriarchal family, which historically represented a site of oppression for black women.

In addition the following chapters explore the ways that agency was enacted on a physical level, that is through the use of bodily presence or absence, as when mothers occupied welfare offices and refused to leave until they received immediate assistance. These actions were significant for the ways they embodied both persuasive and coercive elements. Participants were involved in more than a "controversy" or "difference of opinion"; rather they were engaged in a "genuine conflict" in which "talk between parties" was not enough (Simons 1972). Time and again welfare rights activists expressed frustration upon realizing they gained little ground and often nothing in the way of necessary resources when they employed the usual persuasive means—for example appeals to rights or to emotions—with social workers or welfare department bureaucrats. On many occasions they saw it was imperative to use coercive tactics that were effective at forcing the hand of welfare administrators.

For example in Baton Rouge, Louisiana, welfare rights activists organized other poor people in the area for a direct action on August 10, 1970. One hundred and fifty people occupied the welfare department and made various demands, most of which were met. The report written by one of the activists noted that "persons who had been denied the right even to apply for aid, applied in such numbers that an extra worker had to be assigned to help handle the applications" ("Southern Caravan Success" 1970, 2). Welfare mothers' occupation of a public space was significant for at least two reasons. First the sheer presence enabled them, as a collective, to place pressures on the welfare bureaucracy (for example by filling out applications en masse) in a manner that one person acting alone might not have been able to accomplish. In these instances mothers were drawing on a history of activism in labor and civil rights struggles, in which men and women successfully made use of collective actions such as sit-ins and walk-outs in order to win demands.

Second their actions held symbolic value to the extent that they brought the supposedly personal experience of mothering out of the home and into the public, thus calling attention to ways in which public decisions impacted their personal lives. In short they politicized motherhood. Furthermore their steadfast refusal to leave the office until they received necessary aid underscored their dire situations and thus undermined the stereotype of the welfare queen or the notion that recipients were lazy mothers who were ill-equipped to care for their own children and who relied on public assistance monies to live extravagantly.

The rhetorical strategies and direct actions welfare rights activists engaged in order to create agency were in many respects a response to prevailing myths and stereotypes of welfare recipients that circulated in popular and political discourses during this period. Hegemonic political discourses were themselves shaped in part by economic interests that had a stake in welfare legislation that would potentially impact the availability of a pool of unskilled, cheap labor.

This view of agency as cultivated through awareness, collectivization, and public engagement recognizes that the development and articulation of agency is not always carried through to the point of public engagement. For instance one may critically reflect on her experiences of degradation or want but fail to see a connection between these experiences and a broader socioeconomic system. Or individuals may in fact recognize the collective nature of their experiences but lack the time or motivation to express their concerns publicly. Indeed mobilization of a group of like-minded individuals is perhaps one of the most formidable tasks facing movement leaders. Furthermore to frame agency as a process grounded in a dialectical view of reality and language allows for complexity. The view promoted in this essay concords with Campbell's observation that "authors/rhetors are materially limited, linguistically constrained, historically situated subjects; at the same time, they are 'inventors' in the rhetorical sense" (2005, 5) who hold the capacity for reflection, organization, and action.

The study that follows looks at how individuals (welfare recipients) with similar experiences acted collectively in public spaces in order to confront and change material and political circumstances that impacted their abilitiy to control their lives and raise their children in a humane way. This book also discusses the insights to be gained from locating theoretical accounts of oppression and agency in case studies that I believe can bring us closer to understanding the ways that ordinary people affect the world around them. In Leff's words, we should keep our theory moving "along the broken ground covered by the specific material of the discipline" (1980, 347). Our "theoretical precepts attain meaning only as they are vibrated against the particular case and are instantiated in an explanation of it." This examination of the rhetoric of welfare rights activists contributes to the body of productive research on "vernacular discourses" and the ways that marginalized "others" give voice to their concerns in wider publics governed by dominant interests and worldviews.* Particularly in the context of academic debates

---

* The literature on vernacular discourses is very broad and includes studies with a variety of emphases (Avant-Mier and Hasian 2008; Delgado 1999; Flores and Hasian 1997; Hauser, 2007, 2008; Ono and Sloop 1997; Triece 2001, 2007). In their 1995 article Ono and Sloop study vernacular discourses, or the discourses of disempowered

regarding the status of reality, truth, and claims to truth, the following chapters explore what it means—in a rhetorical and philosophical sense—for subaltern groups to make epistemological claims of knowing. In sum examining the rhetoric and direct actions of welfare rights activists of the late 1960s and early 1970 enables us to examine the ways that marginalized groups shape public discussions, in part by challenging widespread misconceptions and giving presence to their lives as they see and experience them. In addition and not least important, the study provides an entry into debates on the nature of agency within the context of global capitalism. As Villadsen (2008) suggests, we need more studies that examine "rhetorical agency as it is played out in fairly familiar rhetorical forms" (29) so as to contribute to what Leff (1980) refers to as "conceptual thickening" (347) or a deeper understanding of the implications of our theories.

---

groups, as they are constructed from bits and pieces of popular culture. Relevant to my own study is Collins's work on the importance of self-definition for African American women who struggle to counter "controlling images," that is dominant racist images (1991).

2

Critical Reflection and Consciousness Raising

> There's one good thing about welfare. It kills
> your illusions about yourself, and about where this
> society is really at. It's laid out for you straight.
> Tillmon, "Welfare Is a Women's Issue," 1972

In this statement welfare recipient and activist Johnnie Tillmon spoke to the power of firsthand experience in shaping one's perceptions; she spoke to the importance of standpoint. Through struggles with poverty and racism, Tillmon got a "straighter" view of power relations and inequalities. And in their efforts with the welfare rights movement, Tillmon and other recipient-activists sought to "set society straight" when it came to perceptions of women and poverty.

The previous chapter discussed standpoint and the role it plays in the dialectical process by which oppressed groups come to critically interpret and understand their experiences. Standpoint theory sheds light on the rhetoric-reality dynamic by noting that knowledge is perspectival and is derived in part by one's position within economic, political, and cultural systems of power. Furthermore some groups—particularly those in marginalized positions— gain "epistemic advantage" (Alcoff 2006, 96), or a keener insight on oppression through their very experiences of being denied access to necessary resources.

The dialectic between objective structures and discourses about those structures—both hegemonic and counterhegemonic—creates the conditions by which oppressed groups come to a critical understanding of their experiences and potentially act upon them. First when descriptions of events, groups, and so forth found in political and popular discourses do not concord with the perceptions of those who have firsthand experience with such events, groups, and so on, a contradiction or "reality gap" arises, which may prompt critical inquiry as to why prevailing discourses—for example popular explanations of poverty, descriptions of motherhood—do not ring true with one's own experiences. Second the rhetoric of marginalized groups—from daily conversations with neighbors and friends to publicized arguments in the form of pamphlets and speeches—contributes to the shaping of a critical consciousness, particularly when such personal and public messages speak more aptly to or fit better with one's daily experiences.

In their extensive study of social dissent, Piven and Cloward (1979) note that the "emergence of a protest movement entails a transformation both of consciousness and of behavior" (3). This chapter explores how welfare rights activists developed critical awareness and gained a sense of the collective nature of their experiences as poor black women, two processes that catalyzed their public speaking and extradiscursive actions aimed at changing the welfare system. The following pages look at the role that *firsthand experience, reconstitution* and *consciousness raising* played in the development of a critical orientation necessary for public speaking and direct actions aimed at disrupting a racist welfare system.

Hegemonic Images of Poor Black Women

Welfare controversies in the early 1960s—the events in Newburgh, New York, and Senator Byrd's 1962 welfare fraud hearings—spurred public discussions surrounding race, poverty, and public assistance and secured the image of the welfare chiseler in the mind of the general public for decades to come. Stories of welfare scandal were scattered throughout the pages of popular newspapers and magazines (Patterson 2000, 106) and found a ready place in political discourses. During congressional hearings in the 1970s, Senator Russell Long (Democrat from Louisiana) decried welfare cheats, some of whom, according to Long, received as many as ten checks. In perhaps his most infamous statement—that he would not stop fighting welfare until he could find someone to iron his shirts ("The Long and the Shirt of it," Patterson *America's Struggle*)—Long evoked dual images of the employable black woman who, by refusing to work, took advantage of the system. Nixon invoked the image of the welfare chiseler in his 1971 State of the Union address when he asserted that the country must "stop helping those who are able to help themselves but refuse to do so" (227).

Images of the "welfare queen" and the "matriarch," also readily evoked by politicians, offered a specifically gendered take on recipients who allegedly took advantage of the system. These two images tapped into racist narratives of motherhood extending back to slavery, which at one and the same time contrasted the notion of the "deserving" white mother, domestic and pure, with the black mother, employable, promiscuous, and greedy. Echoing the slave-era brute commodification of black women, the early 1960s Louisiana governor Jimmie H. Davis worried about "the existing policy regarding public assistance to unwed mothers who have proved by their past conduct that they engage in the business of illegitimacy in the same way that a cattleman raises beef" (qtd. in Neubeck and Cazenave 2001, 72). A few years later, in similar crude language, Senator Long referred to mothers receiving AFDC as "brood mares" (Steiner 1971, 53).

The 1965 report "The Negro Family: The Case for National Action," written by Daniel Patrick Moynihan, who was at the time a U.S. Labor Department official, secured the image of the matriarch in the public imagination through reference to the dysfunction of "black matriarchy" and the "culture of single motherhood" characteristic of black families (76). The ideological effect of such rhetoric was to uphold traditional definitions of motherhood, work, and the work ethic and by extension to dissuade qualifying low-wage female workers from applying for aid, particularly when the labor market was tight (Neubeck and Cazenave 2001, 108). Schram (2005) explains, the "'black welfare queen' has been constructed out of need for an 'other' to legitimate the middle-class white man of virtue who practices personal responsibility and has no need for assistance from the government" (274). Oftentimes welfare rights activists saw through such constructions. NWRO chairperson Johnnie Tillmon (1972b) expressed what thousands of recipients knew from firsthand experience: "The truth is a job doesn't necessarily mean an adequate income. A woman with 3 kids—not 12 kids, mind you, just 3 kids—that woman, earning the full Federal minimum wage of $1.60 an hour, is still stuck in poverty. . . . Society needs wom[e]n on welfare as 'examples' to let every woman, factory workers and housewife workers alike, know what will happen if she lets up, if she's laid off, if she tries to go it alone without a man" (par. 13).

The predominance of controlling images aimed at keeping black women "in their places" has made the issue of self-definition crucial for black women's survival (Collins 1991). The disconnect between their firsthand experience with struggles to get by on public assistance and the prevailing image of the "lazy" welfare recipient provided poor black women an "outsider-within" perspective, a unique "angle of vision" that led to a sharper critique of the ways black women have been positioned economically, politically, and culturally (94).

Cultivation of Critical Awareness

Chapter 1 introduced the idea of agency as a process that emerges as individuals come to think and act on their own behalf within a context of real structures that motivate, limit, and delimit social action. Agency is initiated by way of a critical awareness that is cultivated through firsthand experience and a rhetorical process called reconstitution.

The Role of Firsthand Experience

Feminist scholars have done significant work in bringing to light the ways that critical reflection upon one's life experiences may provide the impetus for social change (Collins 1991; Kraus 1993; Taylor and Whittier 1992; Triece 2003). In my work on the early twentieth-century labor activist Leonora O'Reilly, I argued for the importance of recognizing how firsthand experience can "interact with, accompany, or even precede rhetorical intervention" (2003, 10). Young working women often described an "aha" moment in which their immediate circumstances of want or workplace abuse "'spoke volumes'" and "did much to motivate them even in the face of recalcitrant bosses and repressive gender norms" (8). Collins (1991) similarly notes that "concrete experiences" of black women "can stimulate a distinctive Black feminist consciousness concerning that material reality," which can in turn lead to direct action (24). Annie Adams described a poignant workplace experience that sparked her involvement in the civil rights movement: "When I first went into the mill we had segregated water fountains.... Same thing about the toilets. I had to clean the toilets for the inspection room and then, when I got ready to go to the bathroom, I had to go all the way to the bottom of the stairs to the cellar. So I asked my boss man, 'What's the difference? If I can go in there and clean them toilets, why can't I use them?' Finally, I started to use that toilet. I decided I wasn't going to walk a mile to go to the bathroom" (Collins 1991, 28).

Las Vegas women who formed the Clark County Welfare Rights Organization pointed to the ways their experiences on welfare prompted anger, which then motivated them to confront the powers that be. Alversa Beals almost lost her children due to the 1967 amendments to the Social Security Act, which empowered welfare departments to remove children from "homes with low standards including multiple instances of illegitimacy" (Abramovitz 1988, 338). From her interview with Beals the historian Annelise Orleck (2005) concluded, "Beals was tired of being threatened and feeling powerless. Nearly losing her children changed something inside her" (97). Shortly after the incident Beals joined the Clark County WRO.

Mary Wesley of the Clark County WRO spoke of a similar awareness that came from her frustrations with the welfare system. She stated that the welfare administrators "knew damn well that the money they was giving us was not going to pay your rent and then pay for food. . . . But they was telling us we couldn't have jobs. You couldn't make it unless you did something illegal. You had to do something—some work on the side—because you couldn't pay your rent, your utilities and have enough to feed your kids. I guess that's what keeps the rich richer and the poor poorer. All that stuff finally started to dawn on me then. It finally started to dawn on all of us" (Orleck 2005, 101).

Mildred Calvert's "aha" moment, which came as she participated in a welfare rights protest, demonstrates the dynamic relationship among the phases of agency development. The experience of protesting further honed her critical consciousness. Once she was at the state capitol in Madison, Wisconsin, for the protest, Calvert explains: "That's when I really started learning. I had been learning little by little, but that's when I really learned how bad the system is, how we are really hated, and how people could make you feel degraded and how humiliating it really is to be a welfare recipient to a person who just really doesn't understand. I sat there and listened to the legislators determining that we had taken over their assembly and that they would not listen to us and that they were going to call in the National Guard and this, that, and the other, and I had to cry. My children didn't understand why I was crying but, all of a sudden, I realized what we were up against, and then I was determined to fight. I was determined" (1972, 29).

Oftentimes recipients' experiences of "coming around" to a critical view of their life situation was prompted through comparison to more privileged peers. The sociologist Margaret Archer (2000) explains that as children, we reflect upon the "day-to-day manifestations of objective and externally determined life-chances. The most basic of these reflections is an early recognition of constraints and enablements" (264). Recipients' descriptions of their childhood experiences illustrate Archer's point. In 1971 the NWRO's official paper, the *Welfare Fighter,* explained that activist Jennette Washington's "ideas of what is right come from many years of intimate association with what she knows to be wrong" ("Profile of a Welfare Fighter: Jennette Washington" 11). In the article "Profile of a Welfare Fighter: Jennette Washington," Washington explained that as a child she "saw white kids riding bicycles to school and laying them on the green lawns of the school, and we just had dirt all around our school. . . . Within myself I felt some kind of disservice; I felt my family was in fear, bowing down, passive" (1971, 11). Explaining how school officials abused her at her school, Georgia Phillips, daughter of welfare rights activist Ruby Duncan, said, "We never saw white children mistreated, just us" (Orleck 2005, 221). Because of her experiences, Phillips and fellow junior high classmates led a sit-in. "We got tired of being treated like nothing, . . . so we demanded respect" (221).

Echoing Washington and Phillips, Mildred Calvert (1972), chairperson of the Northside Welfare Rights Organization in Milwaukee, shared the way that her experience with poverty—particularly vis-à-vis images of wealth—angered her and motivated her to act. "When I see money being wasted—sending men to the moon . . . dumping nerve gas in the ocean, burning potatoes . . . and then I see hungry and raggedy children running around, this is the kind of country that we live in, and this is what just burns me up. I feel the only way changes will be made . . . is through poor people, welfare people, organizing and raising a lot of hell" (30).

Reconstitution

Motivation to think or act in resistant ways was spurred not only by concrete experience but also by a rhetorical process called reconstitution. Jensen and Hammerback (1998) define reconstitution as the "process by which audiences redefine themselves" in empowering ways (128). Reconstitution occurs when a "message merges the rhetor's thought and character" so as to create a strong identification with the reader/listener. Through identification readers discover "latent qualities in themselves" (128). Reconstitution was a particularly important transformative process for female welfare recipients who, by way of restrictive gender norms and a degrading welfare system, were not encouraged to act—indeed were punished for acting—on their own behalf. A similar process is captured in the idea of a "rhetoric of possibility," which "addresses [audiences] in terms of their capacity to become what they are not, and brings to their attention things they do not already feel, know, or understand" (Poulakos 1984, 223). Narrative provides a particularly apt mode of communication for conveying potential states of being since through stories "rhetors can confront the states of awareness and intellectual beliefs of audiences" and "through [them] can show [audiences] previously unsuspected ways of being and acting in the world" (Kirkwood 1992, 32).

Articles and regular features in the *Welfare Fighter,* such as Profile of a Welfare Fighter, The States Report, and letters to the editor, provided sites where recipient-activists could share their experiences as individuals and as members of their local WROs.* These spaces enabled not only self-definition but also redefinition in much the same way that Watson (1999) describes the function of women's autobiography: "In writing their life stories . . . women were expressing the possibility of a new kind of womanhood for others; in recording their life stories, these women were redefining womanhood and personhood for their contemporaries" (2).

The process of redefinition was often prompted by hearing stories of others in similar positions. For women who felt subjected to the whims of the welfare system, learning about other recipients who took charge and led community efforts for welfare rights may have encouraged readers to see themselves similarly as actors rather than as those acted upon. For instance in one installment of Profile of a Welfare Fighter, readers learned about Geraldine Smith, who initiated a minimum standard drive in her community ("Profile of a Welfare Fighter: Mrs. Geraldine Smith"); in another they learned about Marian Kidd, who formed a welfare rights group in her hometown of Newark, New Jersey ("Profile of a Welfare Fighter: Marian Kidd"); and in another they learned about Angie Matos, who moved to New York from Puerto Rico in 1952 and became a community activist five years later ("Profile of a Welfare Fighter: Angie Matos"). In her profile Annie Smart, the southern representative on NWRO's executive committee, spoke encouragingly when addressing the issue of becoming a welfare rights activist. "I never had any trouble speaking my mind," she noted. "But it's wonderful to see with a lot of the others that they're getting very verbal, and aren't afraid to speak out. And they're asking questions; if a person starts asking, that

---

* The regular feature The States Report was originally called State Action. Profile of a Welfare Fighter was first called Profile of a WRO. The States Report appeared in every issue of the *Welfare Fighter.* Profile of a Welfare Fighter was featured less consistently, appearing in fewer than half of the issues between 1969 and 1972.

means they're interested. I always tell people not to apologize for not knowing something, just be proud they're learning" ("Profile of a Welfare Fighter: Annie Smart," 11).

In addition to inspiring readers with stories of determination of other re-cipients "just like" them, the *Welfare Fighter* urged readers to share their own perspectives in the paper. In these instances the very act of writing one's story authenticated one's experiences and provided an important outlet for self-definition for the writers and for rethinking poverty for readers. "By author-ing, [women] author-ized their experiences" (Triece 2007, 85). In her study of women's autobiography, Watson (1999) explains that "the mere act of [women's] writing distinguishes them from many of their predecessors and contemporaries. Some feminist critics have claimed that women do not so much record their lives as write themselves into existence" (1). Toni Morrison (1971) notes that black women in particular "had nothing to fall back on: not maleness, not whiteness, not ladyhood, not anything. And out of the profound desolation of her reality she may very well have invented herself" (63).

In the *Welfare Fighter*'s second issue in October 1969, NWRO chairperson Johnnie Tillmon seemed to intuit the importance of narrating one's story as she urged readers to contribute more to the paper in the way of articles and updates. Tillmon wrote, "I . . . had hoped to see more of the paper written by YOU. I won't get discouraged because I know the next issue will be filled with articles and comments written by Mr. and Miss Welfare client" (1969a, 2). Later issues reminded readers to send in updates of their local affiliates' activities. Readers could "send newspaper clippings" covering their events, but the paper especially wanted "to hear your own version of what happened" ("Of Note to All Groups," 5; "Do You Feel Left Out?" 6).

Bertha Cavanaugh (1969) wrote a letter to the *Welfare Fighter* in December 1969 explaining how she became a state representative to the NWRO. With a husband out of work and six children to care for, Cavanaugh went to her local welfare department to receive assistance. There she learned of the local welfare rights organization; she attended her first meeting that night and was active thereafter. Cavanaugh concluded her letter on an optimistic note. "I hardly ever spoke before I joined NWRO, now, I never shut my mouth," she reported (2). Her story is one of transformation. She acknowledged her feeling of unease at speaking out—a feeling common to many recipients especially when they risked losing benefits for overtly challenging the system. But she points out that once she spoke, she gained a sense of power, and she never let up. Her story conveys a sense that if she could do it, the reader could too.

Recipient Betty Jones, chairperson of the Parent-Welfare League in Akron, Ohio, wrote a letter also appearing in the *Welfare Fighter* in 1969. Jones appealed directly to recipients as mothers. By linking welfare activism to the conventional duties of motherhood, Jones placed the risky behavior associated with welfare activism within a sphere—motherhood—recipients were arguably more comfortable in. Jones declared, "We must stand tall and speak up, since we have nothing to fear." Jones linked voice with the responsibilities of parenting and citizenship when she explained that as a parent you "must speak out, since you have no other way of taking care of your children. You must have strength and courage to be willing to work together and fight for ou[r] place in this so-called Model Society" (3).

The November 1971 issue of the *Welfare Fighter* featured an article by Jackie Pope, an assistant field director in the NWRO office in Washington, D.C., who eventually found full-time employment that enabled her to get off welfare. In her article Pope recognized that being a black woman on welfare was the "worst of all hells" in the United States, but she underscored organization as the key to pulling oneself out of the "pit of despair and the cave of ignorance" (7). When recipients join a local WRO and demand rights alongside other recipients, she explained, they take control over their lives. Pope was aware of the role that she and other recipient-activists—whom she calls "models"—played in motivating poor women to fight for their rights. "We models in Welfare rights . . . hold our heads high, our shoulders back; our eyes are clear. All of us are always hoping that some welfare recipient who is steeped in despair and hopelessness will look at us or hear about us and think to himself or herself, 'If they can do it—so can I'" (7).

Likewise Katie B. Harris, a mother of nine and chairperson of the Flint WRO, recognized the important role she played in organizing women in similar positions. Of her fellow recipients she stated, "They know I'm just like they are. . . . I can get closer than a person from an office or with a white collar" ("Grandmother Organizes New York Poor" 1972, 19). Harris also realized the collective nature of welfare recipients' experiences. She asserted the importance of organizing, noting that "without that we're going to be washed downstream. . . . The only thing the government will listen to is numbers" (19).

Collectivization of Experiences

Successful social protest geared toward substantial socioeconomic change requires not only critical awareness of individuals but also attentiveness to the collective nature of oppression and recognition of the need for resistance in collective terms. Reconstitution is a process that takes place at the level of the individual; for example reading an account in the *Welfare Fighter* may lead to redefinition, or a recipient's writing her own account in the paper may lead to self-transformation as described above. In addition concrete experiences of black women often prompts critical reflection on those experiences and in turn often leads to the development in these women of a "distinctive group consciousness," which may in turn lead to collective action (Collins 1991, 25). As Jackie Pope

(1971) explained, "The only real hope for survival for Welfare mothers is to be 'organized'" (7). Black women have historically created and sought out numerous avenues through which they could define themselves and assert their needs and concerns as a group, including through personal relationships, in church groups, in black women's clubs, as well as through black women's writings and blues (Collins 1991). Collins also notes that these "safe spaces" are a "necessary condition for Black women's resistance" (95).

One place where welfare mothers developed strength and courage was in relationships with friends, family, and neighbors, which oftentimes led to the formation of local WROs. A study conducted of recipient-activists in Minnesota pointed to the "importance of personal networks" in motivating women to become involved in the cause of welfare rights. Recipients who did not move frequently and who were involved in other social groups such as clubs and church groups were more likely to join a WRO (Nadasen 2005, 27). Sociological studies confirm that interpersonal contacts provide crucial impetus to join a movement (Friedman and McAdam 1992, 158; see also Bolton 1972; McAdam 1986). Recipients such as Joyce Burson learned about welfare activism and the minimum standards campaign in Brooklyn, New York, from a flyer she received at the grocery store in her Bedford-Stuyvesant neighborhood. Reflecting on her first welfare rights meeting, Burson noted, "I was hearing people say that you can do something . . . you don't have to be ashamed because you're on welfare . . . it's not your fault" (Kornbluh 2007, 56). At the very least casual meetings with friends and neighbors at the supermarket, on sidewalks, or in churches provided an outlet for venting one's frustrations with stingy or intrusive caseworkers (Orleck 2005, 96). Johnnie Tillmon asserted that the idea of welfare rights came from "welfare mothers finding out that no matter where they live, the problems are the same, and they are treated no different" ("Profile of a Welfare Fighter: Johnnie Tillmon" 1971, 3).

The NWRO acknowledged the challenge of organizing recipients but urged locals to continue their efforts particularly after the successful 1966 Walk for Decent Welfare, when organizational momentum was still at a peak ("Bi-weekly Letter"). The historian Deborah Gray White (1999) recounts the experiences of Jennette Washington, a welfare recipient and organizer of the West Side Welfare Recipients League (WSWRL) in New York. Washington "got involved in organizing poor people in New York when, after losing her factory job, the seventh she had held in a year, welfare officials forced her to live in a hotel room with her three children" (226). Washington "recalled how meeting collectively helped individual recipients overcome the shame attached to welfare" and recognize the rights they were afforded by law (226). A WSWRL organizer explained, "Many people had the same feelings but never expressed them in a unified way. Suddenly they began to admit that they were on welfare and they were relieved and willing to go out and express the community feeling to the state and city. They said they were sick of conditions on welfare and were now ready to band together and fight welfare" (Jackson and Johnson 1974, 63).

Prompted by nuns at Our Lady of Victory Catholic Church, Jackie Pope and fellow recipients in her Bedford-Stuyvesant neighborhood formed a support group that initially enabled the women to exchange stories of struggle with the welfare department. It was in these meetings that Pope realized she was not alone and she was not to blame for her circumstances (2011). By attending the meetings mothers learned that "other people just like themselves have the same problems with the Welfare Department" (1971, 7). The nuns watched the children during meetings so that Pope and other recipients could devote energy to garnering new members, establishing their needs, articulating demands, and politicizing the support group, which became the Brooklyn Welfare Action Council (B-WAC). Pope (1971) also noted the winning effect on new members when they saw women like themselves chairing meetings, "meeting high officials, making demands and getting demands met" (7).

The formation in 1963 of Aid to Needy Children–Mothers Anonymous (ANC–Mothers Anonymous) grew out of recipients' common frustrations as they lived in a housing project in the Watts section of Los Angeles. Johnnie Tillmon, who would go on to chair the National Welfare Rights Organization, had no previous organizing experience but mustered the courage to send a letter out to over five hundred recipients in her area calling them to a meeting to discuss concerns with the welfare department (see figure 2.1). The turnout at the initial meeting was overwhelming. The women immediately got to work. They elected officers and decided to name their group "ANC–Mothers Anonymous because the dictionary definition of anonymous was 'nameless'" (White 1999, 225). Tillmon explained, the women "understood that what people thought about welfare recipients and women on welfare was that they had no rights, they didn't exist, they was a statistic and not a human being" (White 1999, 225). Tillmon and her fellow activists were aware that as poor black women they were invisible to the rest of society. However they used that awareness as a foundation upon which to launch challenges to the system. Maintaining the title "anonymous" enabled the women to work out of sight of suspicious case workers and landlords who could easily retaliate by withholding assistance. As one of the first local WROs, ANC–Mothers Anonymous remained active in blocking evictions and helping women receive aid. The group was successful at getting recipients "to believe that they could have some control over their lives" (White 1999, 225).

Organizers of Nevada's Clark County Welfare Rights Organization first met in a sewing class, a job-training class they were required to take in order to receive AFDC. Sewing side by side, the welfare mothers, including Ruby Duncan, Emma Stampley, Essie Henderson, Alversa Beals, Mary Wesley, and Eddie Jean Finks, forged ties, exchanged stories, and shared "bitter complaints about the welfare system" (Orleck 2005, 101). Soon the women started convening regularly, first

Fig. 2.1
Johnnie Tillmon, founder
of Aid to Needy Children–
Mothers Anonymous and
the first to chair the National
Welfare Rights Organization.
Records of the National
Welfare Rights Organization
(NWRO), Moorland-Spingarn
Research Center, Howard
University.

in living rooms then in a church meeting room. Out of these meetings the Clark County Welfare Rights Organization was born.

In many ways local WROs served as consciousness-raising groups, safe spaces where women could share the experiences and frustrations associated with being a black woman in a racist patriarchal society. Yet the historical positioning of poor black women at the intersection of capital and care calls up the need to expand understandings of consciousness raising as articulated in early 1970s scholarship on the issue. Campbell (1973) explains that as a "persuasive campaign" consciousness raising speaks "to women in terms of private, concrete, individual experience, because women have little, if any, publicly shared experience" (79). Furthermore in consciousness-raising groups the "participants seek to understand and interpret their lives as women, but there is no 'message,' no 'party line.' . . . If action is suggested, no group commitment is made; each must decide whether, and if so which, action is suitable for her" (79).

Poor black women did indeed have shared public experiences as underpaid and exploited domestic and agricultural workers throughout the nineteenth and twentieth centuries. Their workplace experiences also helped them understand their experiences of "motherwork" (Collins 1994, 47) as collective. Black mothers have historically labored side by side with their children in fields or have been separated from their children either by slavery or in their role as domestic workers cleaning the homes and caring for the children of white families (50, 51). In addition minority women worked to ensure the survival not only of their own children but of their communities at large (50).

When women in the Clark County WRO got together, they discussed the hurt they felt at being branded "lazy mothers" (Orleck 2005), a label that applied to them specifically as poor black women. And they, along with the hundreds of other local WROs across the country, developed a clear message about poor black women's place within the economic system, and they strategized direct actions aimed at welfare departments and political institutions. These two functions are discussed in subsequent pages.

This chapter discussed the initial processes by which individuals come to critically reflect on their circumstances and recognize the collective nature of their oppression. Through firsthand experience, reconstitution, and consciousness raising, welfare recipients began the cultivation of a collective agency directed at legal and economic systems that discriminated against them.

Furthermore, as suggested earlier, agency formation includes public engagement whereby groups direct their arguments to broader publics, both sympathetic and hostile. The next chapter looks at the ways recipient-activists brought their experiences as workers to the fore in an effort to create "presence" in public debates on welfare policies.

3

Credible Workers

What do I think about the welfare? It ought to be cut back.
The goddamn people sit around when they should be working
and then they're having illegitimate kids to get more money.
You know, their morals are different. They don't give a damn.

Chicago cab driver, quoted in May, *The Wasted Americans,* 1965

We have organized NWRO to get the money we need to raise our
families. . . .We have organized NWRO to fight for opportunities for
decent jobs with adequate pay. We have organized NWRO to
participate in this country, to be a part of this country.

Beulah Sanders, *Social Security and Welfare Proposals,* 1969

All facts to the contrary, popular sentiment during the 1960s cast welfare recipients as lazy, immoral, and undeserving of help. This popularly held image was no doubt further inspired by speeches of politicians throughout the 1960s and early 1970s (Feagin 1975, 4–7; Komisar 1977; Patterson 2000, 167, 168; Neubeck and Cazenave 2001). In a 1961 speech Joseph Mitchell, city manager of New-burgh, New York, decried the "moral chiselers and loafers" who "squat on the relief rolls forever" (214). Ten years later Louisiana senator Russell Long stated in a congressional debate: "The welfare system as we know it today is being ma-nipulated and abused by malingerers, cheaters, and outright frauds to the detri-ment . . . of the American taxpayers" (Patterson 2000, 167-168).

Statistics from the decade tell a quite different story. Public aid did not in fact provide a lifestyle worthy of compelling thousands to remain "on the rolls forever." The average payment for an AFDC family of four in 1966—$1,728 per year—was not even half of the official poverty line of $3,355 for a family of four. In fact notes Patterson (2000), "Despite rising case loads . . . the costs of public assistance in the United States represented a fairly stable percentage of the federal budget" during the 1960s (172). The outcome of such paltry handouts could be seen in the average recipient's home. In 1967 nearly a quarter of AFDC fami-lies did not have running water in their dwellings, 30 percent lacked beds, and nearly 1 in 5 had children who at times did not attend school due to inadequate clothing (Abramovitz 1988, 336). In addition birthrates among AFDC recipients contrasted sharply with claims that women had many children in order to receive larger checks. Only about 35 percent of AFDC mothers in the 1960s had four or more children (Steiner 1971, 41; Neubeck and Cazenave 2001, 139).

Perhaps the most insidious myths surrounding welfare concerned race. Welfare was and continues to be framed as a "black problem" when according to statistics a majority of AFDC recipients in 1967 were white (Steiner 1971, 41; see also Gilens 1999; Neubeck and Cazenave 2001). The disproportionate representation of black people on welfare rolls was the legacy of racist discrimination in the workplace and crumbling neighborhood infrastructures and schools. The same can be said of joblessness both then and now (Wilson 1996). More recent statistics (from early 2011) are revealing: among white workers, the unemployment rate was 8 percent; among black workers unemployment was double that number at 16 percent (Bureau of Labor Statistics). Yet NWRO leaders such as Johnnie Tillmon seemed to have it right when they repeatedly asserted the organization worked for all poor people regardless of race (Tillmon 1969b, 1970a, 1970b). In Tillmon's words, "POOR knows no color" (1970a, 2).*

The "durability" of racist welfare images indicates that such stereotypes "serve important racial control functions" (Neubeck and Cazenave 2001, 141). Yet such attempts to discipline and constrain the lives of welfare recipients were not lost on the welfare recipient-activists themselves, who directly confronted policy makers through rhetorical efforts of their own. It is worth noting again that poor black mothers occupied a conflicted position at the intersection of capital and care from which they at times rhetorically negotiated in contradictory ways. First speaking as women discriminated against by a capitalist welfare state that positioned them exclusively as (failed) mothers (Fraser 1989, 153), they established themselves as credible workers deserving of decent jobs, which is the focus of this chapter. Furthermore from their position as black women living under the slave-era legacy of forced employment, they established themselves as deserving mothers who had a right to remain home with their children.

The following pages discuss the rhetoric of welfare rights activists in the NWRO who challenged stereotypes of the welfare "chiseler" by establishing themselves as credible decision makers and as actual or potential workers exploited by a larger economic system. I begin the chapter with a discursive backdrop to point to the role of the term *opportunity* as it was used rhetorically in order to personalize poverty and publicly condemn the poor.

---

* Tillmon further noted: "Organized clients know better than most people that all poor people are oppressed by the system in this country so that it is extremely important for Chicanos, Puerto Ricans, Indians, Whites and Blacks to join in this fight for power" (1970b, 2).

Narratives of <Autonomy> and <Opportunity>

In order to appreciate the arguments offered by recipient-activists, it is worthwhile to understand prevailing ideologies surrounding work and success in the broader culture during the late 1960s and early 1970s. The welfare chiseler represented one narrative element in a larger American story where "autonomy" and "opportunity" figure prominently. Both terms cut a wide course through longstanding political mythology (see Fineman 2004). Both function as ideographs, words that encapsulate the political commitments of a culture. Ideographs— denoted by < >— "function as guides, warrants, reasons, or excuses for behavior and belief" (McGee 1980, 6). Describing their persuasive force, McGee notes that ideographs are "more pregnant than propositions could ever be" (7). As part of our everyday discourse, ideographs go unquestioned, unexamined. For instance "everyone is conditioned to think of 'the rule of law' as a logical commitment just as one is taught to think that '186,000 miles per second' is an accurate empirical description of the speed of light even though few can work the experiments or do the mathematics to prove it" (McGee 1980, 7). Likewise Fineman (2004) explains that political myths are "difficult to examine critically," but examine we must since such discourses tend to operate conservatively and often to the detriment of "healthy social programs" (16).

For example <autonomy> privileges the supposed self-sufficient "man" who on his own merit achieves success. Less apparent is the way that <autonomy> works in tandem with notions of "dependency" to stigmatize those unable to pull themselves up by their bootstraps. Indeed the folding of <autonomy> into the mythology of American equality occurs so flawlessly as to obscure the varying ways that all citizens are dependent. It's just that some forms of dependence are sanctioned and thus called by different names, for example subsidy, tax credit, and so on. Other labels for dependence, such as welfare, connote laziness and unworthiness, and thus these forms are less likely to be rewarded with government funds. To understand how deeply these myths resonate, consider that in 2002, $93 billion were directed to corporate welfare, according to the Cato Institute ("Government Spends More"). This number includes everything from corporate farm subsidies to tax breaks and land subsidies given to large corporations such as Wal-Mart and McDonald's. In contrast federal and state spending on Temporary Assistance for Needy Families (TANF) in 2006 was $26 billion. Despite the disparity in spending on corporate and social welfare—which has been consistent at least since the late 1990s—a 2011 Rasmussen poll found that 71 percent of respondents believe that the "bigger problem with the welfare system . . . is that there are too many overqualified recipients rather than not enough," that is too many people get welfare who shouldn't ("71% Say").

Much like <autonomy>, <opportunity> embodies assumptions of freedom and choice; it calls forth the well-known Horatio Alger or "bootstraps" story wherein any person regardless of racial, ethnic, and economic status can achieve success in America, the "land of opportunity." Stories of <opportunity> necessarily preclude recognition or examination of systemic barriers (for example institutionalized racism, rigid gender roles, chronic unemployment) that delimit choices. In short ideographs such as <autonomy> and <opportunity> short-circuit nuanced reasoning and operate hegemonically to preserve the status quo. They encourage a "Well, of course!" response that makes further inspection of the issue an apparent waste of time.

In the case of welfare policy discourses, the term *opportunity* provided a framework for understanding the nature of and solutions to poverty, one that concorded with deeply held beliefs of what it means to be an "American," that is hard working and self-reliant. In his message to Congress on the Economic Opportunity Act, which was passed in 1964, President Lyndon Johnson narrated the familiar story of <opportunity> in America: "With the growth of our country has come opportunity for our people—opportunity to educate our children, to use our energies in productive work, to increase our leisure—opportunity for almost every American to hope that through work and talent he could create a better life for himself and his family" (223). And Americans heard nearly the same story of <opportunity> five years later when Nixon (1969) vowed to push "toward full opportunity for every American to share the bounty of this rich land" (319).

The Johnson and Nixon administrations did not completely ignore barriers such as race discrimination and obstacles to decent education. As Patterson (2000) notes, the War on Poverty "reflected a conservative application of structuralist observations" (131). Administrators emphasized government programs as a "hand up, not a hand out" as evidenced in the words of a War on Poverty administrator, Sargent Shriver, who described the Job Corps' purpose as "altering society so poor people are able to raise *themselves* above the poverty level through their *own* efforts" (Zarefsky 1986, 165). Likewise when Nixon introduced his Family Assistance Plan to the nation in 1969, he stressed "this nation became great not because of what government did for people, but because of what people did for themselves" (314).

Indeed the ideograph <opportunity> is closely associated with <responsibility>, and politicians increasingly highlighted that connection into the late 1960s as some War on Poverty programs were proving unsuccessful. Zarefsky (1986) explains that rather than address the solution to poverty by making jobs more available for those who entered the Job Corps program, Johnson decided to redefine the prevailing understanding of poverty so that it was in line with the solution already in place. "The problem of the poverty cycle was reinterpreted so that only some of the poor—those with proper motivation and without antisocial tendencies—could escape. But that view made the exit from poverty seem to depend more on individual personality traits than on cultural conditions, and it strongly implied that those who remained behind were poor because something was wrong with them" (169). In this way then the notion of the welfare chiseler found a ready place in prevailing stories of opportunity in America.

Welfare rights activists responded directly to charges of cheating the system by establishing their credibility as spokespersons for their own needs and concerns. And they created presence for their experiences as workers *within a system* where jobs were lacking and the wealthy benefited at the expense of those on welfare. Historical materialism, explained in an earlier chapter, provides a viable theoretical framework for understanding activists' use of reality referencing to ground their claims to knowing in the context of an economic system based on disparity.

"We have lived it, we know": Establishing Credibility

Welfare rights activists challenged the stereotype of the welfare chiseler by redefining themselves as workers and emphasizing the extent to which their poverty was rooted in a larger economic system and shaped by welfare policies. They established their credibility to speak on welfare issues by pointing to a reality that could serve as a gauge when assessing competing narratives of work and opportunity within welfare policy debates. Activists referenced lived reality as a way to make the case that they, not politicians, were experts on welfare policy and how resources should be distributed. At root these discussions were about how needs would be interpreted—what Nancy Fraser (1989) theorizes as the "politics of needs interpretation" (146).

Welfare righters persisted in efforts to define their own needs in welfare debates dominated by politicians and administrators who they saw as distanced from the "reality" of the situation. In these instances reality referencing provided a necessary tool for making the argument that their own conceptualization of needs was the one that should serve as a basis for formulating policies regarding the distribution of money. Joy Stanley, the president of the Los Angeles WRO, put the matter this way when testifying before Congress in May 1967: "We in the community believe we could more effectively plan and implement programs for our communities so that we can lift ourselves out of poverty. The people in Watts, the people in East Los Angeles, the people in Venice, know their communities, know their people, and know their needs. . . . I don't know how you expect to know the real effect that the war on poverty has made unless you talk to all these people sitting out here today. . . . Only the people can tell you what you want to know, for they are the *only ones who really know*" (Examination of the War on Poverty 1967, 3956, emphasis added).

Simone St. Jock and Betty Meredith expressed the same sentiments in hearings on the War on Poverty the following month. At the June 1967 session St. Jock reminded Senator Edward Kennedy, "We are not all dumb dodos" and continued to speak to the importance of lived experience when it came to running programs for the poor. "How can somebody 150 miles back or 50 miles away even tell us what we need here? Why do they put low priority on our programs? We have fine ongoing programs here. . . . We know what we want. We want more money. We want jobs" (Examination of the War on Poverty 1967, 4674, 4675). Likewise in her testimony to Kennedy, Meredith asserted, "We know [about poverty issues] because we and our friends and neighbors live with them, and with a lot of other things too, and we feel we should have the right to decide what the greatest needs in our community [are] and what to do about them" (Examination of the War on Poverty 1967, 4521).

Two years later, in 1969, welfare rights activists testified before Congress, with Beulah Sanders providing frank replies to congressional members' queries (Social Security and Welfare Proposals 1969; "Sanders Testifies" 1969). Calling attention to the ways that lived reality buttresses claims to knowing, Sanders exclaimed, "We know how the present inadequate welfare system perpetuates poverty because we have to live under it. We know how our children's future is damaged by not having proper food, clothing and medical attention. We believe we can provide the best understand[ing] of what is wrong and what needs to be done" ("Sanders Testifies" 1969, 6). In an exchange about the types of programs most useful to recipients, Sanders asserted, "If you want to save some money, and this is really what you are talking about . . . I would suggest that you consult with people, because I constantly tell the administrator in New York City, 'If you want the program to work, go out and ask those people what do they want.' . . . Hire those recipients to go out in the community and knock on doors and find out what the people want, what do they feel is best for them. They have brains. All of them are not dumb and uneducated as you think they are. They do have sense enough to sit down and come up with an intelligent answer and I am quite sure you won't waste so much money" (Social Security and Welfare Proposals 1969, 1033).

NWRO activists also expressed frustration at politicians' and bureaucrats' lack of experience with poverty. As they saw it, firsthand experience with poverty granted one a degree of authority on the issue. For example at a March 28, 1972, demonstration at the capitol building in Madison, Wisconsin, the deputy director of Health and Human Services, Fred Hinickle, expressed a "deep-seated concern" for families on welfare. One protesting mother responded, "Don't tell me you care. I know you don't because it doesn't affect you or your family" ("Sixteen Cities Join" 1972, 11). A few months earlier mothers in Maryland met with the lieutenant governor of their state to discuss raising welfare payments. One mother became so frustrated she walked out of the meeting. She explained, "He ain't saying nothing but 'YES,' 'how absurd,' 'OH, that's awful'" ("The States Report, Maryland" 1972, 10). Another mother who walked out stated with similar frustration, "When he said, 'I have eight children of my own,' that's as much as

I could take." This example shows how welfare activists interpreted politicians' attempts at sympathy—as superficial rhetoric that held no weight because such claims were not back by references to lived experience, as were their own claims.

The Rhode Island welfare rights group Fair Welfare employed the often used tactic of trying to get middle-class folks to live on a welfare budget for a week. The activists, who were part of a government-established task force, two-thirds of which was comprised of middle-class folks, were turned off by the "self-righteous" attitude of the other members and their "point-blank refus[al] to experience what it's like to be poor by trying to live on a welfare budget for a week" ("Fair Welfare Wins" 1970, 4).

In Virginia and Cleveland activists showed up uninvited to official meetings to demand their voices be heard. They were clear in asserting they had a more accurate view of poverty and should therefore be given a say in the development of poverty programs. Virginia welfare rights activists targeted the U.S. Department of Agriculture at its National Agricultural Outlook Conference in February 1971. Uninvited, the group of twenty-five "took over" the opening day of the meeting and read a position paper that demanded the USDA "work with poor people in establishing a policy-making body including poor people and their representative organizations" ("We're Tired of Coming Away" 1971, 8). The group also "blasted the Agriculture Department, calling it colonial governor for the rural colonies" to ensure profits for agribusinesses (8). One member of the group, a mother on welfare, asserted, "We are tired of being taught to live on air and peanut butter by people who've never had to do that. Let me refute the myth that the poor are miraculously happy. If you see us smiling, it's because we're organizing" (8).

The group of Virginia welfare rights activists also showed up at a follow-up meeting held by White House delegates in Williamsburg, Virginia. They presented a "list of 20 resolutions and case histories to bring the delegates into focus with reality" ("We're Tired of Coming Away" 1971, 8). In turn the activists were told to trust in the government's good intentions. Writing about the event, the *Welfare Fighter* noted, "Good intentions look delicious, but are very low in protein, vitamins and calories" (8).

Cleveland welfare rights activists walked into the Ohio Welfare Conference held by the state welfare department. Minnie Player reported the event in the *Welfare Fighter,* stating that the "rich administrators had planned to sit around and discuss 'the problem' (that is, welfare recipients). Recipients around the state, mostly from Cleveland, went to the Conference for the purpose of teaching the so-called professional what welfare is all about" ("The Fight Goes On" 1970, 7).

Beulah Sanders and others in the national office were incensed at New York governor Nelson Rockefeller's planned conference on public welfare where presidents of the 150 largest corporations would have a hand in shaping welfare policy. The November 1967 issue of *NOW!*— the NWRO's official paper—stated that "some NWRO folks might just be at this conference anyway, to *tell it like it is*" ("Rockefeller Welfare Conference" 1967, emphasis added).

Activists in Kansas City and Washington, D.C., took creative approaches aimed at the general public as a way to establish the credibility of their claims to knowledge about poverty. The Kansas City group, League for Adequate Welfare, produced a play, *Struggle*, which was performed by recipients without a script. "They are personal experiences," noted Ruth Miller, the chairperson of the group. "We are saying it the way we have lived it" ("Kansas City WRO Goes On Stage" 1970–1971, 5). Marie Ratagick, member of D.C. Family Welfare Rights, created a game called "Shoe on the Other Foot," with rules similar to that of Monopoly ("Shoe on the Other Foot" 1972, 15). The *Welfare Fighter* article that described the game noted that "nothing can completely transfer the degradation of being on welfare to a person who has never experienced it," but the game "forces the player to deal with many of the problems welfare recipients face" (15). Although the game may have confirmed recipient expertise and garnered sympathy from the middle class, there is little evidence to suggest that this tactic had any long-term impact on altering public misconceptions, which circulated widely in media and political discourses.

The previous examples illustrate with striking similarity the extent to which welfare recipients referenced a more or less reliable reality that could be used as a basis for comparing competing narratives of work and welfare. To put it differently, in order to link evidence to their claims of knowing—which is the role of a warrant—activists employed reality referencing. In addition to establishing their expertise on welfare issues, activists gave presence to their experiences as workers within a larger system of class disparity.

Creating Presence As Workers

Chapter 1 introduced Perelman's (1982) concept of presence. Speakers create presence when they "single out" or amplify particular ideas or experiences. Without presence some ideas remain abstract or nonexistent. It was clearly crucial for welfare rights activists to establish presence for their experiences as black women in poverty given how distanced their audience of mostly white, well-to-do males was from the lives of these women. Indeed it would be difficult to overestimate how remarkable it was that poor, mostly black women—many of whom were maligned in political and popular discourses for receiving public assistance—testified before Congress, an audience characterized by convention and elitism. For some women the trip to Washington, D.C., was an achievement in itself, given their extremely limited resources and the demands they faced as caretakers in their homes. Given his status as a well-known civil rights leader (in the Congress on Racial Equality and Poverty/Rights Action Center), middle-class ally George Wiley likely arranged some of the earlier congressional testimonials.

By 1970 recipients organized access to political officials by forming the Legislative and Lobbying Committee, which arranged meetings with Health, Education, and Welfare secretary Elliott Richardson ("NWRO's Legislative and Lobbying Committee" 1971, 10).

Boston area community activist Betty Meredith noted in her testimony to Congress in June 1967, "All the degrees in the world can't help someone who's never been really hungry to know how much an empty stomach hurts, or what it's like to live in a fourth-floor, cold-water walkup flat with no heat, no plumbing, and rats and roaches" (Examination of the War on Poverty, 1967). Despite this fact welfare rights activists still struggled to garner the understanding of politicians through their testimony to congressional leaders between 1967 and 1972. Recipients related their own version of reality—one developed from lived experience—in order to counter outrageous and mean-spirited stereotypes such as that of the welfare "chiseler" who was "shiftless and undeserving of help."* The following examples illustrate the emphasis women placed on their workplace history in an attempt to define themselves as workers.

In 1972 a group of welfare recipients, their children, and leaders of the NWRO testified before Congress on Nixon's Family Assistance Plan (FAP). The NWRO stood in strong opposition to FAP, which would guarantee $1,600 per year for a family of four and would require all able-bodied adults, except mothers with pre-school-aged children, to work or be in training in order to receive benefits. The NWRO pointed out that were the $1,600 minimum passed, benefits would rise in only eight states. In all other states recipients would lose benefits. The NWRO proposed their own plan, which would provide a family of four $5,500 per year, the figure determined by the Bureau of Labor Statistics to be a minimum adequate income for a family of four ("Up the Nixon Plan" 1970; "This Is How the Nixon Plan Would Affect You!" 1970; "NWRO-Guaranteed Adequate Income" 1970).[†] Given the controversial nature of FAP, it is not surprising that recipients' testimonies were punctuated by expressions of frustration and at times antagonism. Typical was the testimony of Elaine McLean: "I have worked 10 years as a telephone operator . . . and many other jobs [including] setting pins in a bowling alley, waitress, in a laundry, a candy factory, a mortuary, a florist shop, cleaning offices and motels . . . housewife, mother. . . . I wish you knew why my family went on welfare and just how many ways and how many times we tried to get off" (Social Security Amendments of 1971 1972, 2245, 2246, 2247). In her testimony Elizabeth Perry responded directly to welfare stereotypes by referencing her own work experiences both in and outside of the home. "I have been following Mr.

---

* Senator Robert Byrd of West Virginia made this comment during congressional hearings in 1962 on the issue of welfare fraud (qtd. in Neubeck and Cazenave 2001, 103.
[†] See Quadagno (1994) for details on how FAP would benefit recipients primarily in southern states.

Long's [Senator Russell Long of Louisiana, chairperson of the Committee on Finance] statement now. He talks about welfare bums. I am a mother with 11 children; I worked and took care of my children until 1967 came with a chronic ailment, worked for the District government, cannot draw any disability because an inadequate city hospital did not keep a record ... and I wonder what you guys are talking about when you call people bums, people who work cannot even draw their money" (Social Security Amendments of 1971 1972, 2067).

Chairperson of the NWRO Johnnie Tillmon related her own experiences of work in an article appearing in *Ms. Magazine* in 1972. Tillmon's article, "Welfare As a Women's Issue," provided an incisive critique of the racist and sexist dimensions of the welfare system. It is significant that Tillmon began the piece by alluding to the importance of self-definition in the face of demeaning labels. "I'm a woman. I'm a black woman. I'm a poor woman. I'm a fat woman. I'm a middle-aged woman. And I'm on welfare. In this country, if you're any one of those things[,] poor, black, fat, female, middle-aged, on welfare[,] you count less as a human being. If you're all those things, you don't count at all. Except as a statistic" (1972a, par. 1, 2). Tillmon continued by recounting her own experiences of work as a way of demonstrating the falsity of prevailing ideas of welfare recipients. Here she is proposing her experiences as a more accurate picture of the experiences of those receiving public assistance: "I have raised six children. I grew up in Arkansas, and I worked there for fifteen years in a laundry, making about $20 or $30 a week, picking cotton on the side for carfare. I moved to California in 1959 and worked in a laundry there for nearly four years. In 1963 I got too sick to work anymore." In the remainder of the article Tillmon exposed the many ways the welfare system punished women who received public assistance.

Tillmon's account of her life experiences raised awareness of many as indicated in the letters she received from individuals whose lives were far removed from the welfare system. "I have just finished reading your article. . . . I now realize . . . that I know very little about the welfare system in this country and those who make up its roles," wrote a woman from New York (Johnson letter). A man from Princeton, New Jersey, stated, "I was very disconcerted by my failure to perceive many of those obvious contradictions and injustices prior to reading the article. Whatever the reason for that blindness, I would now like to open my eyes even more" (Frascella letter). Such feedback indicates the importance for marginalized groups to give presence to their experiences. Describing the life of a welfare recipient from the standpoint of one who lived it—that is referencing one's reality—was key to "opening the eyes" of a public whose understandings of welfare were shaped primarily by prevailing racist assumptions and images.

As evidenced by the amount of energy directed at dispelling myths about welfare, activists were well aware of the need to foreground a different reality of welfare. Local groups such as the Welfare Rights Organization of Allegheny County distributed literature that called forth and then debunked popular misconceptions about welfare recipients ("Who Gets Welfare?" pamphlet). In their own report members of the National Welfare Rights Mothers of Rapid City stressed the importance of "making the public aware of the problem regarding welfare and changing the image of the ADC recipients" ("Public Control in America" 1970, 12). At the national level George Wiley distributed a letter to NWRO friends and allies in 1971 stating that the group "has intensified its effort to combat the pervasive public prejudice and misinformation which makes repression possible" (Wiley letter). Accompanying the letter was a brochure, "Six Myths about Welfare," which allies were encouraged to distribute widely. The following year the national organization drew up a "Candidates' Contract with the People" in an effort to commit presidential candidates to addressing the needs of the poor. Among those items deemed most important for candidates to work towards was "exposing and combating the myths about poor people" ("Candidates' Contract" 1972, 8). This section of the contract urged candidates to "work to end the cruel myth that a government that has thrown away billions upon billions of dollars on a war against the poor of Indochina somehow has been bankrupted by poor people."

In sum through public speeches, articles, and NWRO literature, recipients constituted themselves as former and present *workers* as a way to combat the chiseler stereotype. Testimonies of work and myth-busting literature provided recipients an opportunity to detail their lives in contradistinction to widespread stereotypes or to, as they put it, "tell it like it is." Through statements such as "I wish you knew" and "I wonder what you are talking about," McLean and Perry lay claim to a clearer view of life as a poor woman on public assistance. Avant-Mier and Hasian (2008) explain that testimony provides among other things a "sense of autobiographical truth and voice" for individuals on the margins of society (330). For black women in particular, testimony—through pen or voice— provided a means for "inventing" themselves (Morrison 1971, 63) and thus breaking the silence surrounding race, poverty, and womanhood in America.

Indeed statements echoed in activists' speeches and writings such as "tell 'em where it's at" and "tell it like we have lived it" imply a reality that one experiences and can refer to in making a case for more resources. Such a perspective does not mean that people's perceptions of their own lives are unmediated or uncomplicated by other factors. It is simply to say that individuals who experience scarcity (of food, safety, adequate shelter) are in a better position to articulate what that experience is like; they hold "epistemic advantage."

Welfare rights activists did not stop at detailing their own experiences. They thought it important and took great pains to link seemingly individual problems to a larger system. The fact that there was "too much month left at the end of the money" ("Too Much Month" 1972, 15) was not due to an abdication of responsibility on their part, they pointed out. Rather it had more to do with an economic system that directed money to wars and moon walks rather than its citizens.

Collectivizing Experiences of Work

Repeatedly in NWRO literature and congressional hearings, recipient-activists framed themselves as willing workers who were unemployed due to lack of jobs not lack of motivation. It is important to note that welfare recipients alternated between casting themselves as present or potential members of the workforce and as mothers deserving to stay home with their children. The dual—and dueling—frames represented fitting responses to the obstacles facing poor black women. Race discrimination, which denied them the protections of "ideal motherhood," meant that if poor black women chose to remain at home to perform care work, they would be labeled "welfare queens." In this chapter the analysis focuses on the ways women countered the stereotype of the "chiseler," an image that called up the legacy of racism, which saw black women as "employable" regardless of their motherhood status and which buttressed economic exploitation by using poor black women as a ready pool of cheap labor.

Welfare righters gave lie to the idea that recipients were lazy or unwilling to work through the oft-repeated refrains of "Jobs or income now!" ("Who Gets Welfare?" pamphlet); "Adequate income and/or jobs with dignity and justice" ("Welfare Rights of Montclair"; "Welfare Bill of Rights"); and "Payrolls not relief rolls" ("5000 March" 1971, 1). In contrast to the idea of the "welfare chiseler" who didn't want to work, their rhetoric underscored their readiness to work and shifted responsibility to the government to ensure that jobs were available. At a news conference in 1968 Beulah Sanders, then leader of New York's City-Wide Coordinating Committee of Welfare Groups welfare rights organization, proclaimed the group's "bread, justice, and dignity campaign," asserting, "It's not a question of lazy, shiftless women. It's a question of decent jobs" (Kifner 1968c, 7). And in congressional testimony the next year, Sanders pointed out the two-fold problem with Nixon's welfare reform plan, that "there are no jobs available," and "people will be given the menial jobs" (Social Security and Welfare Proposals 1969, 1018). Sanders demanded "adequate jobs be given to mothers that want to go to work and that adequate training be given to that mother" (1018).

A cartoon with accompanying text in the November 1971 *Welfare Fighter* made a similar point. The picture shows a large fist coming down on Nixon's desk as the president sits looking somewhat intimidated. The fist represents welfare recipients, the caption reading, "We need jobs not double talk." Countering the idea that recipients don't work because they are lazy, text below the cartoon cites the 5.8 percent unemployment rate and notes that finding jobs for trained recipients is "nearly impossible" ("Now Let *ME*" 2). "It is inhuman[e] to train welfare recipients, who want to get off welfare, for jobs that do not exist. It only adds to the frustration of being poor."

Local WROs were clear in their demands for jobs. On the organization's fact sheet, ANC–Mothers Anonymous stated as their objective: "To obtain decent jobs with adequate pay for those who can work, and to obtain an adequate income for those who cannot work—an annual income to properly include the poor in our democratic society" (ANC–Mothers Anonymous). The WRO of Allegheny County also distributed a pamphlet demanding "decent jobs with adequate pay for those who can work, and adequate income for those who can not" ("Who Gets Welfare?" pamphlet). In response to demands to "go get a job," organizers responded flatly, "There are no jobs," then offered statistics on unemployment in major cities to prove their point ("Notes on Welfare"). Activists' demands were straightforward as indicated by what protesters told Los Angeles welfare administrators. According to Tillmon, the group's leader, the women told city officials, "We didn't want any more welfare—we wanted jobs. . . . But if they couldn't come up with jobs, then they should leave us alone, and put some more money in the checks. It's just as simple as that" ("Profile of a Welfare Fighter: Johnnie Tillmon" 1971, 3).

In her article "Welfare Is a Women's Issue," Johnnie Tillmon (1972b) was specific about where the blame for lack of jobs rested: "Nobody denies, least of all poor women, that there is dignity and satisfaction in being able to support your kids through honest labor. We wish we could do it. The problem is that our country's economic policies deny the dignity and satisfaction of self-sufficiency to millions of people—the millions who suffer everyday in underpaid dirty jobs—and still don't have enough to survive."

Men and women in the NWRO were often at odds with regards to who should be targeted for employment. When the group began organizing the Poor People's Campaign in 1968, the NWRO's male-dominated staff developed a platform that called for "a minimum guaranteed income of $4000 [annually] for every American family" and "three million jobs for men" (West 1981, 86). They emphasized the "desperate need for jobs in the ghettos for men to permit them to assume normal roles as breadwinners and heads of families" ("NWRO Demands").

In contrast women's demands often reflected their combined needs for well paying employment outside the home and decent child care for their children. The history of black women's work outside the home—for instance the necessity of their wages to subsidize the low income of black men and the prevailing belief that black women were more employable than white women—in addition to their need and desire to care for their own children in their own homes shaped black women's conceptions of work. Jacqueline Jones (1985) notes that "black women had incorporated both traditional (homemaking) and nontraditional (paid employment) roles into their personal ideologies of work, without needing to identify themselves exclusively in terms of either one role or the other the way white wives often did" (305). Thus when it came to shaping the platform for the Poor People's Campaign, women recipients "listed their major needs as higher welfare benefits for women, more jobs and training, and child care, rather than jobs for men and more funds for 'intact' families" (West 1981, 86).

In short, poor black women demanded the same choices their white well-to-do sisters had. They expressed a desire to work when meaningful opportunities were available; yet they also placed care for their children as a top priority (West 1981, 89). Calling attention to the ways race and economic position affected their workplace opportunities and mothering experiences, Tillmon (1972a) pointed out, "If you're a society lady from Scarsdale and you spend all your time sitting on your prosperity paring your nails, well, that's okay." But if you are a woman on welfare, society accuses you of being "lazy" and "immoral."

A heated exchange between NWRO leaders and Senator Martha Griffiths, chairperson of the Subcommittee on Fiscal Policy, during hearings in 1968 further illustrates the ways that race, sex, and class shaped the differing arguments activists provided regarding the status of black women in the workplace. In a discussion on the welfare department's ability to provide jobs for recipients, George Wiley, the NWRO's executive director, stated that the "important thing is that the men, that the people who are able to be heads of households or ought to be legitimate heads of households be the ones that get those jobs" (Income Maintenance Programs 1968, 77). In response Senator Griffiths, who described herself as the "most dedicated feminist we have in Congress," asserted that mothers on welfare should "have a choice" whether to work outside the home or not. Her description of the typical welfare mother's home life was surely one of the more sympathetic responses from congressional members. She stated, "Imagine being confined all day every day in a room with falling plaster, inadequately heated in the winter and sweltering in the summer, without enough beds for the family . . . the furniture falling apart, a bare bulb in the center of the room . . . no hot water most of the time . . . with only the companionship of small children who are often hungry and always inadequately clothed" (qtd. in Steiner 1971, 49).

In a bold move Beulah Sanders, then the second vice chairperson of the NWRO, pushed Griffiths's middle-class sympathies aside and called into question the existence of the "choices" mentioned by the senator. First Sanders appealed to Senator Griffiths based on the commonality of sex: "Could I say one thing before you go, woman to woman?" (Income Maintenance Programs 1968, 78). Then she promptly called out the limitations of Griffiths's middle-class, white feminist viewpoint. Sanders pointed out that although she had a high school degree and skills, she and others like her were often pushed into low-paying domestic positions (78, 79). Furthermore Sanders noted that like their well-to-do counterparts, welfare mothers were concerned about the lack of available child care should they decide to take a job outside the home. In other words what appeared to be "choices" for well-off white women were not available to poor black mothers on welfare.

Wiley's position was typical of responses in the black community to the ways that black masculinity has historically been undermined, a response that challenged white male privilege but that left intact traditional gender roles. Senator

Griffiths's mention of "choice" evoked the white privilege accompanying the widespread belief in <opportunity> and the notion that people could act unconstrained by barriers such as race discrimination. Yet her assertion that women should be targeted for jobs upended the traditional associations of femininity with the domestic sphere. It is interesting to note that from her position as a poor black woman Sanders articulated a response that brought to light the ways that poor black women were exploited in the workplace and denied the resources needed to care for their children adequately in the home.

The complexities of race, sex, and poverty also surfaced in debates surrounding Nixon's proposed welfare legislation, the Family Assistance Plan (FAP), which would guarantee a family of four $1,600 per year. The NWRO noted that FAP represented "guaranteed poverty, guaranteed cheap labor, destruction of the family unit and elimination of the human rights of welfare recipients" ("H.R. 1 Has Contempt" 1971, 1). The organization responded with a demand for a guaranteed adequate yearly income of $5,500, the amount determined by the Bureau of Labor Statistics as the minimum necessary for a family of four to live (Press release). The NWRO was vocal in its denunciation of FAP, particularly in the pages of the *Welfare Fighter,* where beginning in the early 1970s the paper regularly proclaimed, "$5500 or Fight," "Zap FAP," and "Up the Nixon Plan." The paper's March 1970 special edition summarized the organization's position: "Poor people—working and non-working people—need more money. We don't need caseworkers, we don't need food stamps, or surplus food . . . we need an Adequate . . . Income!" ("Adequate Income NOW!" 1970, 1).

The NWRO's responses to FAP called up the ways that the welfare system exploited poor black women, first by denying them viable opportunities in the workplace and second through control of their home life and personal relationships. Although recipient-activists argued for more jobs for men and women as we will see in subsequent sections, they often underscored the urgency of finding jobs for men as traditional breadwinners and providing income for mothers who were "needed in the home" ("Up the Nixon Plan" 1970, 3). On the face of it these two emphases appear to reinforce traditional gender roles and expectations. Yet in the context of a long history of racist welfare legislation based on the notion of the "employable black woman" and the "welfare chiseler," activists' appeals represented a challenge to racist economic exploitation. For instance an article in the paper's special edition on FAP expressed concern regarding "forcing welfare recipients to work without providing either jobs or safeguards against creating a new slavery" and "forcing men to support their families when there are not enough jobs" ("Up the Nixon Plan" 1970, 3). The organization also believed that all mothers (not just mothers of preschool-aged children) should be exempt from forced work, and should they choose to work, they should have access to adequate daycare as did more well-to-do mothers who chose work outside the home ("Adequate Income NOW!" 1970, 1). Arguments for black women's right to choose domesticity countered the notion that black women were more "employable" than white women and that they, therefore, leeched off the system when they chose to stay home with their children.

By mid-1971 the NWRO was demanding "$6500 or fight" in their offensive against FAP. In April welfare rights activists from nine states went to Washington, D.C., to present a "Poor People's Bill of Particulars" on the steps of the capitol. Among the items they demanded was the "creation of 200,000 jobs . . . with priority given to Black and poor people" and the "right of the working poor to organize" ("And the Wall Came" 1971, 2). As part of their rally welfare rights activists along with a supportive employee from the Department of Health, Education, and Welfare (HEW) attempted to enter the HEW building to speak to other employees who supported the demand for $6,500. A temporary wall built to keep them out blocked the protesters. The group summarily tore down the wall and told the police they were taking it to Nixon ("And the Wall Came" 1971, 2).

After three years of struggle welfare recipients saw a small victory as the House and Senate voted to eliminate FAP from the Social Security bill. Those supporting the efforts of welfare righters included liberal congressional members, the United Auto Workers, the AFL-CIO, the Leadership Conference on Civil Rights, and even the League of Women Voters ("Congress Kills FAP" 1972, 3). Elaine McLean's 1972 testimony to senators summed up the groups' position: "We don't want FAP. We don't need FAP. If you and President Nixon want it—you take it, live on it and let us know how it was" (Social Security Amendments of 1971 1972, 2246). In the tradition of "verbal aggressiveness" in which black women have historically "used their sharp tongues as weapons against menacing whites" (J. Jones 1985, 287), McLean turned the tables on congressional leaders and figured herself and other recipients as the directors of welfare policy.

When recipient-activists did argue explicitly for jobs for women, they were astute to the ways that assumptions regarding race and sex shaped understandings of what constituted "work," who had to work, and who got what jobs. Indeed white politicians readily invoked the popular notion that black women were more suited to hard labor than white women, as illustrated in a Georgia representative's response to a proposed bill that would qualify more single black mothers for aid. The man lamented, "There's not going to be anybody left to roll these wheelbarrows and press these shirts" (Quadagno 1994, 130). Democratic Louisiana senator Russell Long was known to have made a similar statement, asserting he would not stop fighting welfare until he found someone to iron his shirts.

Activists provided more or less direct responses to such dubious notions. In a speech to the Pima County WRO, Johnnie Tillmon stated simply, "The best way to get me to work is to pay me a decent salary. Folks tell us we have to be making an honest living—what's so honest about slinging a mop for $1.25 an hour?"

("The States Report: Arizona" 1970, 9). In her 1968 testimony before Congress, Beulah Sanders responded this way to Representative Martha Griffiths's assertions that recipients be given the "choice" to work outside the home: "One of the things we are concerned about is being forced into these nonexisting positions which might be going out and cleaning Mrs. A's kitchen. I am not going to do that because I feel I am more valuable and can do something else. This is one of the things these people are worrying about, that they are going to be pushed into doing housework when they can be much more valuable doing something else" (Income Maintenance Programs 1968, 79).

Sanders's testimony in subsequent years resounded with the frustrations that come with repeating demands for dignity amidst political discourse laced with gender, race, and class stereotypes. At unofficial congressional hearings held by Senator Eugene McCarthy in 1970, Sanders referred to Senator Ribicoff as a "nut" for his proposal to have women cut off New York City welfare rolls and be put to work cleaning streets. Sanders proclaimed to Ribicoff that she "would be the first welfare recipient to volunteer to clean up New York's streets if your mother and your wife were beside me" (qtd. in Kornbluh 2007, 156–57). She maintained that "welfare reform must not be a vehicle for subsidizing slave wage employers at the expense of poor people" (156). Four years later Sanders expressed similar irritation in congressional testimony over amendments to Social Security. After explaining her difficulties getting dental care for her children, Sanders declared "there are other children who [have] to go through the same problem in New York, and Rockefeller is trying to force us to clean some doggone pee-ery. He has got nerve" (Social Security Amendments of 1971 1972, 2071).

Activists repeated concerns over black women being exploited as laborers in white women's homes. Speaking before the Democratic Platform Committee in 1968, Indiana welfare activist Juliet Greenlaw (1968) invoked a history of race exploitation in her condemnation of forced-work provisions: "We think the real reason for this bill [the 1967 welfare amendments] is to force black people to take the maid and hardman jobs that no one else wants to do and that don't pay enough to support a family. We have our own kitchen floors to scrub and our own children to look after!" The December 1971 *Welfare Fighter* ran an article about the organization of household workers, which quoted Ms. Edith B. Sloan of the Household Technicians of America who asserted, "Unless there are some changes made, Madame is going to have to clean her own house and cook and serve her own meals because everyone is going to quit" ("Aunt Jemima Ain't" 1971, 4). And at a protest of over three hundred members of the Philadelphia WRO in August 1972, Louise Brookins told welfare officials that "welfare recipients are not going to scrub floors and clean kitchens at slave wages" ("The States Report: Philadelphia" 1972, 16).

Similarly calling up the ways that traditional "womanhood" relied on the exploitation of black women's labor, Faith Evans, the NWRO eastern regional representative condemned the League of Women Voters for support of the Ribi-coff amendment to FAP that would allow $3,000 a year per family of four. Evans, a black man who had firsthand experience living on welfare, was an NWRO ac-tivist who believed in vesting organizational power in poor women (West 1981, 122). Of the League of Women Voters, Evans stated, "That tea-circle group finds it easy to tell other families to live off that, and they need to have guaranteed annual poverty, they need poor folk to iron their husband's shirts, clean their houses and cook their food for menial wages so they can have tea parties" ("Ribi-coff Attempts" 1971, 4). Evans astutely called out the dimensions of race and exploitation within a capitalist system that work in tandem with a welfare state to ensure a pool of workers desperate (or forced) to take any available job (see Marx 1906). To their credit recipients often refused being economically cornered and instead demanded their right to respectable work.

Brookins' words illustrate the ways activists at times called up the legacy of slavery in their denunciations of welfare reform. In a speech given in Pittsburgh in October 1971, Beulah Sanders decried FAP, calling it a "brazen attempt to enslave the poor people of this country" (Draft of speech). In a November 1967 press conference held by George Wiley, Johnnie Tillmon, and Etta Horn, Wiley asserted that the "welfare department is an extension of the big white plantation which decided what was best for a family" (Press conference).

In sum through congressional testimony and NWRO literature, welfare right-ers upended the image of the welfare chiseler, an image that figured prominently in stories of <opportunity> and that justified the personalization of poverty, the idea for example that if opportunities are available, it must be the individual's fault that she is stuck in poverty. Welfare legislation depended on the image of the "undeserving" poor—chief among that group, the "employable black woman"— in order to maintain a ready pool of low-paid labor. Through demands for de-cent jobs with fair pay, activists redefined themselves as (potential) members of the workforce, and they challenged black women's relegation to low-paying domestic positions.

Giving Presence to Class Disparity

To give further force to their worker persona, activists called attention to the ex-istence of class division, thus giving presence to an economic reality often elided in commonplace understandings of life in America, "the land of opportunity." Although activists did not make explicit reference to "capitalism" as the source of the many problems they faced, they used confrontational language to point out the ways the current system perpetuated poverty in the midst of wealth. Militant rhetoric can be viewed as a necessity given the ways that prescriptions for deco-rum can act hegemonically to discipline the civically marginalized who may be labeled "unruly" when expressing defiance or anger in elite settings.

Beulah Sanders was aggressive in establishing her humanity in a speaking context marked by race, class, and sex power disparities. In response to the charge that she made personal attacks on Long during Senate hearings on amendments to Social Security, Sanders responded: "I am talking to him as a woman and I think he should talk to me as a man. He could protect himself. He got a mouth. Let him speak" (Social Security Amendments of 1971 1972, 2062). The exchange between Long and Sanders continued:

> Long: Well, you people, the witnesses here today—
> Sanders: You people—my name is Mrs. Sanders, Mr. Long.
> Long: Well, lady, whatever your name is—
> Sanders: Don't say lady, I have a name. I call you Senator Long; you call
>   me Mrs. Sanders.

Sanders's verbal volley with Long is remarkable on a number of levels. Her exchange is an unequivocal example of "talking back" as black feminist scholar bell hooks describes it (1989). "Moving from silence into speech is for the oppressed, the colonized, the exploited, and those who stand and struggle side by side a gesture of defiance that heals, that makes new life and new growth possible. It is that act of speech, of 'talking back,' that is no mere gesture of empty words, that is the expression of our movement from object to subject—the liberated voice" (9). With defiance ("Don't say lady") Sanders spoke herself into existence; she demanded respect and the right to self-representation. One can imagine the smiles that crossed the faces of fellow recipients who were there to testify with Sanders that day. Furthermore the formal context of the exchange—a Senate hearing—ensured Sanders a captive (albeit hostile) audience of powerful decision makers, and her words were preserved in the congressional record for scholars to repeat and reaffirm.*

Verbal aggressiveness also provided the means for giving succinct framings of the economic woes facing poor black people: "We need jobs. We need food. We need houses. But even with the poverty program we ain't got nothin' but needs" (J. Jones 1985, 287). In June 1968, speaking before Congress, Sanders took the New York state welfare bureaucracy to task for deliberately creating delays and headaches for potential recipients. She said, "We [welfare rights activists] have been accused in New York [of] killing the goose that laid the golden egg and I am still trying to find where in the hell that goose is. I have not seen him yet, because if he laid a golden egg, I want to know why did I not get my share of it, why did not my brothers and sisters get their share?" (Income Maintenance Programs 1968, 76). In this statement Sanders made visible a system of wealth (the "goose") and established solidarity with her "brothers and sisters" who have been unfairly

---

* Whether or not access to the political elite should be a goal for marginalized groups was the subject of debate within the NWRO.

excluded from resources that are rightfully theirs. Her statement challenged the widespread notion that poor black mothers constituted the "undeserving poor."

In her testimony the following year Sanders stated, "This country is too rich for any of us to be sitting here saying that we don't have enough money to give to poor people in order to maintain their livelihoods. It is too rich for that and the fact that you are saying rather than give them more money they should be going and get a job when you know for a fact that this country has failed to provide the jobs that poor people need. . . . These are the things you need to be thinking about" (Social Security and Welfare Proposals 1969, 1033). She continued by pointing out that government spends "more for dog food, the blind people's dogs, than they spend for human beings. These are the kinds of things that we are fighting and everybody in this country has a right to share this wealth. It was not set up for just one class of people and this is what we have. One class is getting all the wealth and the second class is getting nothing" (1033, 1034).* Sanders concluded by summoning the solidarity of the poor. "Either you include us in decision making that is going to govern our lives, or . . . we are going to disrupt this State, this country, this capital and everything that goes on" (1034).

Echoing Sanders's sentiments Elaine McLean emphasized the lack of available jobs as a primary reason for the increasing welfare rolls. She concluded her prepared statement by setting up a divisive relationship between those in her position and those in privileged positions: "What about all the people who will not be eligible for welfare and who still cannot find jobs? Don't you worry that what you are creating is a still lower—lower class? Are you selling our bodies and souls and the future of our children under the guise of saving a few dollars? It is not *our* fault that the economy is in the shape that it is in—*our* money goes back into the economy within 30 days. We do not put our money in Swiss banks—it goes to landlords, to buy oil, American beef, to pay tithing, utilities, for medical care, soap and keep our kids in school. Because for most of us the LAST thing we want is for our kids to end up on welfare" (Social Security Amendments of 1971 1972, 2247). Both Sanders and McLean highlighted economic exploitation in an attempt to challenge the personalization of poverty and to cultivate group identity based on economic position.

Welfare rights activists also called attention to the ways legislation perpetuated class disparities. Maryland WRO member Lucille Iuzollino-Gitten minced no words when she pointed out that the "poverty situation in Maryland is bad because the government keeps it that way. This is called *institutionalized* poverty. . . . 'Welfare Cadillac' is a myth. The average recipient in Maryland can barely scrape together the money for her child's school shoes" ("Md. WROs Push Increase" 1971, 4). With regards to farm subsidies and tax credits, Hope Hardin,

---

* In this statement Sanders was referring to the fact that Nixon reportedly spent thousands of dollars a year to feed his dog.

a community activist in Rochester, stated, "This isn't free enterprise, this is free-loading. The poor are getting peanuts and the rich are getting caviar" ("The States Report: Rochester" 1972, 17). An organizational document published in 1970 outlined the "welfare" received by the rich that results in "poverty for the poor" ("Welfare for the Rich"). The paper compared the average amount a family of four received from welfare ($2,460 per year) with subsidies and tax exemptions received by farmers, oil companies, and stockholders. To put the welfare figure in perspective, the annual poverty line set by the Social Security Administration in 1970 was $3,968 per year (G. Fisher 1992). And a flyer passed out at food stamp centers by the Detroit WRO noted that money distributed to farmers and businesses is called "subsidies," but when it goes to "ordinary folks" it is called "welfare" ("Food Stamps for GM Strikers" 1970, 5).

In a June 1971 pamphlet on the organization's "Adequate Income Plan," the NWRO relied on statistics to make their point. "We call upon the government to stop subsidizing the rich and the corporations who need it least and start assuring an adequate income for all Americans (through wages, welfare, or both). The richest 20% of the population today has 43% of the income while the poorest 20% has only 6%. We demand that the government move now to assure EVERYONE an adequate income" ("The NWRO Adequate Income Plan" 1971, 3).

Recipients also took aim at Nixon, figuring him as a benefactor of class privilege and as a perpetuator of poor people's oppression. A NWRO flyer dated around 1970–1971 showed Nixon's dogs sitting on the front lawn of the White House and asked: "Who Gets Welfare?" The flyer proceeds to explain, "This family of three has a yearly budget of $2,700. Their Master, who lives in that white mansion, believes that a family of three *people* can live on $1,300 a year ($1,600 for a family of four) . . . for food, clothing, housing . . . everything!" ("Who Gets Welfare?" flyer). Sanders similarly called attention to the fact that Nixon's dogs received better treatment than the nation's poor in her 1972 testimony before the Senate on proposed amendments to Social Security. To Senator Russell Long, the presiding chairperson, Sanders asserted, "You might be able to tell Nixon if he stops spending so much money on war that he can deal with [her children's] future and if he stops spending so much money on feeding his dogs he could spend money to feed [her children], to see they get the proper food, the decent medical care and they would grow up to be healthy children and might get that education so that they could take your place" (Social Security Amendments of 1971 1972, 2061). At an April 15 rally in 1970, Etta Horn, chairperson of the D.C. Citywide stated, "Mr. Nixon is doing everything in his power to keep black and poor people down, hungry, starving, and oppressed" ("April 15th Rallies" 1970, 1). She warned that if Nixon's FAP passed there would be "no peace nowhere as far as poor people are concerned." Likewise Sarah McPherson, chairperson of the D.C. Family Rights WRO asserted that "poor people would never accept" FAP and advised Nixon to "get on the ball unless he wants poor people to take their problems to the streets" because if they did it would "surely be hell" (1).

Poor people on welfare did indeed take it to the streets, and women leaders repeatedly spoke of the benefits gained by organizing the poor.* Upon winning a repeal of Nevada's cuts in aid to recipients, Ruby Duncan, the chairperson of the Clark County WRO stated, "We have demonstrated that when poor people stand up for their rights, speak up for their rights, march for their rights, go to jail for their rights, and organize for their rights, they can win their rights" ("Total Victory in Nevada!" 1971, 5). With regards to the Nevada victory, Johnnie Tillmon (1971), the national organization's chairperson, reminded *Welfare Fighter* readers, "We had to fight for this victory with our lives and the lives of our children. . . . We should have learned from this fight if we hadn't learned before, that we have strength if we are together and if we are organized. Alone, we have no voice, no power at all" (12). Their sentiments echoed those of early twentieth-century labor activists who spoke to the importance of "sticking capacity" (solidarity) in struggles against bosses.†

The NWRO forged ties with other social justice organizations throughout its history, including SNCC, SCLC, and Martin Luther King's Poor People's Campaign (Kornbluh 2007; West 1981). As early as 1969 welfare rights activists made efforts to organize with workers, and such efforts became more of a centerpiece of the organization in 1971 and 1972, at the urging of George Wiley. For example in late 1969, when social workers attempted to force recipients to break two strikes, recipients refused, explaining that it would result in "musical chairs," with those on strike becoming the newest folks on welfare ("State Action, Virginia" 1969, 4). And when General Electric workers went on strike, local WROs in Massachusetts, Virginia, and New York assisted strikers in getting public assistance. In exchange strikers supported welfare rights activists' campaign for a minimum guaranteed income of $5,500 ("GE Strikers" 1969, 3).

Throughout 1971 the national organization made several moves to broaden the welfare rights struggle, giving further impetus to the group's emphasis on class. Beulah Sanders stated unequivocally, "We are about a 'Guaranteed Adequate Income' for all Americans; and that means a true redistribution of this country's resources in such a way as to guarantee the right to a decent life to all Americans, be they man, woman, child, black, white or red, working or nonworking" ("Beulah—From the Chair" 1971, 3). That year the *Welfare Fighter* ran a column called Movement Spotlight, which highlighted the actions of others struggling for workplace justice, such as domestic workers, trade unions,

* The NWRO's "street strategy" (West 1981, 292) is discussed in chapter 5.
† In 1915 Melinda Scott used the phrase "sticking capacity" to describe women of the hat-making industry who stood by male comrades during a six-month struggle for workplace rights.

university employees, and peace groups. In October the NWRO's annual convention held panels on "the Movement," with speakers representing the Tenants Union and National Household Employment and others who emphasized the "need for all groups struggling for a decent living to recognize their common goals and to find ways to support one another" ("Convention '71" 1971, 7). The convention also held workshops on Black Power, blue-collar power, and La Raza.

In February 1971 the NWRO joined forces with the Southern Christian Leadership Conference to demand "adequate paying jobs or an adequate guaranteed income for all Americans . . . an end to white, racist domination of education . . . the guarantee by law of the right of the working poor to organize themselves and bargain collectively for decent pay and working conditions . . . an immediate end to all forms of repression against poor people" ("SCLC Links Up" 1971, 1, 9). Leaders of the two groups, George Wiley and Ralph Abernathy, formed the People's Lobby against poverty, war and repression and encouraged mass demonstrations across the country, which were coordinated from April 2 to April 5, 1971. On April 5 over five thousand marched down Wall Street "to force the nation's attention to the failure of people who worry every day about nourishing their money while millions around them are unable to nourish their children" ("The Spring Offensive" 1971, 2). At the rally Jennette Washington spoke to the power of solidarity among the poor: "You are not going to kill leaders anymore like you did to Martin Luther King. Because if you kill me, you haven't killed a leader. There are another 150,000 people who will take my place" (2; see figure 3.1).

Further efforts to join forces with other poor people's groups came in the form of a suggestion to fold the *Welfare Fighter* into a proposed paper, *Economic Justice*, which would cover the efforts of household workers, tenants, farm workers, migrants, and so on. The paper would "bring unity of information and possibly some unity of action to various poor people[']s groups" ("New Direction for Fighter").

As Wiley attempted to broaden welfare rights to include other poor people's organizations, black female recipients who represented the grassroots of the welfare rights movement worried about their own positions. From Wiley's perspective welfare rights needed to broaden its base to garner more support from other groups in poverty, for example unemployed and working poor (West 1981, 116). Wiley also believed that emphasis on welfare should be replaced by the goals of jobs and employment, which were more clearly aligned with the traditional values of self-reliance and hard work. In contrast women leaders "feared that attention to their unique problems as female heads of household would be diminished" (116). And some felt their leadership positions would be threatened by expanding the organization.

Gender tensions came to a head in the early 1970s as poor black women on the executive committee expressed dissatisfaction with the amount of control

Fig. 3.1
Jennette Washington, recipient
and organizer of the West Side
Welfare Recipients League
in New York. Records of the
National Welfare Rights Organization (NWRO), Moorland-Spingarn Research Center, Howard
University.

wielded by Wiley (West 1981, 113). At an August 1972 meeting on state and regional development, local recipient-leaders noted that among other things national leaders held too much power and that "welfare recipients should be the paid staff in their own office" (Gross 1972). In addition paid field organizers should be welfare recipients. In her notes of the meeting, Rita Gross also noted the "ego problem" of NWRO staff. "The people in control (males) at NWRO have egos which require an empire—regardless of whether it be at the expense of poor people" (2). Brooklyn organizer Jackie Pope similarly noted the condescending approach that some staff members took. "The sexism was there," although recipients did not use that term at the time (2011).

Other tensions within the national organization centered on the group's relationship to the political establishment. Women leaders, including Johnnie Tillmon, believed that even as they took aim at the system they should make attempts to negotiate within it. The "Tillmon model," as West (1981) called it, was an organizational approach that emphasized "traditional political and legal strategies . . . such as voter registration, running for elected office, and the use of established political processes and the courts" (102). Beulah Sanders led a group to the 1972 Democratic National Convention, where they presented the Poor People's Platform, which stated, "All Americans must be guaranteed the right to an adequate income" of $6,500 annually, and "All Americans should have their economic security assured." Expressing the seeming ambivalence women had in efforts to accommodate the political system, Sanders explained, "We . . . will go to the Democratic National Convention in the same manner we have always dealt with the unjust system—with representation on the inside but our real strength on the outside in the streets" ("NWRO Marches" 1972, 8).

Thus in their efforts to call attention to disparities based on class, women in the NWRO faced a number of challenges both in and outside of the organization, which shaped their goals and strategies between 1969 and 1972 and ultimately led to a decline in militancy. Notable is that external "political and economic conditions impinged on and aggravated the tensions within the NWRO" (West 1981, 78). As government officials and welfare administrators tinkered with the welfare system in response to sit-ins and massive demonstrations and tightened controls over the poor, the NWRO shifted to negotiating within the system, but not without criticism from middle-class allies, such as Frances Fox Piven and Richard Cloward, who provided leadership for the welfare rights movement from its inception. Piven asserted, "When WRO leaders are willing to wander into these higher realms and sit down and negotiate with the Secretary of HEW, with members of liberals in Congress, and don't stay with the grassroots, time and money are wasted. Nothing changes" (West 1981, 304).

The stereotype of the welfare chiseler, particularly prominent during historical moments of welfare debate and reform, helped to perpetuate the belief that some poor people were "undeserving" of public assistance. The image of the welfare chiseler worked in tandem with racist beliefs surrounding women, work, and mothering. Poor black women, viewed as a ready pool of domestic workers and field hands, were labeled lazy if they received public assistance.

As Collins (1991) notes, for poor black women self-definition was a matter of survival, and this was especially true when it came to combating stereotypes that impacted their ability to support their families. Welfare rights activists responded to the myth of the welfare chiseler by redefining themselves as motivated and capable workers who were part of a larger economic system that failed to provide adequate jobs.

Besides being stereotyped as "welfare chiselers" in regards to their work lives, poor black women were stereotyped as "welfare queens" in their domestic lives, an image that illustrates the ways that race shapes women's experiences of mothering. Together the two stereotypes controlled women's experiences in and outside their homes and placed them in a double bind. Welfare policies sought to push poor black mothers into wage-earning work and to control the types of work available to them even as the image of the stay-at-home mother remained a societal ideal. When recipients attempted to remain home to care for their own children, they were labeled "welfare queens" and endured invasions into their personal lives as a condition for receiving public assistance. Welfare rights activists responded by affirming their capability as mothers who deserved state assistance to help them raise their children, which is the subject of the next chapter.

4

Deserving Mothers

Not just one man hangs around—but two or three men frequent
the home. The children don't know who their fathers are. These
mothers and their paramours are breeding future citizens
who are going to have no conception of law and order.
Senator Robert Byrd, quoted in Neubeck
and Cazenave, *Welfare Racism*

If you think that I'm gonna have a baby—and watch that child
grow up with no food or clothing; and . . . see him go into the
army and get really shot up in there—if you think I'm gonna
go through all that pain and suffering for an extra $50, or
$100, or even $500 a month, why you must be crazy.
Mrs. Anne Henderson, welfare mother, quoted in
Tarantino and Becker, *Welfare Mothers Speak Out*

Throughout the 1960s "body-centered attacks on childbearing black women,"
specifically in the image of the "jezebel" or "calculating breeder for profit," represented a continuation of slave-era stereotypes and were used to justify racist
welfare legislation from the 1950s through the 1980s (Solinger 2000; see also
Collins 1991; Morton 1991; Mullings 1995). The degradation of black mothers
was reinforced in the postwar writings of sociologists and criminologists who
blamed women of "literally giving birth to the nation's . . . social problems," including poverty, juvenile delinquency, and gang violence (Orleck 2005, 82). Such
views were further reinforced by Senator Daniel Patrick Moynihan's 1965 report
"The Negro Family: The Case for National Action," in which the author referred
to families headed by black women as a "tangle of pathology."

In the face of racist discourses that justified or legitimized economic exploitation and political discrimination, black mothers have worked to ensure the men-
tal well-being and physical survival of their children as well as their communities
(Collins 1994; Mullings 2003). Their reliance on the trope of motherhood (Valk
2000) should be understood in the context of poor black mothers' location at the
intersection of capital and care. From slave-era work mandates to forced-work
provisions in welfare legislation of the 1960s and 1990s, legislation has treated

poor black women as "employable" and has denied them the option of decent care for their own families.

This chapter begins with a brief look at prevailing racist discourses regarding poor black mothers as a way to contextualize the resistant rhetoric used by welfare rights activists as they countered the stereotype of the welfare queen. I then turn to an examination of the ways that mothers in the welfare rights movement challenged that stereotype by giving presence to their experiences in the home as they negotiated the contradictions wrought by a racist economic system that relegated them to low-paying jobs and blamed them for not living up to the ideals of middle-class motherhood.

Historical background

Race profoundly shapes the social construction and lived experience of motherhood. From the slave era through the 1960s, public and popular discourses have commodified the black mother and child, condemned black mothers as immoral or hypersexual, criticized them as financial burdens on society, and accused them of creating a culture of delinquency, crime, and perpetual poverty. Racist discourses surrounding the black mother influenced legislation at the federal and state levels and also served to "diffuse" civil rights challenges and to "forestall social change" through the 1950s and 1960s (Solinger 2000, 233).

The practice of slave trade relied on stereotypes that commodified and hypersexualized black women in order to legitimate the brutal treatment and regular sexual assaults against female slaves (Collins 1991). These stereotypes were echoed in early to mid-twentieth-century welfare policy practices that framed the black female as "ill-suited to domestic motherhood by a long history of toil outside the home" in order to justify the exclusion of black women from public assistance (Mink 1995, 51). Such was the case in early configurations of Aid to Dependent Children, which exempted agricultural and domestic workers (primarily poor, black women) from aid—as well as from minimum wage laws and Social Security benefits—when cheap labor was needed by employers and white families (Abramovitz 2000, 64–66; Mink 1995, 132–33; Neubeck and Cazenave 2001, 47–59).

The associations among black women, sex, and money were perpetuated in welfare discourses in the 1960s that understood black women as "in the business of childbearing" in order to collect more public aid (Solinger 2000, 29, 30; see also Orleck 2005, 83). Solinger (2000) explains, "For many white Americans, black women had historically suggested an association between sex and money, as procreating slaves and as prostitutes, profitable or pleasurable for white men" (42). As welfare debates intensified in the 1960s, white politicians reignited these associations by portraying poor single black mothers as a financial burden to white taxpayers. In addition to being portrayed as a financial liability, single black mothers were seen as a threat to the morality of the nation. Popular and professional commentators in the era following World War II studied white out-of-wedlock pregnancy in psychological terms, as maladjustment to family or societal mores. In contrast black out-of-wedlock pregnancy was understood as purely biological; that is black women were deemed naturally sexual and thus immoral and sexually out of control (43, 44).

The national preoccupation with the supposed biological and moral degeneracy of single black mothers played into "large questions of national life and public policy" in the 1950s and 1960s and was reflected in discussions in newspapers and professional circles (Orleck 2005, 82; Solinger 2000, 45). Alongside theories of biological determinism that scapegoated single black mothers for all that was wrong in the black community, the 1960s saw increasing talk of a "culture of poverty" that supposedly contributed to different familial practices in black communities.* Originally coined by the 1960s anthropologist Oscar Lewis, the term *culture of poverty* was meant to refer to a "defense mechanism adapted by the poor in response to capitalist inequality" (Rosenberg 2008, 46). With the publication of the Moynihan report, the phrase "became a shorthand for black ghetto culture, a defect of the poor" (46). By the late 1960s culture-of-poverty discourses implied a hierarchy of culture—a wholesome white culture, "protective and benign," and an "unwholesome" black culture, "aberrant and dangerous" (Solinger 2000, 61).

A 1965 U.S. Department of Labor report entitled *The Negro Family: The Case for National Action* further legitimated the culture-of-poverty perspective and perpetuated slave-era stereotypes of the black matriarch, the licentious welfare mother, and the "shiftless" black male (Bensonsmith 2005, 247). The then assistant secretary of labor, Daniel Patrick Moynihan, wrote the report in an effort to set a new course for civil rights advocacy into the late 1960s and beyond. Once released to the public, the report set off a firestorm of debate within political, academic, and activist circles, sparked in part by the document's emphasis on the "pathology" of the black female–headed family. In its effort to address the crisis in the black community, the report gave a nod to structural issues, particularly high rates of unemployment among black males. As the report's title suggests however the document pointed to the matriarchal black family as the prime reason for the deterioration of the black community. The report stated that because the matriarchal family structure "is out of line with the rest of American society," it "seriously retards the progress of the group as a whole, and imposes a crushing

---

* Solinger (2000) provides a historical backdrop for discussions of black families and out-of-wedlock births with her discussion of E. Franklin Frazier's 1939 book *The Negro Family in the United States.* Frazier's findings took emphasis off of black women's supposed hypersexuality and redirected it onto environmental factors, for example deteriorated neighborhoods, and so on (Solinger 2000, 59, 60).

burden on the Negro male" (Moynihan 1965, 75). The matriarchal family was described as a "tangle of pathology," with numerous nefarious consequences for black males. In "broken" homes where women lead the family, black males were said to perform more poorly in school, to be more prone to delinquency and crime, in short, to "flounder" and "fail" (Moynihan 1965, 77–86).

It is ironic that the poor black women portrayed as incapable of raising their own children "are thought to be entirely competent at parenting the children of the elite—as mammies during slavery, as domestic workers during segregation, or as childcare workers today" (Mullings 1995, 130), thus underscoring the patriarchal and classist ideological underpinnings of the popular images. Scapegoating poor black mothers for social ills extended into the 1980s and 1990s with female-headed families denigrated as the "underclass" (131). Yet critics had much to say in response to these discourses (Rainwater and Yancey 1967). Dr. Pauli Murray—expressing the sentiments of many black women insulted by the Moynihan report—decried the account for punishing black mothers "for their efforts to overcome a handicap not of their own making and for trying to meet the standards of the country as a whole" (Rainwater and Yancy 1967, 185). Intellectuals emphasized that life in black urban communities was hardly pathological but rather was characterized by "extensive networks of kin and friends supporting, reinforcing each other—devising schemes for self-help, strategies for survival in a community of severe economic deprivation" (Stack 1974, 28; see also Gans 1967, 451; J. Jones 1985, 309).

Welfare recipients, many of whom voiced their concerns through welfare rights organizations, similarly debunked the stereotype of the welfare matriarch through rhetorical efforts that negotiated their incompatible positions at the intersection of capital and care, where simultaneously they were expected to fill low paying jobs in the labor force and were cast as "bad mothers" for failing to live up to a white middle-class ideal of motherhood. The competing demands of capital and care placed poor black women in a double bind—if they chose to stay home to care for their children, they were labeled lazy; if they entered the paid labor force they were considered bad mothers. Just as the demands placed upon them were often in contradiction, welfare recipients' replies to stereotypes varied.

Giving Presence to Home Life

Giving presence to or highlighting their day-to-day experiences—particularly to audiences far removed from the daily routines of welfare recipients—remained an important task for welfare rights activists. Just as women brought to life their workplace experiences, they spoke about what it was like to care for a family on public assistance. Rhetorically speaking, claiming to know the reality of home life better than their interlocutors enabled activists to establish grounds from which to judge competing narratives of the life-on-welfare story. During 1962 congressional hearings on welfare fraud, Senator Robert Byrd of West Virginia relied heavily on gendered and racist "controlling images" of the welfare queen as illustrated in the epigraph that opened this chapter. However a more realistic portrayal of women's lives went unspoken at the 1962 hearings as no recipients were present to testify. Had they been granted the opportunity, no doubt recipients would have given Byrd an earful as they did in subsequent years.

Recipients did testify in May and June 1967 as part of an examination of the War on Poverty and again in 1968 as part of a federal study of rural poverty and hunger. These testimonies provide a window into the ways that welfare recipients gave "presence" to their lives in front of an audience quite distanced from experiences of poverty. Recipients spoke from their position as concerned mothers who did not have enough resources to raise their children. Such appeals stood in direct contrast to prevailing images of the greedy or lazy welfare mother so prevalent in the popular imagination and legitimated by the Moynihan report.

For example in her 1967 congressional testimony, Simone St. Jock, a welfare recipient and board member of the Springfield Action Committee, made this appeal to Senator Edward Kennedy: "We are both parents. I have a son[,] 18[,] who is registered for the draft. When he comes home in 2 weeks, he wants to go [to the Vietnam war].... Now, how am I to feel? Here I have an 18-year-old that wants to go to Vietnam; I have a 5-year-old [at home]; which is the greatest tragedy or the greatest sin—to see my 18-year-old go out there and get killed instantly or to watch my 5-year-old go without every day? ... We need more money for our children" (Examination of the War on Poverty 1967, 4675).

In 1968 Viola Holland, Nancy Cole, and Gussie Davis provided extensive detail of their struggles, which in effect "prolong[ed] the attention given them" and thereby contributed to the presence created "in the consciousness of the audience" (Perelman 1982, 37). Although the race of these three women is not clear from reading their testimony, their descriptions of their struggles are representative of the ways that recipients justified their claims to public assistance and challenged the stereotype of the lazy welfare mother. Although not stereotyped in quite the same way as black mothers were, white women who asserted the right to public aid were considered suspect within the larger discourses of deservedness and motherhood, especially if these women were single and had children out of wedlock.

Giving lie to the idea that mothers on welfare lived a good life off of public assistance, Holland, Cole, and Davis explained the struggles involved in feeding their families and managing a family budget on next to nothing. Holland began her narrative, "Well, I'm a housewife and I have been working with the Appalachian Volunteers for the last 3 years, and the community action, working with the school superintendent of Wolfe County [Kentucky], trying to improve our schools here in this one community in particular" (Rural Poverty and Hunger 1968, 5). She went on, "I don't buy too much food. We usually raise what we eat on the farm. . . . If I had to go to the store and buy all of the groceries for my family even the social security benefits that I draw wouldn't nothing like run us a month" (6). Likewise Cole noted that "the first part of the month we have good meals, up until about 2 weeks of the month, then the rest of the month we live on beans and bread. . . . Sometimes by the last of the month we didn't have bread in our family. We didn't get enough welfare, so life has been hard" (Rural Poverty and Hunger 1968, 7). She continued, "You have to buy books for the children to go to school; you have to buy their clothes; you have to pay their hot lunch bill; you've got your electric bill to pay; you've got all these things to pay and you live off $112 a month for the children, how can you have anything left?" (7).

Davis, who was caring for two children at home after having raised seven others, received $101.60 in assistance per month. She detailed her monthly expenses for Senator Edward Kennedy. "I have to pay $20 a month house rent and pay $15 and sometimes a little more for power bill. I have to buy my coal and it takes at least 2 tons a month, I mean through the cold part of the winter, and takes $10 to get it, if not more, and my baby goes to school and I have to pay 30 cents a day for its lunch . . . and I've got . . . a little life insurance on me—that is $7—so when I get all that stuff there is nothing left for you. I buy food stamps and I have to pay $28 for $40 worth and I have to pay somebody for transportation and pay $5 when I sign up once a year and if I pick them up I have to pay somebody $5 to go down and pick up my food stamps once a month" (Rural Poverty and Hunger 1968, 27).

By detailing household expenses and their struggles to provide basic care for their children, these recipients spotlighted the labor involved in managing family expenses on an inadequate income, what women during the Depression referred to as "making do" (Westin 1976). It is important that they undermined the stereotype of the lazy welfare mom, an image that circulated widely in popular media outlets and in political contexts for decades (Albelda, Folbre, and the Center for Popular Economics 1996).

In addition to testifying before Congress, women formed local WROs and wrote letters to their senators. Margaret McCarty chaired the Baltimore group, Mothers Rescuers from Poverty, which sought basic rights for recipients, including more money for children's school clothes. McCarty asserted that "every woman should know more about politics, more about welfare, more about what their rights are" ("Welfare Mothers–Drive Launched" 1966). She explained the heartbreaking experience of mothers like herself: "One of my boys was told by his gym teacher not to come back to school unless he had his gym clothes. My little girl had to stand on the sidelines at gym period because she didn't have the uniform. The kids come back home, and they look at you, but you can't give them these things."

McCarty was not alone in calling attention to her struggles to provide adequately for her children. At a 1970 NWRO caucus meeting, NWRO officer Nezzie

Willis proclaimed that mothers were "sick and tired of seeing their children go without the little things kids need for a normal existence" (Frauel and Berton 1970, 11). Likewise expressing outrage and sadness, Dorothy Scott sent a letter to her senator, Stephen Young, sharing her opposition to then president Nixon's proposed Family Assistance Plan (FAP), which would provide a minimum income of $1,600 for a family of four—well below the figure determined by the Bureau of Statistics as necessary to feed a family that size. Scott gave presence to her experiences through the use of rhetorical questions that encouraged the senator to imagine her position. She wrote, "My boy is a teenager now and his needs are great—Could you deny yourself so your child could get enough to eat—could you stand to see any spending money you gave him go mostly for something to eat?—could you take seeing him get excited over things other children take for granted?" (D. Scott 1970, 3).

In their angry replies to charges of being lazy mothers who leeched off a bloated welfare system, Scott, Willis, and others were quick to point out how little money was actually spent on public assistance compared to other government programs. Nezzie Willis noted that "money spent on moon shots, air pollution and new highways would be better spent right at home. . . . Clean air is beautiful if there's anyone left to sniff it and the highways are an improvement but who has cars to drive on them" (Frauel and Berton 1970, 11). In her letter to Senator Young, Scott (1970) pointed out, "There is enough money to fight wars that are not even declared . . . and yet . . . you let little children go hungry—right here at home—and wear rags—and even worse" (3).

Recipient-activists also appealed to politicians through live-on-a-welfare-budget events, which sought to "sensitize middle class people to some of the realities of the public welfare system" ("How to Do the NWRO Test"). Note the reference to the "realities" of life on welfare; implied here is the idea that living an experience lends "epistemic advantage" and thus shapes one's understanding of that experience. In 1969 the national organization initiated the Welfare Food Budget week and the Nixon Welfare Plan Test, in which politicians were encouraged to eat on a welfare budget for one week. Activists believed that getting the more well-off to "walk a mile in their shoes" would cause the general public and policy makers to understand their problems in a way that their narratives of making do might not. George Wiley, the NWRO executive director, explained that the "purpose of the test is to educate middle class people . . . and to create an opportunity to translate this education into political action" (Wiley letter 1969). The national organization prepared and sent out to sympathetic organizations materials that included guidelines for participating, statistics on the inadequate weekly budget allotted by the proposed Nixon plan, and suggestions for an evaluation meeting at the end of the week, where participating families could share their experiences ("How to Do a 'Test the Nixon Welfare Budget' Week").

It is difficult to determine what impact these events had on promoting welfare rights. The coordinated national effort combined with coverage from corporate-owned newspapers, including the *Washington Post,* the *New York Times,* and the *Kansas City Star,* spread public awareness of life on public assistance and no doubt encouraged many to rethink the veracity of the welfare queen image. During the campaign launched by New York's City-Wide Coordinating Committee, the food critic for the *New York Times* suggested meals to fit within the welfare budget, no doubt spotlighting the scantiness of poor families' diets. The *Times* also described the experience of Bronx representative Jonathan Bingham and his wife, who stated that during their week on a welfare budget, they were edgy and unable to concentrate on their work (Kornbluh 2007, 140). The *Kansas City Star* quoted sympathetic Missouri senator Thomas Eagleton, who participated in the budget week test: "In a country such as ours, where we can apparently well afford a war, there ought to be a way to feed hungry people, clothe them and house them" ("Eagleton for Welfare Push" 1969, 8A). A *Washington Post* editorial noted that local and federal governments "cruelly ignore the rights and needs of millions of poor people" ("A Week of Welfare" 1969, A16).

Nevertheless negotiating with politicians carried risks as well as gains. Women in the NWRO received public attention and political recognition as when Senator Eagleton met with Evalyn Floyd and others from the Kansas City, Kansas, WRO ("Eagleton for Welfare Push" 1969, 8A). Yet working within the political system represented a strategy of accommodation that took resources away from more confrontational tactics such as those detailed in the next chapter. Furthermore the welfare budget test was inherently limited by its temporary nature; politicians and middle-class citizens went to back to diets of lean meat, fruits, and vegetables at the end of the week while those on welfare continued on commodity foods that barely lasted them through the month. In the end, although Nixon's Family Assistance Plan was eventually defeated, the NWRO's push for a guaranteed adequate annual income of $5,500 never became a reality.

When they were unsuccessful in their appeals to politicians for more resources, poor black women often relied on community organizations and kin and neighbor networking to find their public voice and enable them to make ends meet, if only temporarily. Like other recipient-activists, Simone St. Jock spoke to the importance of her involvement in a community organization. "I am ADC on welfare. Through the block club I was commissioner for a year first at the Springfield Action Committee. Through the block club, they voted me in, which was the first time that I even knew how the mechanism of voting was. I was put on the executive board, and I may be wrong in stating this, but I believe I was the first welfare recipient to sit on a board, a policymaking board.... I have found out that I have a voice" (Examination of the War on Poverty 1967, 4674).

Beulah Sanders, the second vice chairperson of the NWRO, spotlighted recipients' reliance on neighbors to cover expenses for their children: In "New York, we have a series of trips . . . that are taking place for the children because this is the last month of school. I can say today 80 percent of those kids are not going on trips because the parents just do not have the money. Our budgets are so small that to really make it from one check day to the other check day, it is incredible, because she has to borrow from the next-door neighbor. As soon as her check comes, she has to pay it back and that still creates a problem, because when she pays the next-door neighbor the money that she borrowed in order to send her child on a trip, then she has taken money from something that she needed" (Income Maintenance Programs 1968, 67). The historian Jacqueline Jones (1985) explains that exchange processes such as the one described by Sanders "followed the lines of cooperation evident among southern rural blacks immediately after emancipation" and "were no less compelling because they facilitated the use of a car to get to an interview rather than a mule and a wagon to take a cotton bale to town" (309). Cooperative networking continues in the present, as Leith Mullings (2003) notes in her studies of women in 1990s Harlem, New York. "People construct and utilize support systems, primarily women-centered, for garnering and redistributing material and social resources" (191).

In addition to giving presence to their struggles as mothers, welfare rights activists negotiated the competing demands and desires surrounding work and family in a way unique to their positions as black women.

Race, Work, and the Family

Black women have throughout history seen little relevance in white middle-class women's struggles for the right to work in the paid labor force. Black women had always been in the labor force, first as slaves in the fields and homes of white families, then as agricultural and domestic workers segregated by Jim Crowism. Jacqueline Jones (1985) explains that in the post–Civil War south, black families kept women at home when they could afford to. Relieved of the burden of field work, domestic duties, and threats of sexual assault by slave masters, black women prized "emotional fulfillment and a newfound sense of pride from their roles as wives and mothers" (58). In the context of the second wave feminist movement, many black women viewed work outside the home as a dubious freedom. Moreover it was black women's roles as domestics that enabled white women to leave their homes and children for a paid career (316).

Indeed while middle-class white feminists viewed the traditional family as a target for dismantling, black women held their families together "as a locus of resistance against racism" (J. Jones 1985, 403). In the early 1900s poor black mothers were denied aid through mothers' pensions while the welfare reforms of the 1960s disproportionately affected black mothers considered "undeserving" of public assistance, as detailed in the introduction. That is "black women were often viewed as a distinct class of womanhood to which the ideal of domesticity did not apply" (Mink 1995, 142). In this light black women's appeals to the desirability of stay-at-home mothering can be seen as a form of resistance to a white culture's conception of motherhood that denied poor black women the "possibility of nurturing, motherhood and family maintenance" (Boris 1993, 217; see also Mink 1995, 6). Protest signs demanding "Let Mothers Stay Home" (Nelton 1967) highlight poor black women's history of workplace exploitation and family deprivation. When welfare rights activists emphasized mothering and home life they were upending a "social script written for them by the larger culture" that denied their right to create a safe, nurturing home life (Boris 1993, 217).

Welfare rights advocates' responses to a controversial amendment to welfare legislation proposed in August 1967 by conservative House member Wilber Mills of Arkansas provide an insight into the dynamics of race, gender, and family in the context of welfare policy debates. House bill 12080, coined the "anti-welfare bill" by NWRO activists, represented a shift in emphasis from supporting children to punishing mothers, a move that also characterized welfare reforms of the 1980s and 1990s. The bill would freeze AFDC payments at January 1, 1967, levels and force mothers to accept work or training in exchange for benefits. The goal as stated by the amendment was to assure, "to the maximum extent possible, that AFDC recipients will enter the labor force and accept employment" ("Fight the Anti-welfare Bill").

The NWRO's position oscillated between an emphasis on female self-determination and the male-headed familial ideal. The organization denounced H.R. 12080 because it "would mean that the government, not the mother, would decide if she is needed to take care of her children" ("What's Happening?"). The forced-work provision would "take away the right of welfare mothers to decide when it is in the best interests of their children to remain at home as a full-time mother" ("Wanted for Conspiracy" c1968, 3). NWRO literature noted, "Any mother who wants a job should be guaranteed meaningful employment at adequate income with proper child care available" ("Wanted for Conspiracy" c1968, 4). And in their testimony many welfare recipients did not eschew the issue of paid work outside the home altogether; rather they wanted to be able to control the conditions under which such employment was sought. Welfare rights activists protesting in front of the federal building in Detroit in late 1967 explained to the press they wanted "the right to decide [if] it is in the best interest of their children if the mothers remain in the home or take jobs outside" (Nelton 1967). Women in the Massachusetts WRO put the matter simply in their 1970 state report published in the *Welfare Fighter*. The women wanted the "power to get adequate income and dignity, power to keep our children home . . . and power to stop the system from running our lives the way the man wants it; we want to run our own lives" ("Adequate Income NOW!" 1970, 7).

Yet women's claims to deserving a choice to work or stay home sat uncomfortably next to NWRO invocations of the traditional nuclear family ideal. The

Mills bill—as well as Nixon's FAP, which was to be debated just a few years later—was lambasted for destroying the male-headed family. The November 1967 issue of *NOW!*, the NWRO newsletter that predated the *Welfare Fighter*, stated that the anti-welfare bill "continues to attack and divide the families of the poor by allowing states to continue to refuse aid to children until their father is out of the home and by forcing women to work when there are already not enough jobs for men" ("The Anti-welfare Bill" 1967). Another NWRO newsletter stated, "To force women to work at a time when up to 40% of all men in the ghettoes and barrios are unemployed is a serious mistake" ("Wanted for Conspiracy" c1968, 4). NWRO historian Guida West (1981) explains that the "male-dominated [NWRO] staff gave top priority to goals that reinforced the 'intact' and traditional family . . . ignoring the fact that the majority of NWRO's members represented female-headed households" (86).

Similar debate surrounded H.R. 16311, Nixon's Family Assistance Plan, introduced in 1969, which would provide a minimum income of $1,600 for a family four and would exempt mothers of preschool-aged children from work requirements. Although both of these provisions appeared a step in the right direction, welfare rights activists were quick to point out that $1,600 per year was well below the $5,500 minimum determined necessary by the Bureau of Labor Statistics to care for a family of four ("Adequate Income NOW!"; "Up the Nixon Plan"). Furthermore the NWRO called for "protection for mothers with school age children who are needed in the home" as well as for the "right to daycare" should the women desire to work outside the home ("Up the Nixon Plan" 3). Calling up the ways black women have historically been denied the right to remain home to care for their own children, Beulah Sanders told congressional members, the "mother should have the right to say if she wants to work or she should have the right to say whether her children should be put into a government-run center" (Social Security and Welfare Proposals 1969, 1017). And aligning with the national organization's emphasis on work for men, Sanders urged Congress to "provide jobs for the men on the corners first so that they can provide for their families" (1018).

A 1970 special edition of the *Welfare Fighter* delineated specific areas of the bill requiring change and called on readers to "Up the Nixon Plan." The national organization used the battle against FAP as a rallying point and a way to motivate local WROs to demonstrate in conjunction with the group's fourth anniversary on June 30, 1970. In a defiant tone the organization stated, "We in the NWRO have continued to grow in spite of being branded as 'Militants,' 'rab[b]le-rouser' and 'brood mares.' . . . Here we are in 1970 and NWRO is . . . thumbing our noses at those who said 'You're hurting your cause.' Damn them—we'll celebrate in the streets again this year, in the welfare centers, in the state capitols. . . . Our theme will be UP The NIXON PLAN—5,500 OR FIGHT" ("June 30th Birthday" 4).

The NWRO was not without support in Congress. In July 1971 Senator George McGovern introduced a bill in the Senate, the "Adequate Income Act of

1971," which would guarantee a minimum annual income of $6,500. And the Black Congressional Caucus introduced a similar bill in the House ("The Just"). The move was largely symbolic, and neither bill made it to the floor for debate. That same year FAP failed to pass the Senate and was reintroduced as H.R. 1, part of the Social Security amendments of 1971. Welfare rights advocates brought their children to testify before the 92nd Congress in late 1971 and early 1972, a strategic rhetorical move that attempted to stir the emotions of congressional representatives. Indeed the national organization increasingly linked opposition to FAP with child welfare and dubbed 1972 "The Year of the Children" ("NCC Calls for Spring Offensive" 1972). The organization planned a Children's March for Survival to be held on March 25, 1972, with the goal of "highlighting the inadequacies of FAP" (1).

Many welfare righters borrowed a page from the book of earlier feminists who argued that domestic labor was work like any other; therefore, mothers should be paid for it.* Clark County welfare rights activist Alversa Beals explained, "We [mothers] work hard. A lot of people think that raising kids is not a job. But if you gonna raise three or four kids, you got to keep the place clean. You got to wash. You got to cook. Believe me that's a job any way you look at it" (Orleck 2005, 101). This observation was echoed by Clementina Castro (1972), vice chairperson of Union Benefica Hispana WRO and sergeant at arms of the Milwaukee County WRO, who stated that the "mother has got a job all the time, taking care of her children. It's a big job. She has to wash and cook and do everything because she has got to manage the house" (68).

And for their hard work as mothers, some argued, women deserved pay. Bessie Moore of the Milwaukee County WRO had a simple solution. "If the government was smart, it would start calling AFDC 'Day and Night Care,' create a new agency, pay us a decent wage for the service work we are now doing, and say that the welfare crisis has been solved because welfare mothers have been put to work" (qtd. in Tarantino and Becker 1972, 79). Furthermore Johnnie Tillmon (1972a), the former chairperson of the NWRO, noted that if she were president of the United States she would "just issue a proclamation that 'women's' work is *real* work. . . . I'd start paying women a living wage for doing the work we are already doing[,] child-raising and house-keeping. And the welfare crisis would be over, just like that" (429). Betty Niedzwiecki (1972), chairperson of the MOM's WRO and editor of the Milwaukee County WRO newsletter, reasoned this way: "The government owes me because I am raising two boys that I am sure they'll

---

* The place of housework within a capitalist system—and whether or not it constituted productive or unproductive labor—was debated by women in the Communist Party (CP), among other places. In her book *In Woman's Defense*, Mary Inman argued in contrast with other female CPers that housework was productive labor deserving of pay. See Weigand, 2001.

be taking into their armed services one of these days to fight their damn wars. Now I am getting $109 a month plus rent for myself and two children. I should get a lot more than that. I should get paid at least $15 a day, per child, for taking care of my children, because that's what the Welfare Department pays when it has to send a homemaker in if a mother on welfare is in the hospital" (40-41).

Still others adopted a more traditional bent. Lillian Baines (1970), the vice chairperson of the Wyandotte County WRO in Kansas City, Kansas, pointed out that ADC was inadequate to support her family and noted, "The average mother who is head of household would rather stay home and raise her children" (3). She continued, "If farmers are given subsidies for not planting food that would feed hungry children, why shouldn't the mothers of this country be given Federal subsidies for raising good children?" Estella Hightower asserted that "a mother's place is in the home. I don't see punishing a mother with a father's responsibility. I don't think children should suffer with a mother out of the home" (Rudd 1967, 81).

The issues of dignity and self-determination also surfaced in debates over controversial welfare policies that controlled black women's bodies. As the scholar Rickie Solinger (2000) noted, in the 1950s and 1960s the "bodies of black women became political terrain on which some proponents of white supremacy mounted their campaigns" (41). Welfare recipients fought against policies that punished them for bearing "illegitimate" children and waged significant battles against "suitable home" and "man-in-house" policies, which were eventually deemed illegal. In her study of how pregnancy was racialized in the early to mid-twentieth century, Solinger also demonstrates how "black illegitimacy was used to support both arguments about the biological bases of black inferiority and antiblack public policies," which included proposed sterilization and aid cuts (Solinger 2000, 41). Public figures that defended sterilization policies drew on existing racist sentiments by referring to black women as "immoral," "promiscuous," and as "prostitutes" (55). Some worried aloud that black unwed pregnancy represented a threat to the well-being of the nation, as when a member of the Illinois Public Aid Commission stated in defense of sterilization, "We simply need respect for the law and the basic morals that underlie the law if we are to continue as a free people" (qtd. in Solinger 2000, 56).

Welfare rights activists responded to charges of illegitimacy in two ways. In their written testimony before the platform committee of the Democratic National Convention on August 19, 1968, NWRO officials George Wiley, Etta Horn, and Beulah Sanders took a logical approach by drawing on statistics in order to counter public hysterics over the alleged rise in out-of-wedlock births among blacks. The three leaders stated the rate of out-of-wedlock births "among welfare recipients has been roughly constant at about 18% of the children over the past fifteen years" ("Testimony of the National Welfare Rights Organization"). Furthermore they emphasized that, in contrast to politicians' alarm at the rising welfare rolls, they were "heartened by [the rise in relief rolls]. For it simply means that more people in need of public assistance are now getting it."

In 1973 NWRO executive director Johnnie Tillmon testified before Senator Martha Griffiths by appealing to the concerns she shared with Tillmon about sex discrimination. Tillmon framed the relationship between women and the welfare system as a "super-sexist marriage" in order to bring to light the ways poor black women's bodies were controlled through accusations of illegitimacy and proposals for sterilization (Economic Problems of Women 1973, 391). Tillmon related the story of a young welfare recipient with two small children who was misled by her caseworker, who advised her to have her tubes tied "so as to better space her family" (391). The young woman was never told the procedure amounted to sterilization. "The solution to sex discrimination in public assistance is quite simple," explained Tillmon (392). "We must address ourselves to the basic needs of all our citizens" (392). Tillmon bolstered the credibility of the NWRO's proposed adequate income plan by referring to numbers produced by the Bureau of Labor Statistics.

Others approached the issue by assailing the very word *illegitimacy* and the term's arbitrary usage. At a protest by a thousand recipients in Washington, D.C., in August 1967, Kathryn Dunbar, a recipient from Philadelphia, pointed out, "They don't say when they're getting ready to send your children overseas [to war] 'Are you illegitimate?' . . . They don't ask him, 'Are you eligible to fight? Are you able to fight?' They say go" (Honsa 1967, A4). Her observation put the spotlight on the class politics of war, echoing the arguments of Communist labor activist Elizabeth Gurley Flynn, who proposed in 1940, "If Wall Street wants this war [World War II], let the rich, middle-aged bankers and brokers go to war. Let *their* sons go to war—not ours" (8).

In a similar tone of exasperation, Beulah Sanders made this statement before Congress in 1972 as she and other welfare recipients and their children testified against Nixon's Family Assistance Plan: "I can't understand why you want to deal with the whole question of illegitimacy. I don't even know what the word stands for myself. I know what the dictionary says but how can we guarantee that none of you in this room are not illegitimate children. You don't even know whether you was in your mother's womb before she was married so how can you say you are not illegitimate?" (Social Security Amendments of 1972, 2060). Having emptied the term of meaning, Sanders then went on to appeal to the children's future as citizens. To the committee chairperson, Senator Russell Long, she stated, "You need to start dealing with the kids and thinking about their future as a human being . . . because what you have been doing with your committee is just uncalled for. You have not come up with a decent kind of program that would get these kids out of this welfare mess, that would help them to grow up to be decent citizens. . . . I would like to see some of these children sitting at this table take your seat one day. They can't do it if you are not going to help them" (2060).

In addition to addressing charges of "illegitimacy," activists spoke strongly about their right to privacy. Alongside the right to fair treatment and respect, the NWRO's Welfare Bill of Rights listed "the right to receive welfare aid without having the welfare department ask you questions about who your social friends are, such as who you are going out with" ("Welfare Bill of Rights"). Recipients took on the "suitable home" policy, which originated in the mother's pension movement, and the "man-in-the-house" rule. According to the former policy, caseworkers could deem a recipient's home "unsuitable" and thus terminate her benefits if she was believed to inadequately uphold "social and moral standards" characterized by the nation as a whole (Bell 1965, 97).

The "man-in-the-house" policy allowed caseworkers to terminate benefits to any recipient suspected of living or having a relationship with a man, the belief being that such a relationship was indication that she was receiving (unreported) financial assistance from him (Neubeck and Cazenave 2001, 60; Solinger 2000). In Kern County, California, the implementation of the policy was boldly termed "Operation Weekend" and involved caseworkers knocking on the doors of re- cipients Sunday mornings at 7:00 A.M. to search for signs of a man (Kornbluh 2007, 29). Johnnie Tillmon noted that caseworkers were quick to look under the bed for a man but not on top of the bed to see if there were any covers ("Hard Hitting Speeches" 1970).

At a statewide WRO meeting held in November 1967 in Harrisburg, Penn- sylvania, chairperson of the Philadelphia WRO, Hazel Leslie, called attention to recipients' lack of privacy as the audience of 250 delegates shouted, "Tell 'em where it's at!" and "Tell it like it is" ("'New Kind of Welfare Client'" 1967). Mem- bers of the audience, familiar with Leslie's narrative, laughed as she detailed how caseworkers "come in and peek because if the door is open a crack they wonder who's back there. They ask you for a drink of water in the living room and race you to the kitchen" to search for a man ("'New Kind of Welfare Client'" 1967). Des Moines welfare rights activists created a skit to call attention to the injustice of the "man-in-the-house" rule (Szumski 1968). The skit, which put welfare of- ficials "on trial," highlighted the actual experience of Judith Herriott, whose ADC grant was cut from $141 a month to $74 a month because neighbors reported seeing a man in the house to welfare officials. In the skit welfare officials and Herriott's caseworker were "sentenced" "to live for two years on Mrs. Herriott's grant, $74 a month, plus surplus food commodities available through the welfare office" (Szumski 1968).

It was the audaciousness of Mrs. Sylvester Smith, angered by the whims of the welfare system, that led to the withdrawal of her aid, which eventually led to the demise of the man-in-the-house rule. When her caseworker demanded she end her romantic relationship lest her aid be cut, Smith replied, "If God had intended for me to be a nun I'd be a nun" (Goodman 1968, 29). Smith also refused to cooperate with her caseworker, who wanted permission to go to neighbors and grocers to confirm details of her sex life. Outraged at the injustice and humiliation, Smith shared her story with civil rights workers in Selma, who contacted the Center on Social Welfare Policy in New York. The Center's codirector, Martin Garbus, took up Smith's case, which eventually landed in the Supreme Court.

In 1968 the Supreme Court ruled in favor of recipient Smith in *King v. Smith,* putting an end to the practice of withdrawing aid to recipients suspected of having a relationship with a man (Goodman 1968, 28; see also "Man in the House Rule"). The Court's ruling prevented states from dropping children from ADC because their mother gave birth to a child out-of-wedlock. The ruling also restored dignity to recipients whose sex lives were investigated by caseworkers who went to neighbors, friends, and local business owners in search of "evidence" that mothers were "sleeping around." According to the *New York Times,* the court's decision would benefit twenty-one thousand children in Alabama and as many as four hundred thousand nationwide (Goodman 1968, 28).

Still recipients faced an uphill battle. In 1971 the Supreme Court overruled a New York law by declaring that home visits by caseworkers did not constitute a violation of Fourth Amendment rights. Writing for the majority Justice Blackmun (1971) explained, "One who dispenses purely private charity naturally has an interest in, and expects to know, how his charitable funds are utilized and put to work. The public, when it is the provider, rightly expects the same. It might well expect more, because of the trust aspect of public funds, and the recipient, as well as the caseworker, has not only an interest, but an obligation" (par. 3). Blackmun further noted that caseworkers need the right to enter recipients' homes since they have a "profound responsibility" to help those "in need" (par 9). The *Welfare Fighter* called readers' attention to the patronizing tone of the decision by printing the dissenting opinion of Justice Douglas, who wrote, "If the welfare recipient was not Barbara James but a prominent affluent cotton or wheat farmer receiving benefit payments for not growing crops, would not the approach be different? . . . It is a strange [kind of law] indeed which safeguards the businessman at his place of work from warrantless searches but will not do the same for a mother in her home" (qtd. in "Supreme Court Decision" 1970–1971).

Food stamps became a signature issue for women in 1970 as they defended the basic right to control where and how they spent money for necessities. Activists in Texas, Tennessee, Illinois, and Pennsylvania protested various food stamps programs they described as "degrading and insulting" ("Illinois Resolution an Insult"). In Blair County, Pennsylvania, state legislators proposed a program whereby recipients would be paid in scrip rather than real money. The Blair County WRO pointed out the stigmatizing nature of such a proposal. According to Shirley Thompkins of the Blair County WRO, the bill "is aimed at keeping recipients from spending their money in bars. Any state that gives its legislators raises, while giving a welfare family five $59.00 per month for rent, should well be concerned about driving them to drink" ("Fighting Back" 1971, 10).

New York's so-called brownie-point system also struck a nerve with recipients whose home lives and sexual behaviors were scrutinized by caseworkers on a regular basis. The brownie-point system, as proposed in New York, would cut recipients' checks from $3,720 to $2,400 a year and would allow recipients to "earn back" the money through brownie points, which could be obtained by following established measures that disciplined recipients in a variety of ways. Mothers could earn brownie points for vaccinating preschool children, cooperating with school officials, participating in public service jobs such as raking leaves or cleaning toilets, providing "out-of-home day care for a child of another public assistance family," assisting welfare officials in the location of a "deserting parent," "improving housing standard by self-clean-up or self-repair of dwelling," or putting a child in Boy Scouts or "community centers for citizen building activities" (Evans 1971, 1). Given that in 1971 the Bureau of Labor Statistics determined $6,500 per year to be the minimum amount necessary to support a family, the New York proposal was nothing less than appalling. Coined the "Public Service Work Opportunities Project," the New York plan was a bellwether for President Bill Clinton's 1996 welfare reform act, which was dubiously framed as a "work opportunity" act.

The brownie-point plan blatantly invaded recipients' private lives and parenting practices and denied recipients any sense of self-determination. The *Welfare Fighter* asserted that the New York plan would take recipients "back to slavery," where they were forced "to do the bidding of the 'Masters'" (Evans 1971, 14). Highlighting the indignity of the plan, the *Welfare Fighter* wrote, "All mothers of AFDC and Home Relief families are to be treated as irresponsible and non-caring parents (as all slaves were) and must be driven to improve the lot of their families through the familiar contract and stick. In essence, this experience represents a return to pure slavery, where human beings are totally dependent for the very lives of their family members on the good wishes and egotistical whims of a 'Master'" (1). In response to New York's proposed brownie-point plan, the NWRO sued the U.S. Department of Health, Education, and Welfare for access to papers relevant to state and federal discussions regarding the New York plan, since the arrangement would require the waiver of then-current federal guidelines concerning welfare ("NWRO Sues" 1971). In addition in early 1972 the Bay Ridge WRO in Brooklyn, New York, organized over one thousand recipients, unemployed workers, and even some caseworkers to protest the brownie-point plan. The group threatened to close down the local welfare office if the plan were implemented. *Welfare Fighter* coverage of the controversial brownie-point plan indicated that the proposal was never enacted due to public outrage expressed over the issue.

Throughout the 1960s welfare recipients faced the incompatible demands of the marketplace and home front. Poor black women, viewed as the "undeserving" poor, were expected to "earn" their aid by working outside the home to fill low-skill and low-paying positions. As poor mothers, they were accused both of neglecting their children and of defying the mores of the white middle class.

In response to the contradictions wrought by capitalism and care work, welfare recipients gave lie to the image of the welfare queen so widely embraced in the public and political imagination. Through congressional testimony and in the pages of the *Welfare Fighter,* women gave presence to their daily lives and struggled to regain the dignity they were denied through racist and degrading welfare legislation.

The past three chapters have shown the spirited rhetoric employed by welfare rights activists in their struggles for welfare justice. Activists were also quick to express the limitations of talk and the need for direct actions. At the NWRO's first major demonstration in August 1967 in Washington, D.C., Beulah Sanders, vice chairperson of the NWRO, told the crowd they should storm the Capitol and "tear it down if [the politicians] don't listen to you" (Honsa 1967, A4). Fellow protester Margaret McCarty of Baltimore stated the welfare system must be changed "if not by our voices, then by force" (Honsa 1967, A4). Chapter 5 discusses the forceful actions taken by welfare recipients in the late 1960s and early 1970s.

5

Direct Actions

The recovery of black women's literary and public-speaking efforts of the past two centuries remains an important scholarly endeavor (Campbell 1986; Crawford, Rouse, and Woods 1990; Houck and Dixon 2009; J. Jones 1985; Logan 1995; Peterson 1995; Robnett 1997; White 1999). Black feminist scholars have written forcefully about the importance of forging self-definitions and giving voice to their needs and concerns as "acts of resistance," even of survival (Collins 1991; hooks 1989). From the writings of black women of the late 1700s, to the eloquent pleas of Maria Stewart in 1832, to the congressional testimony of welfare righters who condemned racist legislation, black women have "fought with pen and voice" against race, sex, and economic inequalities (Shockley 1989, 110).

The previous chapters discussed the rhetorical efforts of welfare rights activists as they countered the stereotypes of the welfare chiseler and the welfare queen. In congressional testimonies and grassroots writings, black women asserted their rightful place in the workforce and figured themselves as deserving mothers concerned for the well-being of their young children. Yet these women did not rely on "pen and voice" alone. Indeed the realization that talk alone was inadequate—especially in the elitist confines of Congress—often prompted welfare recipients to employ more direct, confrontational tactics. To understand their efforts requires a framework that recognizes the importance of both persuasion and coercion in conflicts marked by race, sex, and class power differentials and for which the desired outcome extends beyond identity recognition (Lozano-Reich and Cloud 2009; Simons 1972; Triece 2007). In other words welfare rights activists spoke loudly *and* carried a big stick as they accompanied their "fighting words with a material presence" (Cloud 2005, 511).

Welfare righters' efforts at "raising hell" represented an extension of their "motherwork," a term Collins (1994) uses to highlight the ways that both public and private influences punctuated black women's roles as mothers. Boris (1993) points out that from the early 1900s black women have "constructed a political voice that refused to be bounded by the separation of public from private, of work from home" (213). This chapter explores the ways welfare rights activists engaged in direct actions that called attention to economic and political influences on their private lives. Welfare recipients faced a unique rhetorical situation when it came to employing bodily actions. Given their tenuous position in the paid labor force, recipients did not have at their disposal the option of withdrawing their labor in the form of a strike or workplace walk-out, the tactic that was so successfully exercised by workers of the early 1900s. Likewise boycotts were not always an option "since refusing the services of the welfare department might jeopardize their survival" (Nadasen 2005, 99). Still recipient-activists were not content to limit their persuasive attempts to polite congressional talk. They were well aware of the inherent limitations of talk, as the opening quote by Sanders indicates. They drew from the storehouse of tools used by civil rights activists of the twentieth century, doing so specifically from the position of "militant mothers" whose motherwork was shaped by both race and class.

Race and the Use of Direct Actions

"Perhaps the best one can do is to avoid the blithe presumption that the channels of rational communication are open to any and all who wish to make use of them" (Haiman 1967, 114). Welfare righters' use of confrontational actions can be better understood with a background on the body of scholarship concerning the links among rhetoric, persuasion, and coercion. Rhetoric has historically been associated with attempts to persuade a change in attitudes, beliefs, or behaviors. In the 1960s, as communication studies scholars widened the net to include movements as part of their studies, some broached issues concerning the relationship, if any, between persuasive and coercive attempts to change social structures (Andrews 1969; Griffin 1964; Haiman 1967; Simons 1972; see also Triece 2001, 2007). Haiman (1967) noted, "If the channels for peaceful protest and reform become so clogged that they appear to be (and, in fact, may be) inaccessible to some segments of the population," then direct actions in the form of civil disobedience "may be more appropriate to the situation than more civilized rules of the game" (105).

Likewise Simons (1972) observed that what is "appropriate for drawing room controversies" may not be effective for "social conflicts, including struggles against established authorities" (236). A distinction must be made between disagreements over "identity and belief" and conflicts over "competing interests" (230). "To resolve a controversy, talk is often sufficient. . . . But in a genuine conflict talk between parties is seldom enough" (231). History abounds with examples of activists who were quick to learn that negotiating with bosses, talking to senators, and pleading with welfare bureaucrats produced limited results. In such instances the speaking situation was marked from the beginning by differences rooted in economic standing, and each party's respective position vis-à-vis access to necessary resources. In other words oftentimes speakers find themselves in situations marked by "genuine conflict."

In contrast contemporary scholars such as Foss and Griffin (1995) have expressed concern over rhetoric's association with persuasion, which on their view is "characterized by efforts to change others and thus to gain control over them" (3-4). According to Foss and Griffin, the traditional definition of rhetoric shares the values of patriarchy, namely those of competition and domination (4). The invitational approach is characteristic of "feminists" who are "united by a set of basic principles" that "challenge the positive value the patriarch accords to changing and thus dominating others" (4). The authors posit a reframing of rhetoric as "an invitation to understanding as a means to create a relationship rooted in equality, immanent value, and self-determination" (5).

Since Foss and Griffin's publication, the concept of rhetoric as invitational has been taken to task on a number of grounds. Fulkerson (1996) questions the conflation of argument and aggressiveness, noting numerous instances—both prosaic and inspiring—where persuasion was imperative and led to increased knowledge and steps toward equality (for example speeches of Martin Luther King Jr. and Susan B. Anthony). Dow (1995) is troubled by the way that invitational rhetorical theory universalizes the term "feminism" and accepts without question feminist "essentialist separatism" (112). Such a stance disregards women's "efforts to work for feminist goals within existing political structures" (113). Likewise Pollack et al. (1996) express concern over the essentializing of the term "persuasion" (149). The authors point out not all attempts to persuade are accompanied by domination as when one persuades a friend not to commit suicide. "By essentializing persuasion (or more accurately the *intent* to persuade), we abstract it from any context of use, ruling out of bounds questions about who speaks to whom, for what reasons, and in what manner" (149).

Lozano-Reich and Cloud (2009) point out the inadequacy of invitational rhetoric when it comes to the numerous real world situations in which powerless groups attempt social change in contexts marked by sex, race, class, and other inequalities. They echo the point Barnlund and Haiman (1960) made thirty years earlier: "When one person or a few people in a group or society possess all the guns, muscles, or money, and the others are relatively weak and helpless, optimum conditions do not exist for discussion, mutual influence, and democracy. Discussion in such circumstances occurs only at the sufferance of the powerful" (12). In addition calls for civility inherent in the invitational framework have historically been exercised to discipline women and other marginalized groups (Lozano-Reich and Cloud 2009). As Scott and Smith (1969) observe, "Civility and decorum" can "serve as masks for the preservation of injustice" (8), silencing marginalized groups and rendering direct actions "out of line" when practiced by marginalized groups who challenge existing power differentials. Lozano-Reich and Cloud (2009) call on scholars to theorize the "uncivil tongue" as a strategy that may be used to challenge hegemonic discourses.

Furthermore cleaving rhetoric and coercion—or in the case of the invitational framework, severing rhetoric and persuasion— tends toward a privileging of polite talk (invitation) as ethically superior and a view of coercion or persuasion or both as practiced only by deviants or radicals (Simons 1972, 233). However rhetoric and coercion (or in Foss and Griffin's terms, rhetoric and persuasion) exist on a continuum, with most debates containing elements on both. In other words persuasion rarely exists without some sort of coercion to back it, and attempts at coercion are often accompanied by persuasive attempts to get listeners on board. Likewise Foss and Griffin unnecessarily dismiss persuasion as ignoring the values and needs of listeners, when the practices of speakers often reflect both persuasion that seeks to change a person and invitation that solicits the mutual understanding between parties.

For example throughout the twentieth century, labor activists relied on more or less traditional channels to argue with supervisors (for example petitions and union negotiations) and to mobilize worker and community support (for example pamphlets, meetings, and speakers). But given the material (coercive) power that supervisors held over workers—that is the ability to fire them—workers found it necessary to collectively withhold their labor power, in the form of sit-ins and walk-outs, to halt production and force the hand of employers in a way that more civil negotiations often could not (Triece 2007). Of equal importance is the recognition that coercion or the threat thereof has been an inherent part of "civil" society. Recall for example the deployment of the Ohio National Guard—who shot and killed Kent State students peacefully demonstrating against the Vietnam War in 1970—and Birmingham police, who used hoses and dogs to halt peaceful civil rights demonstrators in 1963. In "civil" society laws are backed by threat of force, and some laws—as in the case of welfare legislation and laws on marriage—have been used to maintain discrimination.

Indeed the impetus toward dialogue and conversation can foil direct actions that may arguably have a more tangible impact. As Tonn (2005) warns, "Public conversations and dialogues risk becoming substitutes for policy formation necessary to correct structural dimensions of social problems" (408). Welfare rights activists put a great deal of energy into public conversations and dialogue as discussed in the previous two chapters. But frustrated by condescension by welfare bureaucrats and stalling from policy makers, activists engaged in coercive actions that resisted the disciplining effects of "civility." Black women exercised a race-specific militant motherhood (Tonn 1996), which was clearly rooted in the tradition of black women's resistance.

Race and Militant Motherhood

In a seminal essay Tonn (1996) explores the role of symbolic motherhood in agitation efforts, noting that the "nurturing persona" of motherhood can play an important role in protests of the severely oppressed (2). It is worth observing that "agitation and mothering often share two essential dimensions: nurturing and militancy" (2). Tonn explains, "Militant protective love . . . necessarily broadens the maternal 'ethic of care' beyond its genteel mooring to include aggressive confrontation and occasional bodily risk" (5). NWRO leader Beulah Sanders (1971) encapsulated the ethic of militant motherhood when she described the founders of the welfare rights movement. These mothers "brought with them just about all that they had—a love for their children. A love so strong that they were willing to take on the local, state, and federal government with their bare hands, and their bodies and their brains" (1).

Indeed militant motherhood characterizes an essential part of the history of black women's mothering. For women of color a central aspect of motherwork was ensuring the physical survival of their children and their communities (Collins 1994, 49). Black and other ethnic minority mothers have worked to protect their families and communities in the face of constant threats from a racist patriarchal society, from their days as slave mothers to the 1960s civil rights movement. Accounts of the prominent roles played by black women in civil rights demonstrations during the 1960s often recall the ways their involvement was tethered to their identity as mothers (Crawford, Rouse, and Woods 1990; Houck and Dixon 2009; J. Jones 1985; Robnett 1997). Payne's (1990) observation that women ages thirty to fifty were far more likely to participate in civil rights organizations than their male counterparts indicates that for a good many of these activists, experiences of mothering and activism were not easily separable. Jacqueline Jones (1985) writes of the "mama" who held a "legendary capacity to chop cotton all day long, prepare a feast for a dozen folks in the evening, and then sit on her front porch until midnight, a shotgun spread conspicuously across her lap to protect the white and black canvassers lodged in her home" (280). Equally provocative were the stories of Black Panther mothers who had willingly faced imprisonment for militant actions done in the name of their children's futures (Lumsden 2009).

Welfare rights activists carried on the legacy of fierce determination as they advocated for their children through a host of campaigns to secure basic necessities. Adopting a persona of the nurturing mother, welfare rights activists established identification with other recipients who were reluctant to join a local WRO. Chapter 2 discussed the strategies of reconstitution and consciousness raising, which provided a way for activists to engender interest in welfare rights efforts. Securing new members and garnering sympathy from the wider public was just part of the welfare rights effort.

In addition—and specifically from their positions as mother-activists—women engaged in actions outside the bounds of traditional "civility." Their actions fell into a broader effort of direct action outlined in "A Strategy to End Poverty," written by middle-class allies Piven and Cloward (1979, 276). The authors proposed continual disruption of local welfare agencies with a push toward getting all eligible individuals onto the welfare rolls. Expansion of the rolls would create unsustainable pressures on a system intended to keep costs down and individuals unaware of their rights. Piven and Cloward (1979) believed that this tactic would force an overhaul of the system at the federal level with the result being the establishment of a "national income standard" (276).

Exploring direct actions in which welfare activists interrupted, demonstrated, and occupied so-called civil spaces provides an insight into the ways women pushed the bounds of civility, citizenship, and motherhood through confrontation and the "mother tongue" (Stover 2003, 156–57). Not unlike the "uncivil tongue" advocated by the communication scholars Lozano-Reich and Cloud (2009), the mother tongue was a tool used by black women to "talk back" and "challenge the truthfulness of the portrayals" of black women proffered in a society dominated by white people (Stover 2003, 157). By reclaiming labels such as "sassy" and "impudent," black women "nullify the words' power to hurt them while demonstrating that they are a power with which to be reckoned" (156).

Interrupting "Civil" Spaces

As chapters 2 through 4 clearly showed, mothers on welfare made every effort to argue their case for increased funding through traditional means of communication, including testifying before Congress, meeting with welfare bureaucrats including the director of the Department of Health, Education, and Welfare, and writing letters to representatives. Yet recipients often expressed frustration with continual talk, which at times produced little tangible gain. Furthermore welfare policy was crafted behind closed doors in meetings from which recipients were excluded. In these situations the invitational approach to social problems was irrelevant since welfare mothers were most often not invited to such talks in the first place. Unhampered by such exclusions, welfare mothers indicated their willingness to "raise hell" by interrupting meetings, which provided perhaps a quintessential example of militant motherhood, since welfare mothers demonstrated their anger and the lengths to which they would go to obtain money for their families. Although denied a seat at the table, recipients did not let their concerns go unheard. They took an assuredly undecorous route—above referred to as an "uncivil tongue"—as they shouted at meetings and unfurled banners. While such tactics may have produced limited results in terms of tangible gain, recipients often received media attention for their tactics, and they fortified their own sense of militancy and purpose as they employed other tactics.

In New York members of the City-Wide Coordinating Committee of Welfare Groups faced arrest as they banged on the walls of a conference room while officials discussed welfare payments ("Officials Harassed" 1968). Although little came of that incident—aside from the arrest of six members of the committee—subsequent official meetings saw welfare mothers clash directly with welfare bureaucrats, who were none too pleased. Mothers in Des Moines, Iowa, were invited to attend daytime panels at the annual Iowa Welfare Association Conference but were excluded from the evening banquet ("Iowa Welfare Mothers" 1969). Regardless Katherine Bryson and Pat Auch, members of Mothers for Dignity and Justice (the Des Moines WRO), disturbed the unsuspecting diners by shouting, "You sit here eating $6.00 a plate dinners, and our children are home without any food. I asked you earlier in the day for donations for WRO's and there was no response. This is why we returned tonight" ("Iowa Welfare Mothers" 1969). For speaking where uninvited, Bryson was arrested. Pat Auch was maced and handcuffed.

The efforts of activists in Rhode Island Fair Welfare were a bit more coordinated as they disrupted a joint session of the Rhode Island legislature at which Congressman Wilber Mills was to address the assembly regarding the unpopular Family Assistance Plan (FAP). Campaigning against what they called "FAP-OFF," Rhode Island recipients stood up in the balcony of the chambers, and as one activist related, "demanded 5 minutes to let the poor speak for themselves; we demanded that Mills be labeled a fraud and an exploiter of the poor" ("The States Report: Rhode Island" 1971). The group unfurled the Rhode Island state flag and two banners reading "ZAP FAP" and "MILLS IS A FRAUD . . . GIVE MILLS A JOB." As the state governor and legislators "stood in shock," the activists showered them with over seven hundred leaflets that stated, "Wilbur Mills Is Public Enemy No. 1" and included "facts on how FAP-OFF will ruin our lives and rob us of our dignity."

New York's City-Wide WRO likewise employed the tactic of directly targeting welfare officials, disrupting the graduation ceremonies at Albert Einstein College of Medicine on November 21, 1971. As Department of Health, Education, and Welfare secretary Elliot Richardson was receiving an honorary degree for his work in the field, Georgia Ware and George Wiley led one hundred welfare rights activists to the stage, where they presented the secretary with their own "honorary degree"—a "Doctor of Laws in Social Oppression," accompanied by a roll of toilet paper wrapped in a bow. As Wiley attempted to give the "award" to Richardson, Ware read aloud, "For your single minded ability to remain unresponsive to the needs of poor people and to avoid constructive programs of welfare reform which would provide adequate income for all Americans" ("Operation New York Starts" 1971, 1).

The following year, 1972, recipients brought their children with them to the National Governors Conference, held in Washington, D.C. ("Children and

Mothers Confront"). Barred from entering the meeting, the mothers and children "outmaneuvered" the Secret Service by sneaking in a side door. Once inside Marie Ratagick asked Governor Nelson Rockefeller to let the children speak about their experiences living on welfare. The mothers soon found themselves lectured by Rockefeller, who attempted to justify cuts in aid in the name of eliminating welfare fraud, to which recipient Ms. Dotson replied, "The fraud is when people like Reagan don't pay taxes." Governor Ronald Reagan chastised the mothers, whom he accused of "victimizing" their children. Dotson responded in the spirit of "talking back" (hooks 1989) by challenging the perceived benevolence of white leaders. She stated flatly, "You are making them starve, Mr. Reagan" ("Children and Mothers Confront" 1972, 14).

Although their children were never given a chance to speak at the governors conference, it is useful to explore what role that incident and the others mentioned might have played in the activists' larger attempts at achieving welfare justice. Acting publicly as militant mothers, welfare rights activists disrupted business as usual and insisted on their right to participate in the decision making that impacted their lives. In the spirit of participatory democracy, which had been nurtured by the civil rights activist Ella Baker in the late 1950s, recipients opposed the "intransigence of bureaucratic and legalistic obstacles by collective demonstrations of the 'will of the people'" (Mueller 1990, 65). Long a mainstay in the twentieth-century civil rights movement, participatory democracy gave credence to citizens' voices in a "wide range of governmental decisions" (52). Just as Ella Baker insisted that the people be empowered to act on their behalf, welfare rights activists asserted their ability (and credibility) in deciding welfare policy. When excluded from elite forums, women broke with decorum, disrupted meetings, and spoke truth to power.

In addition interrupting formal discussions on welfare policy enabled welfare mothers to publicize the politics of black motherhood. Welfare recipients were accustomed to living under a bureaucratic microscope, subjected to home searches and relentless questioning by social workers. Publicly calling attention to their children at "home without any food" or "starving" at the hands of Governor Reagan's policies enabled these women to bring their personal lives to center stage on their own terms.

Demonstrating at "Civil" Spaces

Welfare rights activists also took measured steps to demonstrate at public locations traditionally marked by processes of government and civility. A perennial issue with welfare rights activists was the ways that established welfare policy restricted their ability to provide adequately for their children. Activists waged minimum standards and special grants campaigns designed to win basic goods for their families and carried their demands directly to decision-making loci, often with children in tow, beginning as early as 1964 (Nadasen 2005, 81). Involving children in public actions has been a part of the history of social protest. Throughout the early 1900s mothers and wives of men on strike put their children on picket lines to call attention to the connections between workplace policies and home life. It is worthy of note that during civil rights marches of the 1950s and 1960s, images of black children protesting peacefully in the face of violent police with dogs and hoses played a key role in garnering sympathy for the cause.

Coordinated efforts were stepped up in the late 1960s as the welfare rights movement gained momentum. In June 1966 recipients walked 150 miles—a "Walk for Decent Welfare"—from Cleveland to Columbus, Ohio, to protest at the steps of the state capitol for fair welfare. Recipients and their children, along with church leaders and a supporter from the county welfare department, sang songs as they set off from downtown Cleveland on June 20. Lyrics to the song "Tramp, Tramp, Tramp" articulated the struggles of making ends meet on meager welfare checks: "The children are in need / With checks to[o] small to clothe and/feed. . . . If we put shoes on the feet, / Then there's not enough to eat. . . . When you pay out all the rent / The utility money's spent, / And you have no heat to keep the / Children warm" ("Walk for Decent Welfare Song Sheet"). Twenty-five individuals made the entire ten-day walk and met over two thousand supporters at a rally in Columbus, Ohio (Brooks 1966). Recipients in eighteen cities, including Washington, D.C., and Boston, held similar rallies ("'Welfare Mothers' Rally" 1966; Richard 1966). All were asking for increases in aid and, of equal importance, dignified treatment by the welfare system. Ohio marchers demanded an end to night searches while Boston women insisted the word "illegitimate" not be used in reference to their children ("'Welfare Mothers' Rally" 1966). Brenda Foster, a protester in Washington, D.C., described the matter this way: Welfare investigators "give you freedom with one hand and take it away with the other. They give you a little money and they treat you as if you were in jail. We are sick and tired of investigators" (Richard 1966).

The following year, in August 1967, activists at the National Welfare Rights Organization's founding convention organized a mock Senate hearing and a "Mother's March on Washington," in which a thousand women gathered on the National Mall and marched to the building that housed the Department of Health, Education, and Welfare Department (Honsa 1967). The women targeted a proposed amendment to Social Security that would "'freeze' the number of children on welfare rolls whose fathers are absent from the home and which would make work and work training a condition of welfare for mothers" (James 1967). The bill would also "require states to set up programs to check illegitimacy" (Honsa 1967). The mock hearing, held in the caucus room in the old Senate Office Building, provided an opportunity for recipient-activists to direct biting words that cut through the otherwise decorous environs. Johnnie Tillmon, the recently elected chairperson of the National Welfare Rights Organization, astutely used the surrounding trappings of civility to her advantage as she lambasted congressional supporters of the amendment. Decrying Congress's excuse that there was a lack of monies to fund welfare, Tillmon pointed to the chandeliers and decorative wall hangings in the caucus room and noted the cost of one chandelier "would feed a recipient for the next ten years" (Honsa 1967). She continued, "That stuff costs money, baby, so they must have some money somewhere."

Following the gathering in the Senate caucus room, the group marched to the National Mall. The presence of outspoken, primarily black female welfare recipients on the mall provided visibility to a constituency often imagined in terms of stereotypes in both the media and in congressional debates. As a group the women created a physical solidarity and were emboldened to speak out at the footsteps of the Capitol. Mrs. Margaret McCarty, a welfare rights leader from Baltimore, decried the "lousy, dirty, conniving brutes" who supported the bill and proclaimed, "I'm black and I'm beautiful and they ain't going to take me back" to slavery conditions (Honsa 1967). McCarty's statement called out the ways the proposed amendment evoked the forced work of slavery and opened black women's personal lives to public scrutiny. Her echo of the slogan Black Is Beautiful challenged hegemonic views that viewed black as dangerous or suspicious (hooks 1992, 18, 19). Contemporary theorist bell hooks (1992) explained the significance of the 1960s catchphrase this way: "Loving blackness as a political resistance transforms our ways of looking and being, and thus creates the conditions necessary for us to move against the forces of domination and death and reclaim black life" (20).

Over the following five years activists would take their demands to city and state government buildings around the country. In September 1969 Wisconsin mothers walked ninety miles from Milwaukee to the state capitol building in Madison to protest the "unlivable cuts in the welfare budget" (Untitled 1969). Meals had been cut from 22 cents to 16 cents per meal. Protesters pointed out that even the monkeys at the Madison Zoo were allotted more than that per meal ("Mothers Sit-In" 1969). On September 30 over two thousand recipients and supporters entered the capitol and listened as mothers told of their struggles. The demonstrators were cleared out by the National Guard later that evening, but undeterred the women returned the following day, five-hundred-strong and, facing armed police and National Guardsmen, sat down en masse on the capitol driveway. Photos of the event appearing in the October 1969 *Welfare Fighter* conveyed the women's resolve. As police ran a hose down the capitol driveway in an attempt to soak the protesters, the women brought in chairs and a picnic table for their children ("Mothers Sit-In" 1969).

Welfare recipients often confronted welfare offices and made their demands in the names of their children ("Complaints against Food Stamps" 1970; "140

Moms and Children Protest" 1970). In May 1970 welfare mothers came to Washington, D.C., from the surrounding areas to participate in a march and protest on the steps of the building where the Department of Health, Education, and Welfare (HEW) was housed. According to the *Welfare Fighter,* the "mothers used a loud speaker to educate new employees and to tell Finch [secretary of HEW] what it was really like to live on welfare" ("Angry Rally Backs" 1970, 1). One participant, Roxanne Jones, "led the Mothers in their telling Finch exactly what they thought of him, welfare, and the war." The article continued, "As time passed the words of the welfare mothers got hotter and more angry. They kept up a steady stream of words, telling Finch what it is like to be poor, black, and hungry" (1).

In Houston, Texas, over one hundred mothers and their children took buses to the state Department of Welfare, entered the building, and demanded food for their children ("140 Moms and Children Protest" 1970). The organization composed a list of demands that were clearly linked to the well-being of their children, including the establishment of "our right to be a part of decisions which affect the lives of our children and ourselves; to be treated with dignity and justice by the welfare authorities" ("The Way It Is" 1970, 7). They also sought "to have Texas declared a welfare disaster" and "to have the state government recognize that we can't feed our children on the welfare checks we are now getting; that this isn't just a welfare problem—the health of our children is being destroyed" (7).

The following year over three hundred mothers placed their demands at the doorstep of the governor of Rhode Island ("The States Report: Rhode Island" 1971, 11). The women condemned the governor's planned welfare cuts, highlighting the ways their children would be hurt. The women "challenged [the governor] to have the courage to tell 300 AFDC mothers and the general public that he would make 29,000 children sleep on the floor and in the cold" (11). The woman also warned that "anything that endangered their children's health and well being will have to confront the recipients of the state head on" (11).

The link between welfare rights and motherhood was cast in sharper relief into the early 1970s and culminated in 1972, which the national organization dubbed the "Year of the Children" ("Children's Issues" 1972, 9). Indeed NWRO executive committee member Frankie Jeter asserted that "children are the basis of the welfare rights movement" ("NWRO Executive Committee" 1972, 20). By 1972 activists had been struggling against Nixon's Family Assistance Plan (FAP) for nearly three years. Chapter 3 detailed recipients' testimony before Congress as to the impact that FAP would have on their families. Beyond their attempts to *talk* to members of Congress, members of the NWRO's National Coordinating Committee, at their February 1972 meeting, planned *action,* a Children's March for Survival, to take place in cities across the country in March of that year ("NCC Calls" 1972, 1). The march provided an avenue for child advocacy that would imagine FAP's impact on families for the broader public and thus raise awareness and garner sympathy in a way that debates in the elite halls of

Congress may not have. Furthermore highlighting the impact of welfare policy on their children did more than arouse sympathy; it provided a way to counter widely accepted misperceptions that able-bodied but lazy men were the primary benefactors of public aid. The January–February *Welfare Fighter* emphasized that children comprised "over 43% of all welfare recipients" and as a result of FAP would have "inadequate food, clothing and shelter" ("NCC Calls" 1972, 1). Tapping into traditional ideals of motherhood, the paper noted that FAP's forced-work provision would hurt children since mothers would have to work "for poverty wages instead of creating a healthy family life" (1).

Despite nearly all media failing to cover the event and obstacles erected at the last minute by the Nixon administration ("Nixon and Friends" 1972, 6), nearly fifty thousand adults and children marched in Washington, D.C., while hundreds more marched in sixteen other cities ("Sixteen Cities Join" 1972, 10). Children held signs, and a few even gave public speeches. In Indianapolis twelve-year-old Nicie Cross called Nixon to task in her speech, asserting that "Nixon had promised to put an end to hunger and war, to reform welfare, but he has escalated the war, cut back in the school lunch program, and created FAP[,] which will depress millions of poor children" (11). Others took the public event as an opportunity to call attention to the ways that direct experience with welfare gave them a keener insight on welfare policy—what earlier chapters referred to as "epistemic advantage." Montgomery, Alabama, marchers—six-hundred-strong—authored a twelve-point program for addressing the conditions of the poor in their state. The list of demands included a neighborhood committee "consisting of 50% poor people by which welfare recipients can assist in determining their own needs" ("Montgomery" 1972, 10). Signs held by Kansas City protesters said, "Poverty was not created by poor people" and "Welfare! Don't knock it, you may have to try it" ("Kansas City" 1972, 13).

Participants of the Children's March for Survival drew attention not only to the need for child well-being but to the greed of the well-to-do in a society marked by class disparities. A report conducted by M.I.T. economists and released around the time of the march revealed an income gap that had nearly doubled in the previous twenty years. The report noted, "Poverty cannot be eliminated by concentrating only on education, training and the like. Only a substantially increased demand for labor," wage increases, and affirmative action hiring programs "can bring about significant income redistribution" ("Income Gap Widens" 1972, 2). In line with the report's observations, protesters in Chicago's Children's March held signs that read, "Higher wages, higher welfare, make the bosses pay"; "Cut Ogilvie, not welfare"; and "Payrolls instead of relief rolls" ("Chicago" 1972, 12).* Marchers in Montgomery, Alabama, demanded economic justice in the form of "jobs that will raise the standard of living" ("Montgomery"

---

* "Ogilvie" is a reference to Illinois' then-governor Richard B. Ogilvie.

1972, 10). And in Columbia, South Carolina, Ms. Louise Hughey, noting that poor people got "warmed over repression" after her state's governor won his election, made demands quite radical by twenty-first-century standards, including the creation of "jobs that will raise the standards of living," "universal child development centers," and "preventative health care" ("Columbia, S.C." 1972, 12).

The story of welfare recipients' confrontations with the state holds significance on a number of levels. In solidarity with thousands of other recipient-mothers and their children, poor black women refused the public image of the negligent and undeserving welfare mother. Standing alongside their children provided a visual that emphasized poor women's roles as mothers. By extension then recipient activists also confronted the centuries-old notion of black women's employability. They demanded the same choice available to middle- and upper-class white women, that is the option to remain home to care for their own children.

In contrast to white women's maternalist discourses of the early 1900s, welfare rights activists' reliance on the traditional trope of motherhood was shaped by the legacy of racism in a capitalist society that relied on poor black women's production and reproduction. Thus recipient-activists enacted a militant motherhood whereby conflict stemmed from care for their children; demands grew from their belief they were deserving mothers. In other words activists recontextualized motherhood through confrontational actions and a quick tongue. Joining with hundreds, at times thousands, of fellow recipients conveyed a powerful message to bureaucrats and lawmakers about the resolve of this group who were otherwise considered incapable of sound decision making.

Public perception was also surely shaped by media coverage of some of these events, oftentimes in ways unfavorable to the cause of welfare righters. Media frames shape common sense understandings through "selection" and "emphasis" (Gitlin 1980) and through repetition, association, placement, and magnification (Entman 1991). In coverage of the Children's March for Survival, the *New York Times* trivialized the organizers' message concerning the impact of poverty and inadequate welfare policy on children. Ignoring the fact that many children gave speeches and held signs during the march, the *Times* noted that the children "turned the protest into a cheerful playtime" ("30,000, Many of Them Children" 1972, 20). The article likewise trivialized protesting adults, who were described as the "Pied Pipers of poverty" by the undersecretary of the Department of Health, Education, and Welfare, who was quoted in the article.

Into the 1970s the national organization continued down the road of political pressuring but not without bitter lessons regarding the shortcomings of this method when seeking tangible gain. In addition to struggles to have meaningful debate in congressional hearings as detailed in earlier chapters, activists expressed profound anger and disappointment when, after garnering support from Democratic presidential nominee, George McGovern, the South Dakota senator refused to support the NWRO's $6,500 Adequate Income plank at the 1972 Democratic National Convention (Young 1972, 4; Colom 1972, 3).

Through demonstrations at symbolic loci of control, welfare activists created a physical presence and spoke truth to power, less constrained in public spaces in comparison to testifying in the halls of Congress. But recognizing the limitations of even this form of protest, activists willingly entered and occupied welfare offices, thus forcing the hand of caseworkers in order to receive much-needed aid.

Occupying "Civil" Spaces, "Lock, Stock, and Playpen"

In these frustrating times, explained Beulah Sanders (1971), "when nothing else worked . . . we invaded the welfare departments, we sat in the offices of welfare directors . . . mayors, governors, legislators, and the secretary of HEW." Sanders was referring to the ways welfare activists used bodily actions to get their point across when words alone fell short. In these instances recipients drew from the inventory of protest tactics successfully employed by labor and civil rights activists of the previous five decades.

In her 1969 testimony before Congress, Sanders announced that welfare rights activists sought jobs with dignity and political voice, beyond their more pressing need for food and clothing for their families. The historian Felicia Kornbluh (2007) locates activists' demands for such goods within a broader history of "consumer politics" in black communities (118–22). From Ella Baker's Young Negroes Cooperative League and the "Don't Buy Where You Can't Work" campaign, both initiated during the Depression, to boycotts and actions of the 1960s, such as "Operation Lambchop," black activists have used their buying power to motivate change in local economies. Within this tradition welfare recipients argued for a minimum income necessary to raise their children with dignity. And as the previous two chapters revealed, their claims to goods were often accompanied by scathing critiques of systems that resulted in widespread disparities between rich and poor.

In the late 1960s the national organization established a special grants campaign that combined rhetorical efforts with direct action. Nadasen (2005) notes that the drive for grants "was one of the welfare rights movement's most visible and successful strategies" (80). The campaign's battles included numerous office occupations directed at disrupting the welfare system. In 1968 women occupied welfare centers in the New York City area in an effort to increase aid to qualified families and to eventually bring the system to a point of crisis ("11 Demonstrators" 1968; Kaufman 1968; "Welfare Clients" 1968). June and July saw welfare recipients occupying offices in the Bronx and demanding funds for basic household items they were entitled to under the current welfare law (Kaufman 1968; Kifner 1968a, 1968b; Kihss 1968d). In Roxbury, Massachusetts, sixty mothers forced the hand of the state welfare commissioner by threatening an overnight sit-in if they didn't receive much-needed furniture and telephones (Creamer 1968). The city-wide protests—numbering somewhere between forty and one hundred—lasted throughout July and were successful in many instances in obtaining "millions in additional aid" (Kifner 1968b). Recipients demanded and received over $13 million in special grants by June, an increase of $10 million over the previous year's grant dispersal, underscoring the initial success of their efforts (Kifner 1968c). The *New York Times* noted that caseworkers often processed claims into the night as protesters refused to leave (Kaufman 1968) and that ultimately activists succeeded in "hampering much of the department's operations and have gained clients millions of dollars in grants for clothing and furniture" (Kifner 1968a).

Although recipients received immediate financial assistance from such actions, welfare administrators in New York reacted punitively by invoking a new "simplified payments" system that would purportedly reduce administrative costs for the welfare department and would also amount to a reduction in aid to recipients (Kihss 1968a, 1968c). Responding to the cuts to be enacted in August 1968, over six hundred people—primarily black women—pushed to get into the barricaded city hall in order to protest the changes that even caseworkers noted would "cut down on the amount of money given to the most deprived segment of our population" (Kihss 1968c). Mounted police responded by dispersing the crowd, but not before eight women, including welfare rights leader Jennette Washington, were arrested along with three children under the age of sixteen (Kihss 1968c). The efforts outside of city hall were buttressed by a series of sit-ins around New York City involving hundreds of recipients in over two-thirds of the nearly forty centers in the area (Kihss 1968b). In some instances activists sustained their sit-in overnight in the welfare center with the support of members of the Black Panther Party. Welfare administrators were forced to respond to the demands by establishing an "emergency communications room" in order to keep tabs on demonstrators and devise rules for permitting the sit-ins. A protest of seventy-five recipients the following month proved particularly confrontational as women overturned desks, scattered papers, and blocked caseworkers from entering a building that housed three welfare centers ("75 Welfare Recipients").

In addition to welfare office sit-ins, activists found their way into the offices of decision makers and demanded they be heard. Although the conversations were held in decorous settings much like congressional testimony described in chapters 3 and 4, the office occupations enabled activists to both physically and symbolically usurp control of a site of decision making. In 1968 New York's City-Wide Coordinating Committee of Welfare Groups staged a three-day sit-in in the office of social services commissioner Jack R. Goldberg, while numerous others camped on the sidewalk outside the building, preventing caseworkers from entering (Kifner 1968a). The protesters were calling attention to the indignities of a welfare program, Operation Compass, that counseled recipients who were supposedly "improperly motivated" to work. Irene Gibbs, one of the protesters,

Fig. 5.1
NWRO chairperson Beulah Sanders sits at the desk of Secretary Robert Finch of the
Department of Health, Education, and Welfare, symbolically taking over his job. She
is joined by other recipient-activists at this May 1970 protest action. Reprinted with
permission of the Washington, D.C., Public Library, Star Collection, ©Washington Post.

asserted that she would send welfare bureaucrats to "Operation Hell" if they
forced her to participate in the program (Kornbluh 2007, 88). Once settled into
the office for the weekend, protest leader Beulah Sanders sat at Goldberg's desk
and appointed herself "Commissioner of People Services" for the weekend (89).

Two years later recipients acted boldly in the Washington, D.C., area. In May
1970 members of the National Welfare Rights Organization, including Beulah
Sanders and George Wiley, burst into the office of Secretary Robert Finch, of
the Department of Health, Education, and Welfare, while he was being interviewed by local reporters. A photograph on the front page of the *Evening Star*
showed the group of black and white women sitting in large leather chairs with
Sanders sitting behind Finch's desk, taking control literally over his chair and
figuratively over his job (Holmberg 1970; see figure 5.1). Calling attention to
the class dynamics common to welfare policy and foreign policy, George Wiley
asserted, "This administration should be fighting for poor people, not killing
them in Southeast Asia" (1). The occupiers were supported by 150 demonstrators
outside the building who held signs reading "$5,500 or fight" and "Nixon unfair
to people." The next month protesters relied on more violent tactics to receive

Fig. 5.2
Mothers in the Washington, D.C., area, fed up with the welfare bureaucracy that made it hard for them to obtain basic necessities, act forcefully and push their way into welfare headquarters in June 1970. Photograph by Charles Del Vecchio/*The Washington Post* via Getty Images.

household items. The *Washington Post* described the five hundred "angry welfare mothers" as storming "city welfare headquarters ... smashing a heavy glass door, breaking windows, tossing rocks and scuffling with police" (Honsa 1970; see figures 5.2 and 5.3). Fed up after having unsuccessfully applied for grants for furniture, the group of mothers forced its way past guards, occupied the building's lobby, and chanted "We want money." Although little came of the event in the way of tangible gain, the women's actions were indicative of the lengths to which they would go to provide for their children.

Recipients were not only forceful but also creative when it came to demanding goods for their families. Jackie Pope and Joyce Burson of the Brooklyn-Welfare Action Council (B-WAC) staged a shop-in in the spirit of sit-ins employed by protesting factory workers and civil rights activists in prior decades. Their fall 1968 action was part of a larger welfare rights campaign for store credit, which would allow mothers to purchase larger durable goods at reasonable prices. As Philadelphia WRO activist Margie Jefferson noted of her organization's successful credit campaigns just months earlier, "No longer are we restricted to buying inferior merchandise at high prices in the ghetto" (Kornbluh 2007, 122). On November 21, 1968, B-WAC activists led by Pope and Burson staged a well-rehearsed shop-in at Korvettes, a large Brooklyn department store. Activists inside the store acted out various roles, including "fake customers (further divided between irate and

Fig. 5.3
Welfare mothers in Washington, D.C., protest outside of welfare headquarters as others force their way into the welfare facilities in June 1970. Photograph by Charles Del Vecchio/*Washington Post* via Getty Images.

sympathetic), real customers, and watchers or crowds (militants and moderates), plus representatives for negotiating with Korvettes' officials" (Pope 1989, 106; 2011). Women who played the "customers" would go from floor to floor of the department store gathering bundles of clothing for "purchase." After being rung up at the checkout counter, the "customer" would hand over her welfare card and tell the cashier to "charge it to the city" (Pope 2011). Meanwhile Pope and other activists played the role of the irate "real customer" who expressed exasperation at having to wait in long lines created by the recipients who refused to pay. Outside the store women handed out leaflets and acted as picketers, messengers, marshals, and spokespersons for the media and passers-by.

These actions resulted in at least three benefits. First major department stores such as Korvettes, Sears, and Abraham and Strauss negotiated credit agreements with recipients. Second these actions attracted new members to WROs; Philadelphia's group doubled its members after its summer campaign (Kornbluh 2007, 122). And third the women who participated in these actions learned a great deal about collective action (Pope 1989, 108). B-WAC members consistently met after each major action in order to discuss strengths and weaknesses of the event and to discuss whether or not goals had been met. Jackie Pope (1989) notes that these meetings became a "key politicizing and organizing tool" (108).

Mothers also waged battles over heating, housing, and clothing, battles that were oftentimes successful at attaining immediate goals. In March 1970 fifty members of the Wyandotte County, Kansas, WRO, led by Ruby Martin, confronted the vice president of the Gas Service Company and demanded their heat be left on in spite of their inability to pay. The VP attempted to "stall" the situation by claiming a company board meeting was required first. The women asserted they would stay until the board came. According to one protester's account, "We brought in sleeping bags and made ourselves comfortable. After serenading them with NWRO songs and spirituals, lo and behold the Board members arrived, one by one" ("Sleep-In" 1970, 8). Refusing to leave until an agreement was signed, the women held fast, and after seven hours of negotiations, they left the gas company at 7:00 P.M. with a guarantee their heat would not be shut off.

The NWRO encouraged locals to get assertive and act collectively by organizing utilities campaigns in their areas ("How to Organize"). The packet sent out by the national office included basic information about the utilities industry and welfare department policy and suggested campaign tactics. A drawing appealing specifically to mothers depicted "Reddi *Kill*owatt" approaching a mother and her young daughter with cup in hand. Strategies for negotiating with utilities companies included paying the company "only what Welfare allows in the budget"; hanging out in utilities offices "where people come with cut-off notices and recruit[ing] new members by getting Welfare to pay their back bills"; and enlisting "friends" (that is middle-class allies) of welfare recipients to delay their own utilities payments while letting the utility company know that it is "out of sympathy with poor people who can't pay the high utility bills on Welfare budgets." Above all the national office encouraged recipients to research utility regulations and customer rights and to "move as a group" in their actions.

In another effort to attain a reasonable standard of living, Ethel Mae Matthews led a group of Atlanta recipients in a sleep-in at the Model Cities headquarters in late 1970. With hot soup, coffee, sandwiches, blankets, clothes and a television set, the women held firm for twenty-six hours. The women pointed out that the officials of Model Cities (part of Lyndon Johnson's War on Poverty) worked "with their fat paychecks and plush chairs" in the midst of a ghetto that housed forty-five thousand people living in thirteen thousand units "of which 6,000 are officially judged 'substandard'" ("The States Reports: Atlanta" 1970–1971, 4). The women's demands were met "when the Atlanta Mayor signed a pledge to . . . open 108 'temporary' mobile home residences immediately and to construct some 500 permanent homes within a year for residents of the area" (4). In Johnson County, Kansas, the mere threat by WRO women was enough to move welfare officials. Asserting they "would move lock, stock and play pens in to the Welfare office waiting room" if left without housing, the women convinced the health department to allow them to temporarily remain in their current substandard rentals until adequate housing could be found. Still the women vowed to press for permanent adequate housing. In language characteristic of the black woman's mother tongue (Stover 2003, 156), the writer of the account noted, "We can't see staying in unsuitable homes when Welfare has plush carpets and leather covered chairs and has done nothing to promote low rent housing for their clients. . . . Right? Right! Go right on, Sisters, because we d—— well shall overcome and sooner than you think" ("WRO Saves 23" 1970, 8).

The issue of inhumane housing conditions came to a head when six children died due to accidents occurring in New York City's "welfare hotels" in late 1970 and early 1971. Welfare recipients were often crammed into the hotels when other public housing was unavailable. Families faced cramped quarters, roaches, and rats. Young children risked lead poisoning or worse, as when a six-year-old fell down an elevator shaft to his death and another child fell down an unguarded stairwell ("Welfare Hotels" 1971). A *New York Times* story on one such hotel, the Broadway Central, suggested that blame rested on residents for whom "squalor is a way of life" (Knight 1971). Rather than garner sympathy for children, the article described them as troublemakers who set fires and ran "wildly" through the halls. Parents, the article suggested, were passive victims of circumstance and unable to control their children.

Recipients saw the situation differently. The *Welfare Fighter* noted that hotel residents were "angry and fed-up, and determined now to pressure the city officials and make their lives miserable until meaningful steps are taken to prove they are going to face the problem with action instead of words" ("Welfare Hotels" 1971, 3). In January 1971 fifty men, women, and children staged a days-long live-in at the offices of the human resources administrator, vowing to "stay until acceptable housing was found" (3). In response administrators acknowledged the hotels were uninhabitable, condemned the building, and provided immediate housing for seventy-five families on the Upper West Side of Manhattan. All of this represented a step in the right direction but still a limited gain since only 10 percent of the units in the building were designated for poor people.

The following month recipients called attention to substandard housing by occupying a nearly completed apartment building on the West Side that was to house middle-income families. The demonstrators moved in with clothing, bedding, and television sets (Fraser 1971, 34). George Wiley explained that the group "did not object to this building. We want welfare people to live in this building." A week later a procession of hundreds of people accompanied to city hall the hearse carrying the body of six-year-old Tyrone Holland—the boy who had fallen down the elevator shaft in the Kimberly Hotel. There speakers rallied for decent housing. Demonstrators then took a bus to the newly constructed apartment building on the city's West Side and occupied it for over three hours, shouting "Right on, right in" and "How many more children will have to die" (Fraser 1971, 34).

Clothing was another issue over which welfare recipients waged pitched battles. Echoing the perspectives of early twentieth-century black women activists, 1960s welfare recipients often viewed education as an antipoverty program, and decent clothing was a necessity in order for their children to attend and learn in school. Gordon (1995) noted that early 1900s black activists' emphasis on education tethered their concerns to traditional gender strictures but also represented a "race uplift strategy," particularly given that most blacks were denied educational opportunities (124). Such thinking was behind the establishment of the Freedom Schools organized in the early 1960s by the Student Nonviolent Coordinating Committee (SNCC) to raise the consciousness of poor black youth in Mississippi (Payne 1995, 302).

Recipients' coordinated efforts to obtain school clothing for their children began as early as 1968, indicating the importance of this issue to welfare mothers active in the early years of the NWRO. In late summer of that year welfare mothers in Ann Arbor, Michigan, threatened to keep their children home from school if they were denied money for school clothing ("Mothers Vow Boycott" 1968). The following month the Ann Arbor mothers interrupted a meeting of the county social services board and demanded $100 to cover school clothing. After refusing the board's offer of $60, the mothers initiated a sit-in in the county services building. Sympathetic University of Michigan students soon joined the group, expanding the number of occupiers to eight hundred (Nadasen 2005, 90). The effort ended with the arrest of two hundred and the board's refusal to meet the mothers' demands.

The following year the NWRO launched a fall campaign for school clothing that involved a series of actions by mothers across the country ("Fall Campaign" 1969). From Warren, Ohio, to West Point, Mississippi, and as far west as Santa Maria, California, mothers occupied and picketed welfare offices and boycotted schools in an effort to obtain money for their children. Nettie McQueen, a mother in Fayetteville, North Carolina, expressed the anger of many mothers when she asserted that recipients were "ready to go to jail rather than allow their

Fig. 5.4
Cleveland, Ohio, activist mothers disrupt a Cleveland school board meeting, forcing
it to be adjourned early. The mothers blocked doorways, preventing board members
from leaving until they agreed to meet to discuss the issue of school clothing with
the mothers. Photographer, Bill Nehez. Cleveland Press Collection, Michael Schwartz
Library, Cleveland State University.

children to attend school dressed in rags" ("Fall Campaign" 1969, 2). In Detroit,
Michigan, mothers entered the welfare office and chained the doors shut behind
them, forcing police officers to pull out their saws in order to remove the women.
Mothers in Cleveland, Ohio, claiming "Mother Power" on their picket signs,
walked from Public Square in downtown Cleveland to the Cuyahoga County
welfare building to demand adequate money for their children's school clothes
("400 Occupy Welfare Bldg." 1969).

Mothers in various states also threatened to keep their children home from
school. One thousand families in Pueblo, Colorado, boycotted their schools and
forced them to close temporarily, while in New York a number of schools vol-
untarily closed in support of the clothing campaign ("Fall Campaign" 1969, 2).
Brooklyn mothers successfully sustained a school boycott well into the fall 1969
school year ("Brooklyn" 1969). Recipients' efforts continued into 1970 with actions in Cleveland, Ohio, and Winnoski, Vermont; and in Brooklyn, New York
("The Fight Goes On" 1970; "Brooklyn Mothers" 1970). In Cleveland 125 mothers
disrupted a Cleveland school board meeting on September 8, 1970, demanding

that the board provide money for their children's clothes as allowed under Title I of the Elementary and Secondary School Act, which was funded by the U.S. Department of Health, Education, and Welfare (see figure 5.4). When school board president Daniel O. Corrigan abruptly declared the meeting adjourned, Cleveland WRO leader Minnie Player fired back, "Oh, no it isn't. We aren't going to let you. You'll sit there and listen to us" ("2 Arrested in School Board" 1970).

The following week welfare rights mothers called for a school boycott. Mrs. Helen Williams was forthright when she explained, "We want to have one day when school children can learn without being sent home from school or be embarrassed because of inadequate clothes" ("Welfare Rights Boycott" 1970). Williams, who was present at the previous week's school board disruption, noted that while board president Corrigan appeared sympathetic to their cause, "we can't spend sympathy."

On September 17, 1970, over one hundred WRO activists and students boycotted a number of schools around the city. WRO leader Minnie Player was on the mark when she noted that "Cleveland is well organized and has some skilled mothers who can help other WRO's around the state" ("The Fight Goes On" 1970, 7). Mothers and their children demonstrated at the school administration building, forcing a shutdown; they leafleted at four schools; and they set up "free" schools at various points around the city where boycotting students could complete school work under the guidance of adult volunteers ("Boycott of Schools" 1970). One volunteer teacher made particularly good use of the alternative school day by having her class of twenty-five write letters to the school board urging them to seek funds for school clothing under Title I ("Boycott of Schools" 1970).

In addition to money for school clothing and supplies, mothers demanded free hot breakfasts and lunches for their children as mandated by the National School Lunch Act, approved in 1946 (Gunderson 1971). In the late 1960s and early 1970s, local WRO activists from Des Moines to D.C., South Dakota to North Carolina, met with mayors, senators, and school boards; filed lawsuits; educated poor people about their right to free lunches; and organized school checks to ensure compliance with federal law ("School Lunch" 1969, 3; "Did Your Child Eat" 1970–1971, 3). In 1970 mothers in Austin and Baltimore spoke before school boards to demand *healthy* free lunches ("not starchy ones"); the Massachusetts WRO even put together a "school packet" to instruct other WROs on how to win free school lunches ("Food Rights Actions" 1970, 9; "School Board Meeting" 1970, 4).

Mothers' claims to the right to have decent school clothes and hot lunches for their children sent a message to the general public that welfare recipients were not lazy or irresponsible parents. In contrast to the images popularized in media accounts and further legitimated by the Moynihan report, these women cared deeply about their children's ability to perform well in school, and they were concerned that their children not be stigmatized by poverty.

Even as these women took extraordinary measures in their roles as mothers, their demands fell into the domain of quintessential Americanism—the right to consume (Kornbluh 1997). In explaining their efforts to obtain store credit at Korvettes, Pope (2011) said, "We wanted to be like everyone else. . . . We wanted to join the mainstream of America." Thus in addition to countering racist stereotypes, recipients "called new rights . . . into being" and associated these rights with citizenship (Kornbluh 1997, 78). Indeed tactics based on protesters' standing as consumers had been used previously by black activists who experienced discrimination in stores, hotels, and mass transportation (Kornbluh 1997, 81). For example in the 1930s and 1940s, African Americans launched a "Don't Buy Where You Can't Work" campaign aimed at white store owners who refused to accommodate black shoppers. And of course the Montgomery bus boycott of 1955–1956 exemplified the leverage to be gained when African Americans collectively withheld their purchasing power.

The right to consume—as in the case of much-needed school clothes—was closely connected to the right to live and raise one's children with dignity, something that welfare mothers believed they were denied by the very welfare system meant to assist them. So for instance mothers in Washington, D.C., refused to accept clothing money in the amount of $10, asserting that it was "inadequate" ("Fall Campaign" 1969, 2). Likewise the chairperson of Milwaukee Welfare Rights, Cass Downer, explained that mothers were "fed up with hand-me-down clothes" ("Milwaukee on the March" 1970, 9). She emphasized mothers wanted money "of [their] own to use" (9). Mothers in San Antonio, Texas, were insulted by a suggestion that Catholic nuns teach them how to sew their own clothes. The *Welfare Fighter* explained, "Mrs. Gutirrez and local welfare recipients were very upset at this ridiculous offer, stating, 'This is what is wrong with this goddamn country.' Most welfare recipients have many disabilities and are not able to sew and besides welfare recipients should be able to buy their children clothes like anyone else" ("Fall Campaign" 1969, 2). Brooklyn mothers similarly noted their children were as deserving as the next child. They wanted to buy their children "proper school clothing" so they could be like "other American children" ("Brooklyn" 1969, 1).

Demands for dignity also extended to treatment in welfare offices. Sixty-five welfare recipients in Vermont held a spontaneous four-day sit-in at their welfare office to show support for a fellow recipient, Mrs. Chafee, who was demanding among other things the "firing of Mrs. Grace Garney," a caseworker who was allegedly so disrespectful, one welfare recipient noted "she could cause Jesus Christ to be violent" ("First Sit-In" 1970, 10). Another hot-button issue, unexpected "home visits" by nosey caseworkers, was the focus of a sit-in staged by women of the Muskogee, Oklahoma, WRO. Washington, D.C., recipients held a day-long sit-in to protest the long waits faced by women needing assistance from their local office. It is interesting to note that services that day were speeded up, and by the end of the day all 117 protesters had been waited on ("D.C. Group Sits-In" 1970).

Much can be made of the direct actions employed by welfare recipients in the mid- to late 1960s, the results of which were mixed. Activists were well aware of the limitations of traditional means of protest when it came to attaining much-needed money and goods for their families. Indeed their insight into the need for confrontation often arose from disappointing experiences communicating with bureaucrats and politicians. As one Rhode Island activist noted after leaving a task force meeting with little gained, "Rational talk alone would not work"; so the group organized a demonstration ("Fair Welfare Wins" 1970, 4). In this situation welfare mothers had reached "rhetorical exhaustion," or the moment "where coercion appears necessary because rhetoric has proven impotent" (Artz and Pollack 1997, 163). Artz and Pollack (1997) explain that when "all possible discussions, arguments, and negotiations have been rallied, deployed, rebuked, and exhausted and prospects for new discourse are lacking," coercion may be justified (163). Justified or not, the interruptions, demonstrations, and occupations by welfare activists were arguably the most pragmatic and readily available form of protest for actors in a rhetorical situation severely constrained by entrenched structures (for example welfare legislation and institutionalized discriminatory practices) and racist images (for example welfare stereotypes).

The examples provided throughout this chapter represent the many victories won by recipients who obtained immediate money for school clothing, increases in special grants, and in a few cases improved housing and heat. Nadasen (2005) notes that the NWRO's special grants campaigns attracted "thousands of new members" and "palpably affect[ed] welfare policy on the local level" (80). In addition the constant "threat of protest and disruption convinced many welfare officials to circumvent bureaucratic regulations and meet the demands of irate welfare recipients" (82). And Brooklyn, New York, organizer Jackie Pope (1989) concluded that members of the Brooklyn Welfare Action Council "won concessions from New York City welfare administrators, and their actions fostered less restrictive policies and services provided in a respectful manner at public assistance offices" (3).

This chapter's examples also highlight the limitations and risk taking inherent in recipients' more confrontational actions. Unlike workers in the paid labor force, recipients lacked the power to halt production, a strategy that "spoke to" company owners in the form of a threat or actual damage to corporate profitability. So for example when hundreds of protesters occupied a county building for three days in Ann Arbor, Michigan, all they got for their efforts were arrests and a statement from the director of the social services department that "we aren't going to put up with this anymore" (Nadasen 2005, 90). The Ann Arbor group was not the only to face arrests; throughout the occupations of the late 1960s and early 1970s, hundreds of others endured police harassment and jail time. Furthermore the issue of arrest was particularly acute for single mothers. Jackie Pope, a single mother of four daughters, recalled her reticence when it came to the possibility of arrest, noting there would be no one to care for her children should she go to jail (2011).

One may also consider the potential impact of mainstream media coverage in shaping public perceptions of the events described in this chapter. By and large commercially mediated stories and images betray an elitist bias that favors powerful groups and status quo public policies (Entman 1989, 1991; Herman and Chomsky 1988; Reese and Buckalew 1995; Triece 2001; L. Williams 1995). The *New York Times*'s coverage of the Children's March for Survival trivialized the marchers' efforts ("30,000, Many of Them Children" 1972), while the paper's stories on welfare hotels portrayed recipients and their families as the cause of their own misery (Knight 1971).* Likewise the *New York Times*'s front-page article covering the mothers' blockade and disturbance at Brooklyn welfare centers characterized the event as a "rampage," which according to WRO leader Hulbert James "did more than any other news story to discredit the movement in New York" (Kornbluh 2007, 108). These examples are not to suggest that media coverage is always the same. The "democratizing potential" (Kumar 2001) of corporate media warrants further study, particularly for the ways that poor people's voices are incorporated into or framed by news accounts, which may give readers a more sympathetic take on such struggles.

The NWRO's decline paralleled the diminishing presence of the black insurgency movement of the 1960s. Civil rights organizations such as CORE, NAACP, SNCC, and SCLC (what McAdam refers to as the "Big Four") lost influence between 1966 and 1970 for a number of reasons, including conflict over strategies and goals; a "proliferation of issues" as opposed to collective rallying around a single issue (that is integration); intergroup competition for resources; and a decline in public concern over civil rights as other issues took center stage, for example the Vietnam War and Watergate (McAdam 1982, 182–201). The NWRO faced similar challenges. Recipient-activists were reluctant to embrace George Wiley's concept of broadening the organization's constituency to include the unemployed and working poor. Members also held opposing positions regarding whether and how to align with establishment figures. Allies Frances Fox Piven and Richard Cloward favored direct disruption of the welfare system, while recipient-activists such as Johnnie Tillmon and Beulah Sanders at times worked within the system by meeting with heads of the Department of Health, Education, and Welfare, with senators, and other powerful government officials. Finally activists then faced and must still deal with the quandary of how to sustain the movement. For welfare righters organizing around special grants campaigns held

---

* Williams's (1995) study of media treatment of public aid recipients living in a Boston area housing project demonstrates that not much has changed in the way coverage of recipient mothers.

inherent limitations (Piven and Cloward 1979, 285–88). Once immediate relief was won, there was little to induce recipients to remain active in the movement.

By and large the early twenty-first century appears to offer little improvement for poor people: welfare recipients, the underemployed, the underpaid. In light of the most recent gutting of the welfare system—the 1996 Personal Responsibility and Work Opportunity Reconciliation Act—we would do well to explore the rhetorical possibilities available to individuals such as welfare recipients and undocumented immigrants whose needs are not always well-integrated by wider social movements that have demonstrated degrees of success throughout the twentieth century. Furthermore challenges facing civil rights groups of the 1960s and 1970s—such as movement recruitment and sustainment, media attention, and goal setting—deserve continued attention as concerned citizens and scholars strategize future movement toward social change.

Conclusion

A historically overlooked element of civil rights struggles of the 1960s, the welfare rights movement launched a significant and oftentimes successful drive for political voice and economic control for poor, primarily black mothers. Racist welfare legislation that prevented women from providing decent care for their children planted the seeds of discontent that prompted recipient-activist Johnnie Tillmon and the many others mentioned in this book to form their own organizations to fight welfare bureaucrats who controlled their pocketbooks and invaded their privacy.

Throughout the 1960s the U.S. economic imperative (for sustained profit) and political exigency buttressed by racist myths positioned poor black women at the intersection of capital and care. Earlier chapters explained the double bind faced by black women who were at once expected to fill low-wage jobs in the marketplace and maintain responsibility for care work in the home. Welfare rights activists countered popular stereotypes of the "welfare chiseler" and the "welfare queen" by establishing themselves as willing workers capable of filling meaningful jobs in the marketplace (chapter 3) and as caring mothers who deserved to remain home with their young children should they choose to (chapter 4). Their negotiated self-definition—as both workers and mothers—was an appropriate response to public policies that placed them in an untenable position.

The previous chapters explored how women in the welfare rights movement responded to public policies they viewed as unfair and racist. In congressional testimony, speeches, and organizational documents, recipients laid claim to a keener view of life on welfare by virtue of their firsthand experience with poverty; that is they relied on "epistemic advantage" (Alcoff 2006). Through reality referencing activists called attention to their experiences as workers and mothers in a context of low-wage work, deteriorated neighborhoods, and widespread unemployment for black Americans. Furthermore women used rhetorical strategies to give presence to their work and home lives, to collectivize their work experiences, and to politicize black motherhood. These activists repeatedly called up the connections among economy, public policy, and the ways they were positioned as poor black women. Not least important was that welfare rights activists deployed "body" rhetoric—direct actions such as mass demonstrations and occupations—particularly upon the realization that traditional channels of communication were often closed to poor people (Rustin 1963).

This study of welfare rights activism has been couched within the larger issue of agency, or the ways marginalized groups act collectively for social change in the context of entrenched structures and policies that delimit the possibilities for discourse and action. Within a theoretical framework of historical materialism, agency can most fruitfully be studied as a process that emerges in the dialectic between subjectivity and structure. Furthermore agency is not static but matures through three phases: cultivation of critical awareness, collectivization of experiences, and mobilization through rhetoric and direct actions in public settings.

The study of agency in the context of welfare rights activism offers two lessons for contemporary students and scholars, one having to do with theory, the second with praxis.

On Theoretical Relevance

Academic debates that continue to foreground influences of language and identity risk shifting conversation away from salient features that impinge on people's quests for equality and decent living conditions. The discursive turn taken by postmodern and posthumanist scholars along with contemporary micromovements' emphasis on identity and Do-It-Yourself (DIY) politics diverts much-needed attention away from class struggle and capitalist exploitation, arguably still relevant in the twenty-first century.*

What are the implications and consequences of holding to one theory or another? When theory is kept moving "along the broken ground covered by the specific material of the discipline" (Leff 1980, 347), we keep our studies relevant and we may begin to shed light on questions relating to real-life implications and therefore theoretical relevance. A look at the struggles of marginalized groups reveals a number of important reasons for grounding studies in traditional Marxism with its spotlight on class (consciousness, interests, exploitation, and struggle) and emphasis on a dialectical relationship between real conditions and discourse pertaining to those conditions. Chapter 1 introduced the terms "reality gap" (Triece 2007) and "reality test" (Cloud 2006) and the ways these concepts home in on the process by which ordinary people come to understand the "mechanics" of their oppression (whether it be in the form of workplace exploitation, patriarchal relations, racism); formulate a method for challenging that oppression; and then judge whether or not equality has been achieved. A "reality gap" is "the space between prevailing, widely accepted ideologies . . . and the reality of

---

* See McRobbie (2009) for her incisive critique of third-wave feminism's preoccupation with identity. See Baumgardner and Richards (2004) for a good example of identity politics promoted in the form of what the authors refer to as "girlie feminism."

people's day-to-day existence," which gives "rise to contradictions or paradoxes that . . . provide an opening for social critique and change" (Triece 2007, 2). Likewise a "reality test" provides a way to judge "political discourses and ideologies from the standpoint of ordinary people" (Cloud 2006, 331). Both concepts stress the idea that assessments (of what is fair or unfair, just or unjust, equitable or inequitable, racist or antiracist, and so on) can be made only by making comparisons to lived experience. To accept otherwise is to fall into the "rabbit hole of relativism" (Cloud 2006), wherein there are no referents outside of discourse and thus no way to judge whose version of reality (for example as expressed in public policy, political debate, and popular narrative) is the more accurate and thus more appropriate as a basis for the formulation of public policy, movement struggle, workplace arrangements, and so on.

Chapter 1 also elaborated on the importance of standpoint as discussed by Marxist scholars such as Lukács (1968) and Hartsock (1983b), a concept that directs scholars to examine the voices and lives of marginalized groups as they are situated within and shaped and motivated by systems of material production and distribution. Negt and Kluge (1993) refer to the "materialist instinct" to indicate the centrality of lived experience in ordinary people's lives. "The masses live with experiences of violence, oppression, exploitation, and, in the broader sense of the term, alienation. They possess material, sensual evidence of the restriction of possibilities in their lives, of their freedom of movement. Accordingly, the resistance to this restriction has a sensual credibility" (43). Indeed welfare activist Jackie Pope's (1971) observation underscores how experiences as a poor black female awakened her to the need to organize: "To be black, a woman, and a Welfare recipient is the worst of all hells in these United States in the year 1971. The only real hope for survival for Welfare mothers is to be 'organized'" (7).

For a study of the resistance struggles of mothers, housewives, or welfare recipients—groups that remain outside of though integrally related to workplace relations and conditions—Marxist concepts remain relevant even as we recognize the importance of figuring the role of immaterial labor (for example domestic work) into our understandings of class exploitation and struggles. Recent scholarship of a postmodern, posthumanist, or post-Marxist bent has emphasized capitalism's supposed shift toward immaterial labor or work that involves information exchange, problem solving, and affect over and above traditional commodity production (Hardt and Negri 2000). Greene (2004) notes that by examining labor that is "associated with care, affect, and consumption" we can better understand how these forms of labor are gendered and raced (199). Certainly it is of paramount importance to examine how experiences in the workplace are affected by racism and sexism and how women—particularly women of color— experience work differently than, say, white males. However to acknowledge the role that immaterial labor (in the form of care work) played in poor black women's lives does not require us to "reconceptualize the idea of production" (Greene

2004, 199) or alter our understandings of exploitation and struggle in the context of global capitalism.

Indeed one may argue that claims of the centrality of immaterial labor are exaggerated (Cloud, Macek, and Aune 2006), particularly when we look globally at the work performed by women of color. In her study of female workers in Thailand, Mills (2005) notes that "women constitute the primary workforce for most of the labor-intensive industries [such as] textiles, electronics, food products" and that "similar patterns of feminized labor recruitment are common around the world, a by-product of globalizing capital's unending search for ever cheaper and more flexible labor" (117).

An examination of the experiences of poor black women in the welfare rights movement points to the driving force of capitalist production in their lives—particularly as it was intimately tied to the formation of welfare policy and their ability to control their work and family lives. The history of welfare legislation in the context of expanding corporate capitalism throughout the early to mid-1900s underscores the intimate relationship between welfare legislation and the needs of capitalism. New Deal legislation exempted agricultural and domestic workers (primarily poor black women) from eligibility for aid. And into the 1970s, under the Work Incentive Program, "welfare recipients [were] made to serve as maids or to do day yard work in white homes to keep their checks. During the cotton-picking season no one [was] accepted on welfare because plantations need[ed] cheap labor to do cotton-picking behind the cotton-picking machines" (Quadagno 1994, 128). NWRO activists themselves expressed an awareness of the interrelationship between the economy and state policy, particularly the ways that they as welfare recipients were used to perpetuate class exploitation. As one woman testifying before Congress in 1977 explained, welfare recipients were regularly used as a "club to drive down the wages and working conditions of all workers" (Administration's Welfare Reform Proposal 1977, 38).

This study suggests then that contra some postmodern scholars, the "old distinctions between productive labor and unproductive labor" (Greene 2004, 201) are indeed useful, particularly insofar as the distinctions enable us to theorize how the two are related. When Marx wrote about productive versus unproductive labor he was highlighting a relationship to production, not the nature of a particular commodity produced. Thus some forms of immaterial labor (for example hotel work and piloting), if employed for the purpose of producing surplus value, that is profit, may be considered "productive labor" in the way that making refrigerators is considered "productive labor." Other forms of immaterial labor, particularly unpaid care work, are not synonymous with but rather exist in a symbiotic relationship to commodity production that warrants further exploration by scholars interested in the ways global capitalism positions poor women of color both in terms of production and reproduction. In short a continued awareness of class—in the traditional Marxist sense—keeps us focused on how economic, state, and domestic spheres engaged dynamically with capital, acting as a driving force that impacted poor black women's lives as workers in the paid labor force and caretakers in the home.

Linking Theory and Praxis

"The philosophers have *interpreted* the world, in various ways; the point, however, is to *change* it" (Marx 1888, 145). Marx recognized above all else the importance of linking theory and praxis. Theory must be relevant so that it may be made practical. In a similar spirit recent scholars have confronted the "elitism" characterizing "educational, political, and civic institutions throughout the Western tradition" with concerted attempts to study working-class rhetorics that highlight the existence of "class (and, by extension, class division and class conflicts)" (DeGenaro 2007, 6). Such a scholarly effort, coupled with the efforts of the field of communication studies to become a more "engaged discipline" (Cherwitz and Hartelius 2006),* suggests the continued importance of endeavors exploring how ordinary people get their voices heard in the context of political debates constrained by power differentials between speaker and audience and increasingly shaped by corporate pocketbooks.†

The previous chapters offer one of the few studies examining poor black women's efforts to shape public policy, from their demands made in the elitist halls of congress to their demonstrations in the streets. Such studies remain important as we enter into the second decade of the twenty-first century, thus far a period marked by significant and widespread failures in the global capitalist economy. Now more than ever working people may be poised to recognize the reality gap between the promises espoused in neoliberalist notions of the American Dream and their day-to-day experiences in the workplace and at home. Although productivity is up, workers are earning less now than they were a decade ago, according to recent Census Bureau statistics (Leonhardt 2009). The gap between the wealthiest Americans and those on the middle and bottom rungs has widened, exacerbated by the 2008 recession. And workers in many countries labor in sweatshop conditions making shoes and apparel for U.S. companies such as Nike and Wal-Mart ("Secrets, Lies" 2006).

Within this twenty-first-century "rhetorical situation" (Bitzer 1968), various scholars suggest achieving "escape velocity" (Greene 2006, 92) or mobilizing the

* In 2008 the National Communication Association's annual conference theme was "The Engaged Discipline." The *Quarterly Journal of Speech* featured a forum on Engaged Scholarship in November 2010.

† In the 2010 case *Citizens United v. Federal Election Commission,* the Supreme Court decided in favor of unlimited corporate expenditure to support independent political organizations.

"Soviets of mass intellectuality" (Negri 1996, 220) as fitting responses for ordinary people to muster against global capitalism. Negri (1996) argues that people can construct, "outside of the State, a mechanism within which a democracy of the everyday can organize active communication, the interactivity of citizens, and at the same time produce increasingly free and complex subjectivities" (221). Such suggestions leave scholar and activist alike wondering what "escape velocity" might look like and how ordinary citizens might formulate "complex subjectivities," situated as they are within the structures of state and economy.

Fortunately there exists an inspiring legacy of collective mobilization against oppressive structures pointing toward more just economic and political systems. Throughout the twentieth century labor activists engaged in strikes, walkouts, and sit-ins by the tens of thousands to win basic workplace rights taken for granted today.* Civil rights activists employed boycotts, sit-ins, and mass marches directed at overturning Jim Crow and segregationist laws and winning access to the ballot box. The history of social protest points to the power of ordinary people to alter entrenched systems through mass direct actions that impact the day-to-day workings of economic production and political decision making. Such studies remain important particularly for scholars and activists interested in organizing groups historically left out of mass struggles—for example welfare recipients, paid and unpaid caretakers and domestic workers, migrant workers, and undocumented immigrants—many of whom are women of color and who have a tenuous foothold in the paid workplace.

Although welfare recipients could not (at least very easily) leverage their labor power to force the hands of employers, they used other rhetorical strategies and direct actions with varying degrees of success. The obstacles they ran up against—particularly when it came to political pressuring—suggest the importance of examining the rhetorical possibilities available for establishing solidarity along the lines of class and for exploring the symbiotic relationship between production and reproduction, the workplace and the domestic sphere, and productive and unproductive labor (in the Marxist sense of the terms).

Finally as they related the rhetorical strategies and direct actions of welfare rights activists of the late 1960s, the previous pages proffered a "workable notion" of human agency to shed light on the ways poor women pushed for welfare reform. As posthumanist perspectives maintain traction in academic discussions across disciplines, the words of the sociologist Margaret Archer (2000) provide a particularly poignant call. She notes: "Ordinary people act in undemolished fashion—they confront the world, meaning nature and practice rather than just society, for, as functioning human beings, they cannot endorse the 'linguistic fallacy'; in confronting their environment they feel a continuous sense of the self

---

* The historian Philip S. Foner has published widely on the labor movement from the 1800s through the mid 1900s.

who does so, for they cannot live out their dissolution; they have cares, concerns and commitments which they see as part of themselves, for they cannot accept the 'identity' of demolished men and women; and they have social positions, which most of them would like to rectify, in at least some respect, and are unconvinced that social improvements merely depend upon discursive changes. All this stuff of life needs confirming" (2).

Communication studies will benefit from further examination of the ways poor people have spoken on behalf of themselves in the context of broader policy debates directed by the voices of the elite. We can hope that in an economic and geopolitical landscape of both hope—as in the Arab Spring—and cynicism—born of bailouts for the rich rather than the poor—the seeds of discontent may grow into renewed collective efforts for equality in the spirit of poor people's agitation of the 1960s. If we accept that welfare policy debates are about "what various groups of women really need and whose interpretations of women's needs should be authoritative" (Fraser 1989, 145), we would do well to consider the possibility of asserting and assessing knowledge claims vis-à-vis a material context, particularly for disempowered groups who relied on their own ability to "tell it like it is."

Works Cited

"2 Arrested in School Board Disturbance." 1970. *Cleveland Press,* September 8, n.p.

"11 Demonstrators at Welfare Office Taken into Custody." 1968. *New York Times,* July 1, 66.

"71% Say Too Many People Get Welfare Who Shouldn't." Accessed December 1, 2011. http://www.rasmussenreports.com/public_content/lifestyle/general_lifestyle/august _2011/71_say_too_many_people_get_welfare_who_shouldn_t.

"75 Welfare Recipients Go on Rampage, Closing 3 Brooklyn Centers." 1968. *New York Times,* September 18, 1.

"140 Moms and Children Protest." 1970. *Welfare Fighter,* February, 6.

"400 Occupy Welfare Bldg. Seeking School Clothing." 1969. *Cleveland Press,* September 3.

"5000 March in Ill." 1971. *Welfare Fighter,* November, 1.

"30,000, Many of Them Children, Protest Nixon Welfare Policies." 1972. *New York Times,* March 26, 20.

Abramovitz, Mimi. 1988. *Regulating the Lives of Women: Social Welfare Policy from Colonial Times to the Present.* Boston: South End.

———. 2000. *Under Attack, Fighting Back: Women and Welfare in the United States.* New York: Monthly Review Press.

———. 2002. "Learning from the History of Poor and Working-Class Women's Activism." In *Lost Ground: Welfare Reform, Poverty and Beyond,* ed. Randy Albelda and Ann Withorn, 163–78. Cambridge, Mass.: South End.

"Adequate Income NOW!" 1970. *Welfare Fighter,* special edition, March, 1.

Administration's Welfare Reform Proposal: Joint Hearings before a Task Force of the Welfare Reform Subcommittee of the Committee on Agriculture, Committee on Education and Labor, Committee on Ways and Means, 95th Congress. 1977. Testimony of Melody Abers.

Albelda, Randy, Nancy Folbre, and the Center for Popular Economics. 1996. *The War on the Poor: A Defense Manual.* New York: New Press.

Albritton, Robert B. 1979. "Social Amelioration through Mass Insurgency? A Reexaminatiton of the Piven and Cloward Thesis." *American Political Science Review* 73: 1003–11.

Alcoff, Linda M. 1988. "Cultural Feminism versus Poststructuralism: The Identity Crisis in Feminist Theory." *Signs: Journal of Women in Culture and Society* 13:405–36.

————. 2006. *Visible Identities: Race, Gender, and the Self.* Oxford: Oxford University Press.

"ANC–Mothers Anonymous." Fact Sheet. NWRO Papers Box 2247, unprocessed as of April 4, 2008, Manuscript Division, Moorland-Spingarn Research Center, Howard University.

Andrews, James R. 1969. "Confrontation at Columbia: A Case Study in Coercive Rhetoric." *Quarterly Journal of Speech* 55:9–16.

"And the Wall Came Tumbling Down." 1971. *Welfare Fighter,* August, 2.

"Angry Rally Backs H.E.W. Liberators." 1970. *Welfare Fighter,* June, 1.

"The Anti-welfare Bill." 1967. *NOW!* newsletter. NWRO Papers Box 2101, unprocessed as of April 4, 2008, Manuscript Division, Moorland-Spingarn Research Center, Howard University.

"April 15ᵗʰ Rallies Support Adequate Income, Washington, D.C." 1970. *Welfare Fighter,* April, 1.

Archer, Margaret S. 2000. *Being Human: The Problem of Agency.* New York: Cambridge University Press.

Arthur, Linda B. 1993. "Clothing, Control, and Women's Agency: The Mitigation of Patriarchal Power." In *Negotiating at the Margins: The Gendered Discourses of Power and Resistance,* ed. Sue Fisher and Kathy Davis, 66–84. New Brunswick, N.J.: Rutgers University Press.

Artz, B. Lee, and Mark Pollock. 1997. "The Rhetoric of Unconditional Surrender: Locating the Necessary Moment for Coercion." *Communication Studies* 48:159–74.

Asen, Robert. 2001. "Nixon's Welfare Reform: Enacting Historical Contradictions of Poverty Discourses." *Rhetoric and Public Affairs* 4:261–79.

————. 2002. *Visions of Poverty: Welfare Policy and Political Imagination.* East Lansing: Michigan State University Press.

————. 2003. "Women, Work, Welfare: A Rhetorical History of Images of Poor Women in Welfare Policy Debates." *Rhetoric and Public Affairs* 6:285–312.

Aune, James Arnt. 1994. *Rhetoric and Marxism.* Boulder, Colo.: Westview.

"Aunt Jemima Ain't What She Used to Be." 1971. *Welfare Fighter,* December, 4.

Avant-Mier, Roberto, and Marouf A. Hasian. 2008. "Communication 'Truth' Testimonio, Vernacular Voices, and the Rigoberta Menchu Controversy." *Communication Review* 11:323–45.

Bailis, Lawrence N. 1974. *Bread or Justice: Grassroots Organizing in the Welfare Rights Movement.* Lexington, Mass.: Lexington.

Baines, Lillian. 1970. "Why Not a Subsidy for Mothers?" *Welfare Fighter,* May, 3.

Barnlund, Dean C., and Franklin S. Haiman. 1960. *The Dynamics of Discussion.* Boston: Houghton Mifflin.

Baumgardner, Jennifer, and Amy Richards. 2004. "Feminism and Femininity: Or How We Learned to Stop Worrying and Love the Thong." In *All about the Girl: Culture, Power, and Identity,* ed. Anita Harris, 59–67. New York: Routledge.

Bell, Katrina E., Mark P. Orbe, Darlene K. Drummond, and Sakile Kai Camara. 2000. "Accepting the Challenge of Centralizing without Essentializing: Black Feminist

Thought and African American Women's Communicative Experiences." *Women's Studies in Communication* 23:41–62.

Bell, Winifred. 1965. *Aid to Dependent Children.* New York: Columbia University Press.

Bensonsmith, Dionne. 2005. "Jezebels, Matriarchs, and Welfare Queens: The Moynihan Report of 1965 and the Social Construction of African-American Women in Welfare Policy." In *Deserving and Entitled: Social Constructions and Public Policy,* ed. Anne L. Schneider and Helen M. Ingram, 243–59. Albany: State University of New York Press.

"Beulah—From the Chair." 1971. *Welfare Fighter,* November, 3.

Beverley, John. 2005. "Testimonio, Subalterity, and Narrative Authority." In *The Sage Handbook of Qualitative Research,* ed. Norman K. Denzin and Yvonna S. Lincoln, 547–57. Thousand Oaks, Calif.: Sage.

Biesecker, Barbara. 1992. "Coming to Terms with Recent Attempts to Write Women into the History of Rhetoric." *Philosophy and Rhetoric* 25:140–61.

Bitzer, Lloyd. 1968. "The Rhetorical Situation." *Philosophy and Rhetoric* 1:1–14.

"Bi-weekly Letter." October 31, 1966. NWRO Papers Box 2160, unprocessed as of April 4, 2008, Manuscript Division, Moorland-Spingarn Research Center, Howard University.

Blackmun, Harry. 1971. Dissenting opinion, *Wyman v. James,* 400 U.S. 309. Accessed December 18, 2009. http://supreme.justia.com/us/400/309/case.html.

Bolton, Charles D. 1972. "Alienation and Action: A Study of Peace Group Members." *American Journal of Sociology* 78:537–61.

Bordo, Susan. 1990. "Feminism, Postmodernism, and Gender-Skepticism." In *Feminism/Postmodernism,* ed. Linda J. Nicholson, 133–56. New York: Routledge.

Boris, Eileen. 1993. "The Power of Motherhood: Black and White Activist Women Redefine the 'Political.'" In *Mothers of a New World: Maternalist Politics and the Origins of Welfare States,* ed. Seth Koven and Sonya Michel, 213–43. New York: Routledge.

Bowers, John W., and Donovan Ochs. 1971. *The Rhetoric of Agitation and Control.* Reading, Mass: Addison-Wesley.

"Boycott of Schools Continues." 1970. *Cleveland Press,* September 17, n.p.

"Brooklyn." 1969. *Welfare Fighter,* October, 1.

"Brooklyn Mothers March for Title I." 1970. *Welfare Fighter,* November, 5.

Brooks, Patricia. 1966. "Ohio Welfare March Ends in Rally of 2,000." *National Guardian,* July 9. NWRO Papers Box 2160, unprocessed as of April 4, 2008, Manuscript Division, Moorland-Spingarn Research Center, Howard University.

Brouwer, Daniel C. 2001. "ACT-ing UP in Congressional Hearings." In *Counterpublics and the State,* ed. Robert Asen and Daniel C. Brouwer, 87–109. Albany: State University of New York Press.

Brown, Michael K. 1999. *Race, Money, and the American Welfare State.* Ithaca: Cornell University Press.

Brown, Wendy. 1995. *States of Injury: Power and Freedom in Late Modernity.* Princeton, N.J.: Princeton University Press.

Bureau of Labor Statistics. Economic News Release. Accessed September 2011. http://www.bls.gov/news.release/empsit.t02.htm.

Butler, Judith. 2005. *Giving an Account of Oneself.* New York: Fordham University Press.

Calvert, Mildred. 1972. "Welfare Rights and the Welfare System." In *Welfare Mothers Speak Out: We Ain't Gonna Shuffle Anymore,* ed. Thomas H. Tarantino and Rev. Dismas Becker, 25–30. New York: Norton.

Cameron, Ardis. 1993. *Radicals of the Worst Sort: Laboring Women in Lawrence, Massachusetts, 1860–1912.* Urbana: University of Illinois Press.

Campbell, Karlyn Kohrs. 1973. "The Rhetoric of Women's Liberation: An Oxymoron." *Quarterly Journal of Speech* 59:74–86.

———. 1986. "Style and Content in the Rhetoric of Early Afro-American Feminists." *Quarterly Journal of Speech* 72:434–45.

———. 2002. "Consciousness-Raising: Linking Theory, Criticism, and Practice." *Rhetoric Society Quarterly* 32:45–64.

———. 2005. "Agency: Promiscuous and Protean." *Communication and Critical/Cultural Critique* 2:1–19.

"Candidates' Contract with the People." 1972. *Welfare Fighter,* March, 8.

Castro, Clementina. 1972. "Spanish-Speaking People and the Welfare System." In *Welfare Mothers Speak Out: We Ain't Gonna Shuffle Anymore,* ed. Thomas H. Tarantino and Rev. Dismas Becker, 66–71. New York: Norton.

Cavanaugh, Bertha. 1969. "What NWRO Has Done for Me." *Welfare Fighter,* December, 2.

Cherwitz, Richard A., and E. Johanna Hartelius. 2006. "Making a 'Great "Engaged" University' Requires Rhetoric." In *Fixing the Fragmented University: Decentralization with Direction,* ed. Joseph C. Burke, 265–88. San Francisco: Jossey-Bass.

"Chicago." 1972. *Welfare Fighter,* April, 12.

"Children and Mothers Confront Governors." 1972. *Welfare Fighter,* March, 14.

"Children's Issues Go to Miami." 1972. *Welfare Fighter,* June, 9.

Cloud, Dana L. 1994. "The Materiality of Discourse as Oxymoron: A Challenge to Critical Rhetoric." *Western Journal of Communication* 58:141–63.

———. 2005. "Fighting Words: Labor and the Limits of Communication at Staley, 1993–1996." *Management Communication Quarterly* 18:509–42.

———. 2006. "The Matrix and Critical Theory's Desertion of the Real." *Communication and Critical/Cultural Studies* 3:329–54.

Cloud, Dana L., Steve Macek, and James Arnt Aune. 2006. "'The Limbo of Ethical Simulacra': A Reply to Ron Greene." *Philosophy and Rhetoric* 39:72–84.

Cloward, Richard, and Frances Fox Piven. 1966. "The Weight of the Poor: A Strategy to End Poverty." In *Welfare: A Documentary History of U.S. Policy and Politics,* ed. Gwendolyn Mink and Rickie Solinger, 249–59. New York: New York University Press.

Collins, Patricia Hill. 1986. "Learning from the Outsider Within: The Sociological Significance of Black Feminist Thought." *Social Problems* 33:S14–S32.

———. 1991. *Black Feminist Thought: Knowledge, Consciousness, and the Politics of Empowerment.* New York: Routledge.

———. 1994. "Shifting the Center: Race, Class, and Feminist Theorizing about Motherhood." In *Mothering: Ideology, Experience, and Agency,* ed. Evelyn N. Glenn, Grace Chang, and Linda R. Forcey, 45–65. New York: Routledge.

———. 1998. *Fighting Words: Black Women and the Search for Justice.* Minneapolis: University of Minnesota Press.

Colom, Wilber. 1972. "Lobbying for Minority Plank No. 5." *Welfare Fighter,* August–September, 3.

"Columbia, S.C." 1972. *Welfare Fighter,* April, 12.

"Complaints against Food Stamps." 1970. *Welfare Fighter,* February, 6.

Condit, Celeste M. 1987. "Democracy and Civil Rights: The Universalizing Influence of Public Argumentation." *Communication Monographs* 54:1–18.

Condit, Celeste M., and John Lucaites. 1991. "The Rhetoric of Equality and the Expatriation of African-Americans, 1771–1826." *Communication Studies* 42:1–21.

"Congress Kills FAP." 1972. *Welfare Fighter,* October, 1, 3, 4, 11.

"Convention '71." 1971. *Welfare Fighter,* October, 7.

Crawford, Vicki L., Jacqueline A. Rouse, and Barbara Woods, eds. 1990. *Women in the Civil Rights Movement: Trailblazers and Torchbearers, 1941–1965.* Brooklyn: Carlson.

Creamer, Robert. 1968. "Mothers Win Phones, Furnishings." *Boston Herald Traveler,* July 31. NWRO Papers Box 2160, unprocessed as of April 4, 2008, Manuscript Division, Moorland-Spingarn Research Center, Howard University.

Culler, Jonathan. 1982. *On Deconstruction: Theory and Criticism after Structuralism.* Ithaca: Cornell University Press.

Davis, Martha F. 1996. "Welfare Rights and Women's Rights in the 1960s." *Journal of Policy History* 8:144–65.

"D.C. Group Sits-In at Welfare Dept." 1970. *Welfare Fighter,* May, 9.

DeGenaro, William, ed. 2007. *Who Says? Working-Class Rhetoric, Class Consciousness, and Community.* Pittsburgh: University of Pittsburgh Press.

Delgado, Fernando. 1999. "Rigoberta Menchu and Testimonial Discourse: Collectivist Rhetoric and Rhetorical Criticism." *World Communication* 28:17–29.

"Did Your Child Eat Lunch Today?" 1970–1971. *Welfare Fighter,* December–January, 3.

Di Stefano, Christine. 1990. "Dilemmas of Difference: Feminism, Modernity, and Postmodernism." In *Feminism/Postmodernism,* ed. Linda J. Nicholson, 63–82. New York: Routledge.

Dougherty, Debbie S., and Kathleen J. Krone. 2000. "Overcoming the Dichotomy: Cultivating Standpoints in Organizations through Research." *Women's Studies in Communication* 23:16–40.

Dow, Bonnie J. 1995. "Feminism, Difference(s), and Rhetorical Studies." *Communication Studies* 46:106–17.

"Do You Feel Left Out?" 1971. *Welfare Fighter,* April–May, 6.

Draft of speech. 1971. NWRO Papers Box 2210, unprocessed as of April 4, 2008, Manuscript Division, Moorland-Spingarn Research Center, Howard University.

Droogsma, Rachel A. 2007. "Redefining Hijab: American Muslim Women's Standpoints on Veiling." *Journal of Applied Communication Research* 35:294–319.

"Eagleton for Welfare Push." 1969. *Kansas City Star,* July 13. 8A. NWRO Papers Box 2160, unprocessed as of April 4, 2008, Manuscript Division, Moorland-Spingarn Research Center, Howard University.

Ebert, Teresa L. 1996. *Ludic Feminism and After: Postmodernism, Desire, and Labor in Late Capitalism.* Ann Arbor: University of Michigan Press.

Echols, Alice. 1989. *Daring to Be Bad: Radical Feminism in America 1967–1975.* Minneapolis: University of Minnesota Press.

Economic Problems of Women: Hearings before the Joint Economic Committee, 93rd Congress. 1973. Testimony of Johnnie Tillmon.

Ellingson, Laura L. 2000. "Style, Substance, and Standpoint: A Feminist Critique of Bernie Siegel's Rhetoric of Self-Healing." *Women's Studies in Communication* 23:63–89.

Engels, Friedrich. 1890. "Letters on Historical Materialism." In *The Marx-Engels Reader,* ed. Robert C. Tucker, 760–68. New York: Norton, 1978.

Entman, Robert. 1989. *Democracy without Citizens.* New York: Oxford University Press.

———. 1991. "Framing U.S. Coverage of International News: Contrasts in Narratives of the KAL and Iran Air Incidents." *Journal of Communication* 41:6–27.

Entman, Robert, and Donna R. Leff. 1991. *The Media's Coverage of Poverty.* Chicago: A Report of the Chicago Council on Urban Affairs.

Evans, Faith. 1971. "Back to Slavery?" *Welfare Fighter,* October, 1, 14.

Examination of the War on Poverty: Hearing before the Subcommittee on Employment, Manpower, and Poverty of the Committee on Labor and Public Welfare, 90th Congress. 1967. Testimony of Betty Meredith.

Examination of the War on Poverty: Hearing before the Subcommittee on Employment, Manpower, and Poverty of the Committee on Labor and Public Welfare, 90th Congress. 1967. Testimony of Joy Stanley.

Examination of the War on Poverty: Hearing before the Subcommittee on Employment, Manpower, and Poverty of the Committee on Labor and Public Welfare, 90th Congress. 1967. Testimony of Simone St. Jock.

"Fair Welfare Wins in Task Force." 1970. *Welfare Fighter,* January, 4.

"Fall Campaign—Phase One—School Clothing." 1969. *Welfare Fighter,* September, 2.

Farmer, James. 1965. "The Controversial Moynihan Report." In *The Moynihan Report and the Politics of Controversy,* ed. Lee Rainwater and William L. Yancey, 409–11. Cambridge: M.I.T. Press.

Feagin, Joe. 1975. *Subordinating the Poor: Welfare and American Beliefs.* Englewood Cliffs, N.J.: Prentice-Hall.

"The Fight Goes On . . . " 1970. *Welfare Fighter,* May, 7.

"Fighting Back at Cuts." 1971. *Welfare Fighter,* October, 10.

"Fight the Anti-welfare Bill." 1967. *NOW!* newsletter. NWRO Papers Box 2160, unprocessed as of April 4, 2008, Manuscript Division, Moorland-Spingarn Research Center, Howard University.

Fineman, Martha A. 2004. *The Autonomy Myth: A Theory of Dependency.* New York: New Press.

"First Sit-In in Springfield, VT." 1970. *Welfare Fighter,* April, 10.

Fisher, Gordon M. 1992. "The Development and History of the Poverty Thresholds." *Social Security Bulletin* 55. Accessed September 2011. http://www.ssa.gov/history/fisheronpoverty.html.

Fisher, Sue, and Kathy Davis, eds. 1993. *Negotiating at the Margins: The Gendered Discourses of Power and Resistance.* New Brunswick, N.J.: Rutgers University Press.

Fiske, John. 1986. "Television: Polysemy and Popularity." *Critical Studies in Mass Communication* 3:391–408.

———. 1987. *Television Culture.* London: Methuen.

———. 1989. *Understanding Popular Culture.* London: Routledge.

Flores, Lisa. A., and Marouf A. Hasian. 1997. "Returning to Aztlan and La Raza: Political Communication and the Vernacular Construction of Chicano/a Nationalism." In *Politics, Communication, and Culture,* ed. Alberto Gonzalez and Dolores V. Tanno, 186–203. Thousand Oaks, Calif.: Sage.

Flynn, Elizabeth Gurley. 1940. *I Didn't Raise My Boy to Be a Soldier for Wall Street.* New York: Workers Library.

"Food Rights Actions." 1970. *Welfare Fighter,* February, 9.

"Food Stamps for GM Strikers." 1970. *Welfare Fighter,* November, 5.

Foss, Sonja K., and Cindy L. Griffin. 1995. "Beyond Persuasion: A Proposal for an Invitational Rhetoric." *Communication Monographs* 62:2–18.

Foss, Sonja K., William J. C. Waters, and Bernard J. Armada. 2007. "Toward a Theory of Agentic Orientation: Rhetoric and Agency in *Run Lola Run.*" *Communication Theory* 17:205–30.

Foucault, Michel. 1972. *The Archeology of Knowledge and the Discourse on Language.* Trans. A. M. Sheridan Smith. New York: Pantheon.

———. 1978. *The History of Sexuality: An Introduction.* Vol. 1. Trans. R. Hurley. New York: Random House.

Frascella letter. NWRO Papers Box 2209, unprocessed as of April 4, 2008, Manuscript Division, Moorland-Spingarn Research Center, Howard University.

Fraser, C. Gerald. 1971. "11 Are Arrested in Relief Protest." *New York Times,* February 27, 34.

Fraser, Nancy. 1989. *Unruly Practices: Power, Discourse and Gender in Contemporary Social Theory.* Minneapolis: University of Minnesota Press.

Frauel, Georgiana, and Irene Berton. 1970. "Upstate New York Caucus Meets." *Welfare Fighter,* April, 11.

Friedman, Debra, and Doug McAdam. 1992. "Collective Identity and Activism: Networks, Choices, and the Life of a Social Movement." In *Frontiers in Social Movement Theory,* ed. Aldon D. Morris and Carol McClurg Mueller, 156–73. New Haven: Yale University Press.

Fulkerson, Richard. 1996. "Transcending Our Conception of Argument in Light of Feminist Critiques." *Argumentation and Advocacy* 32:199–218.

Gans, Herbert J. 1967. "The Negro Family: Reflections on the Moynihan Report." In *The Moynihan Report and the Politics of Controversy,* ed. Lee Rainwater and William L. Yancey, 445–57. Cambridge: M.I.T. Press.

———. 1995. *The War against the Poor: The Underclass and Antipoverty Policy.* New York: Basic.

Gaonkar, Dilip Parameshwar. 1997. "The Idea of Rhetoric in the Rhetoric of Science." In *Rhetorical Hermeneutics: Invention and Interpretation in the Age of Science,* ed.

Alan G. Gross and William M. Keith, 25–85. Albany: State University of New York Press.

Geisler, Cheryl. 2005. "Teaching the Post-modern Rhetor: Continuing the Conversation on Rhetorical Agency." *Rhetoric Society Quarterly* 35:107–13.

"GE Strikers and NWRO Support Each Other." 1969. *Welfare Fighter,* December, 3.

Gilens, Martin. 1999. *Why Americans Hate Welfare: Race, Media and the Politics of Anti-poverty Policy.* Chicago: University of Chicago Press.

Gitlin, Todd. 1980. *The Whole World Is Watching: Mass Media in the Making and Unmaking of the New Left.* Berkeley: University of California Press.

Goodman, Walter. 1968. "A Victory for 400,000 Children: The Case of Mrs. Sylvester Smith." *New York Times,* August 25, 28.

Gordon, Linda. 1988. *Heroes of Their Own Lives: The Politics and History of Family Violence, Boston, 1880–1960.* New York: Viking.

———. 1995. *Pitied but Not Entitled: Single Mothers and the History of Welfare.* Cambridge: Harvard University Press.

"Government Spends More on Corporate Welfare Subsidies than Social Welfare Programs." Accessed December 1, 2011. http://thinkbynumbers.org/blog/government-spending/corporate-welfare/corporate-welfare-statistics-vs-social-welfare-statistics/.

"Grandmother Organizes New York Poor." 1972. *Welfare Fighter,* April, 19.

Greene, Ronald Walter. 2004. "Rhetoric and Capitalism: Rhetorical Agency as Communicative Labor." *Philosophy and Rhetoric* 37:188–206.

———. 2006. "Orator Communist." *Philosophy and Rhetoric* 39:85–95.

Greenlaw, J. 1968. Statement of National Welfare Rights Organization to the Democratic Platform Hearing. NWRO Papers Box 2101, unprocessed as of April 4, 2008, Manuscript Division, Moorland-Spingarn Research Center, Howard University.

Gregg, Nina. 1993. "'Trying to Put First Things First': Negotiating Subjectivities in a Workplace Organizing Campaign." In *Negotiating at the Margins: The Gendered Discourses of Power and Resistance,* ed. Sue Fisher and Kathy Davis, 172–204. New Brunswick, N.J.: Rutgers University Press.

Griffin, Leland. 1952. "The Rhetoric of Historical Movements." *Quarterly Journal of Speech* 38:184–88.

———. 1964. "The Rhetorical Structure of the 'New Left' Movement: Part I." *Quarterly Journal of Speech* 50:113–35.

Gross, Rita. 1972. State and Regional Development. (Pre–Task Force Meeting Report). NWRO Papers Box 2209, unprocessed as of April 4, 2008, Manuscript Division, Moorland-Spingarn Research Center, Howard University.

Gunderson, Gordon W. 1971. *The National School Lunch Program.* U.S. Government Printing Office. Accessed September 2011. www.fns.usda.gov/cnd/lunch/About Lunch/NSLP-Program%20History.pdf.

Gunn, Joshua, and Dana L. Cloud. 2010. "Agentic Orientation as Magical Voluntarism." *Communication Theory* 20:50–78.

Haiman, Franklin S. 1967. "The Rhetoric of the Streets: Some Legal and Ethical Considerations." *Quarterly Journal of Speech* 53:99–114.

Hallstein, D. Lynn O'Brien. 2000. "Where Standpoint Stands Now: An Introduction and Commentary." *Women's Studies in Communication* 23:1–15.

Hancock, Ange-Marie. 2004. *The Politics of Disgust: The Public Identity of the Welfare Queen.* New York: New York University Press.

Handler, Joel F., and Yeheskel Hasenfeld. 1991. *The Moral Construction of Poverty: Welfare Reform in America.* Newbury Park, Calif.: Sage.

"Hard Hitting Speeches from Chairman and Director." 1970. *Welfare Fighter*, November, 8.

Harding, Sandra. 1991. *Whose Science? Whose Knowledge? Thinking from Women's Lives.* Ithaca: Cornell University Press.

———. 1993. "Rethinking Standpoint Epistemology: 'What Is Strong Objectivity?'" In *Feminist Epistemologies,* ed. Linda Alcoff and Elizabeth Potter, 49–82. New York: Routledge.

Hardt, Michael, and Antonio Negri, A. 2000. *Empire.* Cambridge: Harvard University Press.

Harris, Tina M., and Deidra Donmoyer. 2000. "Is Art Imitating Life? Communication Gender and Racial Identity. In *Imitation of Life." Women's Studies in Communication* 23:91–110.

Hartsock, Nancy C. M. 1990. "Foucault on Power: A Theory for Women?" In *Feminism/Postmodernism,* ed. Linda J. Nicholson, 157175. New York: Routledge.

———. 1983a. "The Feminist Standpoint: Developing the Ground for a Specifically Feminist Historical Materialism." In *Discovering Reality: Feminist Perspectives on Epistemology, Metaphysics, Methodology, and Philosophy of Science,* ed. Sandra Harding and M. B. Hintikka, 283–310. Boston: D. Reidel.

———. 1983b. *Money, Sex, and Power: Toward a Feminist Historical Materialism.* New York: Longman.

Hauser, Gerard A. 2007. "Vernacular Discourse and the Epistemic Dimension of Public Opinion." *Communication Theory* 17:333–39.

———. 2008. "The Moral Vernacular of Human Rights Discourse." *Philosophy and Rhetoric* 41:440–66.

Herman, Edward S., and Noam Chomsky. 1988. *Manufacturing Consent: The Political Economy of the Mass Media.* New York: Pantheon.

Hertz, Susan Handley. 1981. *The Welfare Mothers Movement: A Decade of Change for Poor Women?* Washington D.C.: University Press of America.

Holmberg, David. 1970. "Protesters Occupy Finch's Office." *Evening Star,* May 13, 1. NWRO Papers Box 2160, unprocessed as of April 4, 2008, Manuscript Division, Moorland-Spingarn Research Center, Howard University.

Honsa, Carol. 1967 "Welfare Bill Called 'Betrayal of Poor.'" *Washington Post,* August 29, A4. NWRO Papers Box 2160, unprocessed as of April 4, 2008, Manuscript Division, Moorland-Spingarn Research Center, Howard University.

———. 1970. "Protesters Storm D.C. Welfare Office." *Washington Post,* June 24. NWRO Papers Box 2160, unprocessed as of April 4, 2008, Manuscript Division, Moorland-Spingarn Research Center, Howard University.

hooks, bell. 1984. *Feminist Theory from Margin to Center.* Boston: South End.

————. 1989. *Talking Back: Thinking Feminist, Thinking Black.* Boston: South End.

————. 1992. *Black Looks: Race and Representation.* Boston: South End.

Houck, David W., and David E. Dixon, eds. 2009. *Women and Civil Rights Movement, 1954–1965.* Jackson: University Press of Mississippi.

"How to Do a 'Test the Nixon Welfare Budget' Week." Pamphlet. NWRO Papers Box 2247, unprocessed as of April 4, 2008, Manuscript Division, Moorland-Spingarn Research Center, Howard University.

"How to Do the NWRO Test of President Nixon's Welfare Proposal." Pamphlet. NWRO Papers Box 2160, unprocessed as of April 4, 2008, Manuscript Division, Moorland-Spingarn Research Center, Howard University.

"How to Organize a Utilities Rights Campaign." Pamphlet. NWRO papers Box 2124, unprocessed as of April 4, 2008, Manuscript Division, Moorland-Spingarn Research Center, Howard University.

"H.R. 1 Has Contempt for the Poor." 1971. *Welfare Fighter,* November, 1.

"Illinois Resolution an Insult." 1970. *Welfare Fighter,* October, 8.

"Income Gap Widens, Report Says." 1972. *Welfare Fighter,* April, 2.

Income Maintenance Programs: Hearings before the Subcommittee on Fiscal Policy of the Joint Economic Committee, 90th Congress. 1968. Testimony of Beulah Sanders.

"Iowa Welfare Mothers Maced." 1969. *Welfare Fighter,* December, 6.

Jackson, Larry R., and William A. Johnson. 1974. *Protest by the Poor: The Welfare Rights Movement in New York City.* Lexington, Mass.: Lexington.

James, Betty. 1967. "Welfare Rally Threatens Riots." *Evening Star,* August 29, A4. NWRO Papers Box 2160, unprocessed as of April 4, 2008, Manuscript Division, Moorland-Spingarn Research Center, Howard University.

Jay, Martin. 1998. *Cultural Semantics: Keywords of Our Time.* Amherst: University of Massachusetts Press.

Jensen, Richard J., and John C. Hammerback. 1988. "'Your Tools Are Really the People': The Rhetoric of Robert Parris Moses." *Communication Monographs* 65:126–40.

Jewell, K. Sue. 1992. *From Mammy to Miss America and Beyond: Cultural Images and the Shaping of U.S. Social Policy.* New York: Routledge.

Johnson, Lyndon. B. 1964. "Message to Congress on the Economic Opportunity Act." In *Welfare: A Documentary History of U.S. Policy and Politics,* ed. Gwendolyn Mink and Rickie Solinger, 223–25. New York: New York University Press.

Johnson letter. NWRO Papers Box 2209, unprocessed as of April 4, 2008, Manuscript Division, Moorland-Spingarn Research Center, Howard University.

Jones, Betty. 1969. "Our Day Is Coming." *Welfare Fighter,* October, 3.

Jones, Jacqueline. 1985. *Labor of Love, Labor of Sorrow: Black Women, Work and the Family from Slavery to the Present.* New York: Basic.

Joseph, Peniel, ed. 2006. *The Black Power Movement: Rethinking the Civil Rights–Black Power Era.* New York: Routledge.

————. 2010. *Dark Days, Bright Nights: From Black Power to Barack Obama.* New York: Basic Civitas.

"June 30th Birthday in the Streets." 1970. *Welfare Fighter,* special edition, 4.

"The Just: NWRO's Adequate Income Bill." 1970. *Welfare Fighter,* November, 4.

"Kansas City." 1972. *Welfare Fighter,* April, 13.

"Kansas City WRO Goes on Stage." 1970–1971. *Welfare Fighter,* December–January, 5.

Kaufman, Michael T. 1968. "Welfare Sit-In Continues in the Bronx." *New York Times,* June 1, 21.

Kifner, John. 1968a. "38 Are Arrested in Relief Protest." *New York Times,* July 2, 18.

———. 1968b. "The Deepening Welfare Crisis." *New York Times,* August 1, 23.

———. 1968c. "Welfare Protest Group Warns Mayor That Drive Will Continue." *New York Times,* July 4, 7.

Kihss, Peter. 1968a. "City Will Simplify Payments System in Welfare Cases." *New York Times,* August 27, 1.

———. 1968b. "Protests Disrupt Welfare Centers." *New York Times,* August 30, 31.

———. 1968c. "Relief Recipients and Police Clash." *New York Times,* August 28, 1.

———. 1968d. "Welfare Protest Ties Up 2 Centers." *New York Times,* July 26, 24.

Kinefuchi, Etsuko, and Mark P. Orbe. 2008. "Situating Oneself in a Racialized World: Understanding Student Reactions to *Crash* through Standpoint Theory and Context-Positionality Frames." *Journal of International and Intercultural Communication* 1:70–90.

Kirkwood, William G. 1992. "Narrative and the Rhetoric of Possibility." *Communication Monographs* 59:30–47.

Knight, Michael. 1971. "Squalor Is a Way of Life at a Welfare Hotel Here." *New York Times,* January 28, 39.

Komisar, Lucy. 1977. *Down and Out in the USA: A History of Public Welfare.* New York: Franklin Watts.

Kornbluh, Felicia. 1997. "To Fulfill Their 'Rightly Needs': Consumerism and the National Welfare Rights Movement." *Radical History Review* 69:76–113.

———. 2007. *The Battle for Welfare Rights: Politics and Poverty in Modern America.* Philadelphia: University of Pennsylvania Press.

Kraus, Celene. 1993. "Women and Toxic Waste Protests: Race, Class and Gender as Resources of Resistance." *Qualitative Sociology* 16:247–62.

Kumar, Deepa. 2001. "Mass Media, Class, and Democracy: The Struggle over Newspaper Representation of the UPS Strike." *Critical Studies in Media Communication* 18:285–302.

Lake, Randall A. 1983. "Enacting Red Power: The Consummatory Function in Native American Protest Rhetoric." *Quarterly Journal of Speech* 69:127–42.

Lears, T. J. Jackson. 1985. "The Concept of Cultural Hegemony: Problems and Possibilities." *American Historical Review* 90:567–93.

Leff, Michael C. 1980. "Interpretation and the Art of the Rhetorical Critic." *Western Journal of Speech Communication* 44:337–49.

———. 2003. "Tradition and Agency in Humanistic Rhetoric." *Philosophy and Rhetoric* 36:135–47.

Leonhardt, David. 2009. "A Decade with No Income Gains." *New York Times,* September 10. Accessed November 2010. http://economix.blogs.nytimes.com/2009/09/10/a-decade-with-no-income-gain/.

Logan, Shirley Wilson, ed. 1995. *With Pen and Voice: A Critical Anthology of Nineteenth-Century African-American Women.* Carbondale: Southern Illinois University Press.

"The Long and the Shirt of it." 1970-1971. *Welfare Fighter,* Dec.-Jan., 11.

Lozano-Reich, Nina M., and Dana L. Cloud. 2009. "The Uncivil Tongue: Invitational Rhetoric and the Problem of Inequality." *Western Journal of Communication* 73: 220–26.

Lukács, Georg. 1968. *History and Class Consciousness: Studies in Marxist Dialectics.* Cambridge: M.I.T. Press.

Lumsden, Linda. 2009. "Good Mothers with Guns: Framing Black Womanhood in the *Black Panther*, 1968–1980." *Journalism and Mass Communication Quarterly* 86:900–922.

Lundberg, Christian, and Joshua Gunn. 2005. "'Ouija Board, Are There Any Communications?' Agency, Ontotheology, and the Death of the Humanist Subject, or, Continuing the ARS Conversation." *Rhetoric Society Quarterly* 35:83–105.

Lyotard, Jean-François. 1991. *The Postmodern Condition: A Report on Knowledge.* Trans. G. Bennington and B. Massumi. Minneapolis: University of Minnesota Press.

"Man in the House Rule." Accessed September 2011. http://law.jrank.org/pages/8412/Man-in-House-Rule.html.

Mansbridge, Jane. 1996. "Using Power/Fighting Power." In *Democracy and Difference: Contesting the Boundaries of the Political,* ed. Seyla Benhabib, 46–66. Princeton, N.J.: Princeton University Press.

Marx, Karl. 1888. "Theses on Feuerbach." In *The Marx-Engels Reader,* ed. Robert C. Tucker, 143–45. New York: Norton, 1978.

———. 1906. *Capital.* Vol. 1. Chicago: C. H. Kerr.

Marx, Karl, and Friedrich Engels. 1846. *The German Ideology.* Part 1. Ed. C. J. Arthur. New York: International, 1970.

May, Edgar. 1965. *The Wasted Americans.* New York: Signet.

McAdam, Doug. 1982. *Political Process and the Development of Black Insurgency, 1930–1970.* Chicago: University of Chicago Press.

———. 1986. "Recruitment to High-Risk Activism: The Case of Freedom Summer." *American Journal of Sociology* 92:64–90.

McBride, Dwight A. 2001. *Impossible Witnesses: Truth, Abolitionism and Slave Testimony.* New York: New York University Press.

McGee, Michael Calvin. 1980. "The 'Ideograph': A Link Between Rhetoric and Ideology." *Quarterly Journal of Speech* 66: 1-16.

McRobbie, Angela. 1994. *Postmodernism and Popular Culture.* New York: Routledge.

———. 2009. *The Aftermath of Feminism: Gender, Culture and Social Change.* Los Angeles: Sage.

"Md. WROs Push Increase." 1971. *Welfare Fighter,* February, 4.

Mills, Mary Beth. 2005. "From Nimble Fingers to Raised Fists: Women and Labor Activism in Globalizing Thailand." *Signs: Journal of Women in Culture and Society* 31:117–44.

"Milwaukee on the March." 1970. *Welfare Fighter,* February, 9.

Mink, Gwendolyn. 1995. *The Wages of Motherhood: Inequality in the Welfare State, 1917–1942.* Ithaca: Cornell University Press.

———. 1998. *Welfare's End.* Ithaca: Cornell University Press.

Mitchell, Joseph M. 1961. "The Revolt in Newburgh: The Failure of the Welfare Reform." *Vital Speeches of the Day* 28:214–20.

"Montgomery." 1972. *Welfare Fighter,* April, 10.

Morrison, Toni. 1971. "What the Black Woman Thinks about Women's Lib." *New York Times Magazine,* August 22, 63.

Morton, Patricia. 1991. *Disfigured Images: The Historical Assault on Afro-American Women.* New York: Praeger.

"Mothers Sit-In." 1969. *Welfare Fighter,* October, 1.

"Mothers Vow Boycott." 1968. *Ann Arbor News,* August 2. NWRO Papers Box 2160, unprocessed as of April 4, 2008, Manuscript Division, Moorland-Spingarn Research Center, Howard University.

Moynihan, Daniel Patrick. 1965. "The Negro Family: The Case for National Action." In *The Moynihan Report and the Politics of Controversy,* ed. Lee Rainwater and William L. Yancey, 45–94. Cambridge: M.I.T. Press.

Mueller, Carol. 1990. "Ella Baker and the Origins of 'Participatory Democracy.'" In *Women in the Civil Rights Movement: Trailblazers and Torchbearers, 1941–1965,* ed. Vicki L. Crawford, Jacqueline A. Rouse, and Barbara Woods, 51–70. Brooklyn: Carlson.

Mullings, Leith. 1995. "Households Headed by Women: The Politics of Race, Class, and Gender." In *Conceiving the New World Order: The Global Politics of Reproduction,* ed. Faye D. Ginsburg and Rayna Rapp, 122–39. Berkeley: University of California Press.

———. 2003. "After Drugs and the 'War on Drugs': Reclaiming the Power to Make History in Harlem, New York." In *Wounded Cities: Destruction and Reconstruction in a Globalized World,* ed. Jane Schneider and Ida Susser, 173–99. Oxford: Berg.

Murphy, John M. 1992. "Domesticating Dissent: The Kennedys and the Freedom Rides." *Communication Monographs* 59:61–78.

Nadasen, Premilla. 2005. *Welfare Warriors: The Welfare Rights Movement in the United States.* New York: Routledge.

"NCC Calls for Spring Offensive." 1972. *Welfare Fighter,* January–February, 1, 6.

Negri, Antonio. 1996. "Constituent Republic." In *Radical Thought in Italy: A Potential Politics,* ed. Paolo Virno and Michael Hardt, 213–21. Minneapolis: University of Minnesota Press.

Negt, Oskar, and Alexander Kluge. 1993. *Public Sphere and Experience: Toward an Analysis of the Bourgeois and Proletarian Public Sphere.* Minneapolis: University of Minnesota Press.

Nelton, Sharon. 1967. "'Humane' Social Legislation Is Goal of Picketing Mothers." *Detroit's Daily Express.* NWRO Papers Box 2160, unprocessed as of April 4, 2008, Manuscript Division, Moorland-Spingarn Research Center, Howard University.

Neubeck, Kenneth J., and Noel A. Cazenave. 2001. *Welfare Racism: Playing the Race Card against America's Poor.* New York: Routledge.

"New Direction for *Fighter.*" c. 1971. NWRO Papers Box 2247, unprocessed as of April 4, 2008, Manuscript Division, Moorland-Spingarn Research Center, Howard University.

"'New Kind of Welfare Client' Confronts State Bureaucrats with Organization." 1967. *Gazette and Daily,* York, PA: November 13, 1. NWRO Papers Box 2160, unprocessed as of April 4, 2008, Manuscript Division, Moorland-Spingarn Research Center, Howard University.

Niedzwiecki, Betty. 1972. "At War with the War on Poverty." In *Welfare Mothers Speak Out: We Ain't Gonna Shuffle Anymore,* ed. Thomas H. Tarantino and Rev. Dismas Becker, 40–45. New York: Norton.

Nixon, Richard M. 1971. "State of the Union Message." *Vital Speeches of the Day*, 37:226-230.

Nixon, Richard M. 1969. "Welfare Reform: Shared Responsibility." In *Welfare: A Documentary History of U.S. Politics and Policy,* ed. Gwendolyn Mink and Rickie Solinger, 313–19. New York: New York University Press.

"Nixon and Friends Try to Sabotage March." 1972. *Welfare Fighter,* April, 6.

"Notes on Welfare." 1970. NWRO Papers Box 2247, unprocessed as of April 4, 2008, Manuscript Division, Moorland-Spingarn Research Center, Howard University.

"Now Let *ME* Make One Thing Perfectly Clear . . ." 1971. *Welfare Fighter,* November, 2.

NOW! Newsletter. 1968. NWRO Papers Box 2160, unprocessed as of April 4, 2008, Manuscript Division, Moorland-Spingarn Research Center, Howard University.

"The NWRO Adequate Income Plan." 1971. Pamphlet. NWRO Papers Box 2247, unprocessed as of April 4, 2008, Manuscript Division, Moorland-Spingarn Research Center, Howard University.

"NWRO Demands for the Poor Peoples Campaign." Flyer. NWRO Papers Box 2160, unprocessed as of April 4, 2008, Manuscript Division, Moorland-Spingarn Research Center, Howard University.

"NWRO Executive Committee Sets Goals." 1972. *Welfare Fighter,* April, 20.

"NWRO-Guaranteed Adequate Income." 1970. *Welfare Fighter.* special edition, 2.

"NWRO Marches on Democrats July 10." 1972. *Welfare Fighter,* June, 8.

"NWRO's Legislative and Lobbying Committee Keeping Tabs on Washington." 1971. *Welfare Fighter,* February, 10.

"NWRO Sues HEW." 1971. *Welfare Fighter,* November, 2.

"Officials Harassed by Welfare Clients." 1968. *New York Times,* July 3, 70.

"Of Note to All Groups." 1971. *Welfare Fighter,* October, 5.

On, Bat-Ami Bar. 1993. "Marginality and Epistemic Privilege." In *Feminist Epistemologies*, ed. Linda Alcoff and Elizabeth Potter, 83-100. New York, NY: Routledge.

Ono, Kent A., and John N. Sloop. 1995. "The Critique of Vernacular Discourse." *Communication Monographs* 62:19–46.

———. 1997. "Out-law Discourse: The Critical Politics of Material Judgment." *Philosophy and Rhetoric* 30:50–69.

"Operation New York Starts Moving." 1971. *Welfare Fighter,* December, 1.

Orleck, Annelise. 2005. *Storming Caesar's Palace: How Black Mothers Fought Their Own War on Poverty.* Boston: Beacon.

Patterson, James T. 2000. *America's Struggle against Poverty in the Twentieth Century.* Cambridge: Harvard University Press.

———. 2010. *Freedom Is Not Enough: The Moynihan Report and America's Struggle over Black Family Life—From LBJ to Obama.* New York: Basic.

Payne, Charles M. 1990. "Men Led, but Women Organized: Movement Participation of Women in the Mississippi Delta." In *Women in the Civil Rights Movement: Trailblazers and Torchbearers, 1941–1965,* ed. Vickie L. Crawford, Jacqueline A. Rouse, and Barbara Woods, 1–11. Brooklyn: Carlson.

———. 1995. *I've Got the Light of Freedom: The Organizing Tradition and the Mississippi Freedom Struggle.* Berkeley: University of California Press.

Perelman, Chaim. 1982. *The Realm of Rhetoric.* Notre Dame: University of Notre Dame Press.

Peterson, Carla L. 1995. *"Doers of the Word": African-American Women Speakers and Writers in the North (1830–1880).* New York: Oxford University Press.

Piven, Frances Fox. 2002. "Globalization, American Politics, and Welfare Policy." In *Lost Ground: Welfare Reform, Poverty and Beyond,* ed. Randy Albelda and Ann Withorn, 27–41. Cambridge, Mass.: South End.

Piven, Frances Fox, and Richard A. Cloward. 1967. "The Weapon of Poverty: Birth of a Movement." *Nation,* May 8. NWRO Papers Box 2160, unprocessed as of April 4, 2008, Manuscript Division, Moorland-Spingarn Research Center, Howard University.

———. 1971. *Regulating the Poor: The Functions of Public Welfare.* New York: Vintage.

———. 1979. *Poor People's Movements: Why They Succeed, How They Fail.* New York: Vintage.

Pollock, Mark, Lee Artz, Lawrence Frey, W. Barnett Pearce, and Bren A. O. Murphy. 1996. "Navigating between Scylla and Charybdis: Continuing the Dialogue on Communication and Social Justice." *Communication Studies* 47:142–51.

Pope, Jacqueline. 1971. "Welfare Means: You Need to Get Organized." *Welfare Fighter,* November, 7.

———. 1989. *Biting the Hand That Feeds Them: Organizing Women on Welfare at the Grass Roots Level.* New York: Praeger.

———. 2011. Telephone interview with the author. November 29.

Poulakos, John. 1984. "Rhetoric, the Sophists, and the Possible." *Communication Monographs* 51:215–26.

Press conference. 1967. NWRO Papers Box 2201, unprocessed as of April 4, 2008, Manuscript Division, Moorland-Spingarn Research Center, Howard University.

Press release. NWRO Papers Box 2124, unprocessed as of April 4, 2008, Manuscript Division, Moorland-Spingarn Research Center, Howard University.

"Profile of a Welfare Fighter: Angie Matos." 1970. *Welfare Fighter,* March, 10.

"Profile of a Welfare Fighter: Annie Smart." 1970–1971. *Welfare Fighter,* December–January, 11.

"Profile of a Welfare Fighter: Jennette Washington." 1971. *Welfare Fighter,* April–Mary, 11.

"Profile of a Welfare Fighter: Johnnie Tillmon." 1971. *Welfare Fighter,* August, 3.

"Profile of a Welfare Fighter: Marian Kidd." 1970. *Welfare Fighter,* April, 3.

"Profile of a Welfare Fighter: Mrs. Geraldine Smith." 1970. *Welfare Fighter,* May, 12.

"Public Control in America." 1970. *Welfare Fighter,* April, 12.

Pugh, Tony. 2007. "US Economy Leaving Record Numbers in Severe Poverty." Accessed April 2008. http://www.commondreams.org/headlines07/0223-09.htm.

Quadagno, Jill. 1994. *The Color of Welfare: How Racism Undermined the War on Poverty.* New York: Oxford University Press.

Radway, Janice. 1984. *Reading the Romance: Women, Patriarchy, and Popular Literature.* Chapel Hill: University of North Carolina Press.

Railsback, Celeste C. 1984. "The Contemporary American Abortion Controversy: Stages in the Argument." *Quarterly Journal of Speech* 70:410–24.

Rainwater, Lee, and William L. Yancy, eds. 1967. *The Moynihan Report and the Politics of Controversy.* Cambridge: M.I.T. Press.

Reese, Stephen D., and Bob Buckalew. 1995. "The Militarism of Local Television: The Routine Framing of the Persian Gulf War." *Critical Studies in Mass Communication* 12:40–59.

"The Report of Workshop 2." 1966. National Welfare Rights Meeting, 1966. NWRO Papers Box 2160, unprocessed as of April 4, 2008, Manuscript Division, Moorland-Spingarn Research Center, Howard University.

"Ribicoff Attempts to Patch-Up H.R. 1." 1971. *Welfare Fighter,* November, 1, 4.

Richard, Paul. 1966. "Marchers Protest Welfare Program." *Washington Post,* July 1. NWRO Papers Box 2160, unprocessed as of April 4, 2008, Manuscript Division, Moorland-Spingarn Research Center, Howard University.

Robnett, Belinda. 1997. *How Long? How Long? African-American Women in the Struggle for Civil Rights.* New York: Oxford University Press.

"Rockefeller Welfare Conference . . . Would You Believe?" 1967. NWRO Papers Box 2160, unprocessed as of April 4, 2008, Manuscript Division, Moorland-Spingarn Research Center, Howard University.

Rosenberg, Tina. 2008. "A Payoff Out of Poverty?" *New York Times,* December 21, 46.

Rosenthal, Rob. 1993. "Skidding/Coping/Escaping: Constraint, Agency, and Gender in the Lives of Homeless 'Skidders.'" In *Negotiating at the Margins: The Gendered Discourses of Power and Resistance,* ed. Sue Fisher and Kathy Davis, 205–32. New Brunswick, N.J.: Rutgers University Press.

Rudd, Edward. 1967. "They Also March Who Stay Home." *Hartford Courant,* November 23, 81.

Rural Poverty and Hunger: Hearings before the Subcommittee on Employment, Manpower, and Poverty, 90th Congress. 1968. Testimony of Gussie Davis.

Rural Poverty and Hunger: Hearings before the Subcommittee on Employment, Manpower, and Poverty, 90th Congress. 1968. Testimony of Nancy Cole.

Rural Poverty and Hunger: Hearings before the Subcommittee on Employment, Manpower, and Poverty, 90th Congress. 1968. Testimony of Viola Holland.

Rustin, B. 1963. "Birmingham Leads to New Stage in Struggle." *New America,* June 18.

Sanders, Beulah. 1971. Draft of speech for PCPJ. NWRO Papers Box 2210, unprocessed as of April 4, 2008, Manuscript Division, Moorland-Spingarn Research Center, Howard University.

"Sanders Testifies before the House." 1969. *Welfare Fighter,* November, 6.

Schneider, Anne, and Helen Ingram. 1993. "Social Construction of Target Populations: Implications for Politics and Policy." *American Political Science Review* 87:334–47.

"School Board Meeting in Austin." 1970. *Welfare Fighter,* March, 4.

"School Lunch Rights Campaign." 1969. *Welfare Fighter,* December, 3.

Schram, Sanford F. 2005. "Putting a Black Face on Welfare: The Good and the Bad." In *Deserving and Entitled: Social Constructions and Public Policy,* ed. Anne L. Schneider and Helen M. Ingram, 261–86. Albany: State University of New York.

"SCLC Links Up with NWRO." 1971. *Welfare Fighter,* February, 1, 9.

Scott, Dorothy. 1970. "Motherhood—A 'Full Time Job.'" *Welfare Fighter,* June, 3.

Scott, Joan W. 1991. "The Evidence of Experience." *Critical Inquiry* 17:773–97.

Scott, Robert L., and Donald K. Smith. 1969. "The Rhetoric of Confrontation." *Quarterly Journal of Speech* 55:1–8.

"Secrets, Lies, and Sweatshops." 2006. *Businessweek,* November 27. Accessed February 2007. http://www.businessweek.com/magazine/content/06_48/b4011001.htm.

Shockley, Ann Allen. 1989. *Afro-American Women Writers 1746–1933: An Anthology and Critical Guide.* New York: New American Library.

"Shoe on the Other Foot." 1972. *Welfare Fighter,* March, 15.

Simons, Herbert. 1970. "Requirements, Problems, and Strategies: A Theory of Persuasion for Social Movements." *Quarterly Journal of Speech* 56:1–11.

———. 1972. "Persuasion in Social Conflicts: A Critique of Prevailing Conceptions and a Framework for Future Research." *Speech Monographs* 39:227–47.

"Sixteen Cities Join National Crusade for Children's Rights." 1972. *Welfare Fighter,* April, 10–11.

"Sleep-In at Kansas Gas Co." 1970. *Welfare Fighter,* April, 8.

Social Security Amendments of 1971: Hearings before the Committee on Finance, 92nd Congress. 1972. Testimony of Beulah Sanders.

Social Security Amendments of 1971: Hearings before the Committee on Finance, 92nd Congress. 1972. Testimony of Elaine McLean.

Social Security Amendments of 1971: Hearings before the Committee on Finance, 92nd Congress. 1972. Testimony of Elizabeth Perry.

Social Security and Welfare Proposals: Hearings before the Committee on Ways and Means, 91st Congress. 1969. Testimony of Beulah Sanders.

Solinger, Rickie. 2000. *Wake Up Little Susie: Single Pregnancy and Race before Roe v. Wade.* New York: Routledge.

Sotomayor, Sonia. 2001. "A Latina Judge's Voice." Accessed August 2009. http://www.nytimes.com/2009/05/15/us/politics/15judge.text.html?pagewanted=1.

"Southern Caravan Success." 1970. *Welfare Fighter,* October, 1–2.

Springer, Kimberly. 2006. "Black Feminists Respond to Black Power Masculinism." In *The Black Power Movement: Rethinking the Civil Rights—Black Power Era,* ed. Peniel E. Joseph, 105–18. New York: Routledge.

"The Spring Offensive Is On!" 1971. *Welfare Fighter,* April–May, 2.

Squires, Catherine. 2001. "The Black Press and the State: Attracting Unwanted (?) Attention." In *Counterpublics and the State,* ed. Robert Asen and Daniel C. Brouwer, 111–36. Albany: State University of New York Press.

Stack, Carol B. 1974. *All Our Kin: Strategies for Survival in a Black Community.* New York: Harper and Row.

"State Action, Virginia." 1969. *Welfare Fighter,* November, 4.

"The States Report: Arizona." 1970. *Welfare Fighter,* March, 9.

"The States Report: Atlanta 'Sleeps-In.'" 1970–1971. *Welfare Fighter,* December–January, 4.

"The States Report: Maryland." 1972. *Welfare Fighter,* January–February, 10, 11.

"The States Report: Philadelphia." 1972. *Welfare Fighter,* August–September, 16.

"The States Report: Rhode Island." 1971. *Welfare Fighter,* October, 11.

"The States Report: Rochester." 1972. *Welfare Fighter,* April, 17.

Steiner, Gilbert Y. 1971. *The State of Welfare.* Washington, D.C.: Brookings Institution.

Stewart, Charles J. 1980. "A Functional Approach to the Rhetoric of Social Movements." *Central States Speech Journal* 31:298–305.

Stover, Johnnie M. 2003. *Rhetoric and Resistance in Black Women's Autobiography.* Gainesville: University Press of Florida.

"Supreme Court Decision." 1970–1971. *Welfare Fighter,* December–January, 1.

Szumski, Jerry. 1968. "Welfare Skit Points Up Plight of ADC Mothers." *NOW!* newsletter February 23. NWRO Papers Box 2160, unprocessed as of April 4, 2008, Manuscript Division, Moorland-Spingarn Research Center, Howard University.

Tarantino, Thomas H., and Rev. Dismas Becker, eds. 1972. *Welfare Mothers Speak Out: We Ain't Gonna Shuffle Anymore.* New York: Norton.

Taylor, Verta, and Nancy E. Whittier. 1992. "Collective Identity in Social Movement Communities: Lesbian Feminist Mobilization." In *Frontiers in Social Movement Theory,* ed. Aldon D. Morris and Carol McClurg Mueller, 104–29. New Haven: Yale University Press.

Testimony of the National Welfare Rights Organization before the Platform Committee of the Democratic National Convention. 1968. NWRO Papers Box 2160, unprocessed as of April 4, 2008, Manuscript Division, Moorland-Spingarn Research Center, Howard University.

"This Is How the Nixon Plan Would Affect You! 1970." *Welfare Fighter,* special edition, 3.

Tillmon, Johnnie. 1969a. "Message from the Chair." *Welfare Fighter,* October, 2.

———. 1969b. "New York, Wage Supplement." *Welfare Fighter,* November, 2.

———. 1970a. "Message from the Chair." *Welfare Fighter,* January, 2.

———. 1970b. "Message from the Chair." *Welfare Fighter,* March, 2.

———. 1971. "Message from the Chair." *Welfare Fighter,* April–May, 12.

———. 1972a. "Welfare As a Women's Issue." In *Major Problems in American Urban History,* ed. Howard P. Chudacoff, 426–29. Lexington, Mass.: D.C. Heath.

———. 1972b. "Welfare Is a Women's Issue." *Ms. Magazine.* Accessed March 2010. http://www.msmagazine.com/spring2002/tillmon.asp.

Tonn, Mari Boor. 1996. "Militant Motherhood: Labor's Mary Harris 'Mother Jones.'" *Quarterly Journal of Speech* 82:1–21.

———. 2005. "Taking Conversation, Dialogue and Therapy Public." *Rhetoric and Public Affairs* 8:405–30.

"Too Much Month at the End of the Money." 1972. *Welfare Fighter,* April, 15.

"Total Victory in Nevada!" 1971. *Welfare Fighter,* April–May, 4, 5.

Triece, Mary E. 2001. *Protest and Popular Culture: Women in the U.S. Labor Movement, 1894–1917.* Boulder, Colo.: Westview.

———. 2003. "Appealing to the 'Intelligent Worker': Rhetorical Reconstitution and the Influence of Firsthand Experience in the Rhetoric of Leonora O'Reilly." *Rhetoric Society Quarterly* 33:1–24.

———. 2007. *On the Picket Line: Strategies of Working-Class Women during the Depression.* Urbana: University of Illinois Press.

Untitled. 1969. *Welfare Fighter,* October, 1.

"Up the Nixon Plan." 1970. *Welfare Fighter,* special edition, 3.

Valk, Anne M. 2000. "'Mother Power': The Movement for Welfare Rights in Washington, D.C., 1966–1972." *Journal of Women's History* 11:34–58.

Villadsen, Lisa S. 2008. "Speaking on Behalf of Others: Rhetorical Agency and Epideictic Functions in Official Apologies." *Rhetoric Society Quarterly* 38:25–45.

"Walk for Decent Welfare Song Sheet." 1966. NWRO Papers Box 2160, unprocessed as of April 4, 2008, Manuscript Division, Moorland-Spingarn Research Center, Howard University.

"Wanted for Conspiracy." c. 1968. *NOW!* newsletter. NWRO Papers Box 2160, unprocessed as of April 4, 2008, Manuscript Division, Moorland-Spingarn Research Center, Howard University.

Ward, Stephen. 2006. "The Third World Women's Alliance." In *The Black Power Movement: Rethinking the Civil Rights—Black Power Era,* ed. Peniel E. Joseph, 119–44. New York: Routledge.

"Washington Welfare Recipients Training Conference." Poverty/Rights Action Center, 1966. NWRO Papers Box 2160, unprocessed as of April 4, 2008, Manuscript Division, Moorland-Spingarn Research Center, Howard University.

Watson, Martha. 1999. *Lives of Their Own: Rhetorical Dimensions in Autobiographies of Women Activists.* Columbia: University of South Carolina Press.

"The Way It Is on Welfare." 1970. *Welfare Fighter,* February, 7.

"A Week of Welfare." 1969. *Washington Post,* July 5, A16. NWRO Papers Box 2160, unprocessed as of April 4, 2008, Manuscript Division, Moorland-Spingarn Research Center, Howard University.

Weigand, Kate. 2001. *Red Feminism: American Communism and the Making of Women's Liberation.* Baltimore: Johns Hopkins University Press.

"Welfare Bill of Rights." Flyer. NWRO Papers Box 2247, unprocessed as of April 4, 2008, Manuscript Division, Moorland-Spingarn Research Center, Howard University.

"Welfare Clients Continue Sit-In at Goldberg's Office." 1968. *New York Times,* June 30, 39.

"Welfare for the Rich—Poverty for the Poor." Document. NWRO Papers Box 2124, unprocessed as of April 4, 2008, Manuscript Division, Moorland-Spingarn Research Center, Howard University.

"Welfare Hotels: A Grim, Tragic Mess." 1971. *Welfare Fighter,* February, 3.

"Welfare Mothers–Drive Launched." 1966. *The Baltimore Afro-American,* July. NWRO Papers Box 2160, unprocessed as of April 4, 2008, Manuscript Division, Moorland-Spingarn Research Center, Howard University.

"'Welfare Mothers' Rally." 1966. *Boston Herald,* July 1, 34. NWRO Papers Box 2160, unprocessed as of April 4, 2008, Manuscript Division, Moorland-Spingarn Research Center, Howard University.

"Welfare Rights Boycott of Schools Due Today." 1970. *Plain Dealer,* September 16, n.p.

"Welfare Rights of Montclair." Pamphlet. NWRO Papers Box 2247, unprocessed as of April 4, 2008, Manuscript Division, Moorland-Spingarn Research Center, Howard University.

"We're Tired of Coming Away from 'Hunger Conferences' with a Belly Full of Empty Promises." 1971. *Welfare Fighter,* February, 8.

West, Guida. 1981. *The National Welfare Rights Movement: The Social Protest of Poor Women.* New York: Praeger.

Westin, Jeane. 1976. *Making Do: How Women Survived the '30s.* Chicago: Follett.

"What's Happening?" n.d. *NOW!* newsletter. NWRO Papers Box 2101, unprocessed as of April 4, 2008, Manuscript Division, Moorland-Spingarn Research Center, Howard University.

White, Deborah Gray. 1999. *Too Heavy a Load: Black Women in Defense of Themselves, 1894–1994.* New York: Norton.

"Who Gets Welfare?" Flyer. NWRO Papers Box 2124, unprocessed as of April 4, 2008, Manuscript Division, Moorland-Spingarn Research Center, Howard University.

"Who Gets Welfare?" Pamphlet. NWRO Papers Box 2124, unprocessed as of April 4, 2008, Manuscript Division, Moorland-Spingarn Research Center, Howard University.

Wiley letter. 1969. NWRO Papers Box 2160, unprocessed as of April 4, 2008, Manuscript Division, Moorland-Spingarn Research Center, Howard University.

Wiley letter. 1971. NWRO Papers Box 2247, unprocessed as of April 4, 2008, Manuscript Division, Moorland-Spingarn Research Center, Howard University.

Williams, Lucy A. 1995. "Race, Rat Bites and Unfit Mothers: How Media Discourse Informs Welfare Legislation Debate. *Fordham Urban Law Journal* 22:1159–96.

Williams, Rhonda Y. 2006. "Black Women, Urban Politics, and Engendering Black Power." In *The Black Power Movement: Rethinking the Civil Rights–Black Power Era,* ed. Peniel E. Joseph, 79–103. New York: Routledge.

Wilson, William Julius. 1996. *When Work Disappears: The World of the New Urban Poor.* New York: Knopf.

Wood, Ellen M. 1986. *The Retreat from Class: A New "True" Socialism.* London: Verso.

Wood, Julia T. 1992. "Gender and Moral Voice: Moving from Woman's Nature to Standpoint Epistemology." *Women's Studies in Communication* 15:1–24.

———. 2005. "Feminist Standpoint Theory and Muted Group Theory: Commonalities and Divergences." *Women and Language* 28:61–64.

"WRO Saves 23." 1970. *Welfare Fighter,* May, 8.

Young, Ginny. 1972. "McGovern Speaks to Welfare Mothers." *Welfare Fighter,* August–September, 4.

Zarefsky, David. 1986. *President Johnson's War on Poverty: Rhetoric and History.* Alabama: University of Alabama Press.

Zucchino, David. 1997. *Myth of the Welfare Queen: A Pulitzer Prize–Winning Journalist's Portrait of Women on the Line.* New York: Scribner.

Made in the USA
Monee, IL
03 January 2023

24326250R00100